T0319356

The Value
of Money

The Value of Money

Prabhat Patnaik

COLUMBIA UNIVERSITY PRESS
NEW YORK

Columbia University Press
Publishers Since 1893
New York | Chichester, West Sussex

Library of Congress Cataloging-in-Publication Data

Patnaik, Prabhat.
  The value of money / Prabhat Patnaik.
      p. cm.
  Includes bibliographical references and index.
  ISBN 978-0-231-14676-0 (hard cover : alk. paper) — ISBN
978-0-231-51921-2 (e-book)
    1. Money. I. Title.
HG220.A2P38 2009
332.401—dc22

                                    2008047974

⊗ Columbia University Press books are printed on permanent and
durable acid-free paper.
This book is printed on paper with recycled content.
Printed in the United States of America

c 10 9 8 7 6 5 4 3 2

For Utsa, Nishad, and Neelabhra

Contents

Preface

EVEN THOUGH THE IDEAS PRESENTED in this book have been with me for a long time and have been presented through my lectures to generations of students at my university, the writing of this book has not been easy. For one thing, it advances two separate though interlinked propositions, one a critique of monetarism from a point of view I christen "propertyist," of which I take Marx and Keynes as the classic examples and that in my view is the superior one, and the other a critique of "propertyism" itself for its incompleteness, for not having made a sufficiently radical break with orthodox economics. Presenting what in effect are two books rolled into one has raised difficulties. When I first started writing the book in 1995, I thought I would just present a set of essays with an introductory chapter that summed up the argument, leaving it to the readers to make the connections. The result turned out to be so reader-unfriendly that I was advised to write the book in a more conventional format and remove the introductory chapter altogether, since stating an argument at the beginning and then developing it at greater length in the course of the book appeared repetitive. When I had done the latter, I was again advised that the core of the argument might get lost because of the two levels of argument in the book and that therefore an introductory chapter stating the entire argument and some of its contemporary implications was in order. This is finally what I have produced—a conventional book with an introductory chapter stating its main themes and their contemporary meaning.

Three people have stood by me and helped me intellectually during this long journey. Utsa Patnaik reacted to my ideas as they developed over the years and critically read through the second draft. C. P. Chandrasekhar read through the entire first draft and is largely responsible for the book's taking its present form. Jayati Ghosh made numerous suggestions for improving the present version. I express my deep gratitude to all of them. Akeel Bilgrami was a source of great encouragement during my writing the latest version of the book. Indira Chandrasekhar of Tulika Books has provided patient and steadfast support throughout this entire project, as has Peter Dimock of Columbia University Press in its later phase. I have discussed my ideas with several colleagues at the Centre for Economic Studies and Planning of Jawaharlal Nehru University, especially Anjan Mukherji, who have left their influence on my thinking. I wish to express my sincere thanks to all of them.

(June 2008)

Introduction

IT IS AN INTRIGUING ASPECT of our daily life that intrinsically worthless bits of paper, which we call money, appear to possess value and are exchanged against useful objects. The purpose of this book is to examine the social arrangement underlying this fact. While this social arrangement is none other than the entire social arrangement underlying capitalism, there is a point in starting our investigation from the "money end." This is because an important part of the overall social arrangement that may not always be apparent when we start from the concept of "capital" emerges with greater clarity when we take money as the starting point of our analysis; this part relates to the fact that capitalism cannot exist, and never has existed, in isolation as a closed, self-contained system, as has been commonly assumed in much of economic analysis. In other words, a better route for understanding the totality of the social arrangement underlying capitalism is to start with a simple question: What breathes value into these intrinsically worthless bits of paper? This question is in turn part of a more comprehensive question: What determines the value of money, irrespective of whether it consists of intrinsically worthless bits of paper or of precious metals?[1] To this question there have been two basic answers in economics. The first proposition of this book is that one of these answers, the one given by what constitutes "mainstream" economics at present, cannot stand logical scrutiny. I therefore begin with a critique of "mainstream" economics and, in particular, the notion of "equilibrium" central to it.

A Critique of the Mainstream Notion of Equilibrium

Mainstream economic theory takes market clearing as its point of reference. In its perception, the flexibility of prices, which characterizes markets in the ideal type of a capitalist economy, ensures the equalization of demand and supply at a set of equilibrium prices. The endowments an economy has and whose ownership is distributed in a certain manner among the economic agents are fully utilized in producing a set of goods whose supply exactly equals the demand for them at this set of equilibrium prices. It follows that there is no question of any involuntary unemployment in such an economy, in the sense of an excess supply of labor at the prevailing wage rate, in equilibrium. Tastes, technology, the magnitude of endowments and their distribution across the economic agents, and the "thriftiness conditions" (to use Joan Robinson's phrase), or what some would call the "time preference" of the economic agents, determine the equilibrium prices and outputs in this world of "rational" agents, where firms maximize profits and individuals maximize utilities.

This mainstream notion of equilibrium, however, is logically tenable only in a world without money, which is why it cannot be a logically valid description for a capitalist economy. This is because in a world with money, according to this conception, the market for money must "clear" at a certain price of money in terms of the nonmoney goods. This can happen only if the excess demand curve for money is downward sloping with respect to the "price of money." For a given supply of money, in other words, the demand for money must vary inversely with the price of money. The price of money being the reciprocal of the price level of commodities in terms of money, this implies that the demand for money must vary directly with the price level of commodities. Mainstream economics took this for granted, because it saw money only as a medium of circulation, so that the higher the value of the goods that have to be circulated, the greater is the demand for money. Since, with output at the full employment level, the value of the goods (and hence the value of the goods to be circulated) depends on their price level, the demand for money has to be positively related to the price level.

The role of money as a medium of circulation ensured this. The problem, however, is that money is a form of wealth, too. It cannot be a medium of circulation without also being a form of wealth, since even the former role requires that money be held, however fleetingly, as wealth. And as the form-of-wealth role of money is recognized, it becomes clear that the demand for money must also depend upon the *expected* returns from other forms of wealth holding. If the demand for money depends upon *expectations* about the future, then there is no necessary reason why the demand curve for money should be upward-sloping with respect to the price level, as required by "mainstream" theory, since any change in the price level cannot leave expectations unchanged.

To get out of this quagmire, mainstream theory has taken two alternative routes. One is to refuse, quite stubbornly, the form-of-wealth role of money and to see money only as a medium of circulation. The other is to recognize the form-of-wealth role of money but to assume that expectations are always of a kind that does not create any trouble for the theory, at least with regard to the existence and stability of equilibrium. The first is the orthodox route of the Cambridge constant, k, or, what effectively comes to the same thing, a constant income velocity of circulation of money (subject to long-run autonomous changes), which is much used even today in bread-and-butter empirical work belonging to the monetarist genre. The second is the route of the "real balance" effect, whose validity depends, among other things, on the assumption of inelastic price expectations.

Both these routes, however, are blocked by logical contradictions. The Cambridge-constant route is blocked by the obvious contradiction that money cannot logically be assumed to be a medium of circulation unless it can also function as a form of wealth.

And if it can, then there is no reason why it should not actually do so. And if it does, then we cannot assume a Cambridge constant k. The second route is blocked by the contradiction that inelastic price expectations presuppose some anchorage to prices, the existence, that is, of some prices that are sticky, and in a world of flexible prices there is no reason why this should be the case. It follows that there is simply no logically tenable way of erecting a theoretical structure in conformity with the "mainstream" perception in a world with money, and hence for a capitalist economy.[2]

Because of this there has been an alternative tradition in economics, which I call the "propertyist" tradition, that has always seen the value of money as being fixed outside the realm of demand and supply. At this value, fixed from outside the realm of demand and supply, individuals habitually hold money balances in excess of what is required for the purpose of circulation: Money constitutes both a medium of circulation and a form of wealth holding. In such a case, Say's law cannot possibly hold. If wealth can be held in the form of money, then the possibility of *ex ante* overproduction of the nonmoney commodities arises. And this *ex ante* overproduction gives rise to actual output contraction, not just of the nonmoney commodities but of money and nonmoney commodities taken together, precisely because the price of money in terms of commodities is fixed from outside the realm of demand and supply, so that price flexibility cannot be assumed to eliminate this *ex ante* overproduction.[3]

It follows, then, that the recognition of the role of money as a form of wealth holding, the recognition of the fact that its value cannot be determined within the realm of demand and supply but must be fixed from outside this realm, and the recognition of the possibility of generalized overproduction or—what comes to the same thing—of involuntary unemployment in the Keynesian sense, are logically interlinked and constitute the propertyist tradition. By contrast, the denial of each of these phenomena, is also logically interlinked, and constitutes the Walrasian-monetarist tradition that remains the mainstream.

Within the propertyist tradition, there are two main contributions. One is of Marx, who had not only explicitly noted the untenability of explaining the value of money in terms of demand and supply, but had also provided an alternative explanation for it through his labor theory of value. He had underscored both the existence of a "hoard" of money at all times as a form of wealth holding in a capitalist society, and had recognized, against Ricardo, who had been a believer in Say's law, the possibility of *ex ante* generalized overproduction as a consequence of this fact. But neither Marx himself nor his followers pursued this fundamental contribution of Marx any farther; they preferred instead to follow exclusively the other major theoretical discovery of Marx, namely the one relating to his theory of surplus value. This is why another three-quarters of a century had to elapse before the same themes had to resurface during the Keynesian revolution through the writings of Kalecki and Keynes, among others, who constituted the second main group of contributors within the propertyist tradition.

There were major differences, of course, between Marx and Keynes in the specifics of their theories. While Marx invoked the labor theory of value to explain the determination of the value of money, Keynes believed that the value of money vis-à-vis the world of commodities was fixed through the fixing of the value of money vis-à-vis one particular commodity, namely labor power (to use Marx's term). The fact that the money wage rate was fixed in the single period, which was Keynes's focus of analysis, is what gave money a finite and positive value vis-à-vis the entire world of commodities. And the fixity of money wages was not a cause for market failure, as has been generally supposed, but the modus operandi of the market system itself in a capitalist economy that necessarily uses money. The superiority of the propertyist tradition in analyzing the functioning of the capitalist economy over the Walrasian-monetarist tradition arises therefore not only from its greater "realism" (for example, the fact that capitalism does witness overproduction crises) but also from its being free of the logical infirmities that afflict Walrasian monetarism.

A Critique of the Notion of Capitalism as an Isolated System

This book advances a second proposition as well. Propertyism, notwithstanding its superiority over monetarism, still remains incomplete. It adduces no convincing mechanism for ensuring that the activity level of a capitalist economy remains within the range that keeps it viable. The proneness of a capitalist economy to generalized overproduction makes it essentially a demand-constrained system (with the supply constraint becoming relevant only in exceptional periods of extremely high demand). But if capitalism is a demand-constrained system, then what ensures the fact that it remains viable, generally earning a rate of profit that the capitalists consider adequate? The spontaneous operations of a demand-constrained system will not ensure that it functions generally above a certain degree of capacity utilization, which constitutes the threshold for its viability. As the Harrodian growth discussion has shown, left to its own devices a capitalist economy does not have the wherewithal to reverse tracks if it starts on a downswing. And as Kalecki has shown in the context of a demand-constrained system, of which the Harrodian universe was one specific example, the long-run trend in such a system in the absence of exogenous stimuli is zero, which would certainly undermine the viability of such an economy.

Now, an isolated capitalist economy operating spontaneously does not have any exogenous stimuli. Innovation, the main exogenous stimulus emphasized by authors as diverse as Schumpeter and Kalecki, is really not an exogenous stimulus, since the pace of introduction of innovations is itself not independent of the expected growth of demand. And state expenditure, the other main exogenous stimulus that can arise in an isolated capitalist economy, is really not a part of the *spontaneous* functioning of capitalism (apart from being a phenomenon that has acquired particular prominence only in more recent years). Hence, even propertyism remains incomplete. Having correctly recognized the capitalist system as being prone to a deficiency of aggregate demand, it offers no explanation of how, despite this, the system has managed to survive and prosper for so long.

There is a second and related issue here. To highlight it, let us assume away for a moment the first issue. Let us accept that exogenous stimulus in the form of innovations always succeeds in keeping up the level of demand and hence the level of activity in the capitalist economy that constitutes our universe. Now, even if the value of money in terms of nonmoney commodities is given from outside the realm of demand and supply in any period, if this value itself keeps moving in an unbounded manner across periods, through, for instance, accelerating inflation, then again the continued existence of a normal monetary economy becomes inexplicable. And if the level of activity has to adjust to keep the "across-period" price movements within bounds, then this level itself may well drop below the threshold that makes the economy viable, in spite of the presence of the exogenous stimulus. It follows that a monetary economy must have not only "outside" determination of the value of money in any period, but also some mechanism, other than through adjustments in the level of activity, to keep price movements across periods within strict bounds. An obvious mechanism is the fixity of some price not only within the period but also across periods. Or, putting it differently, the price that is given from "outside" in any period should also be slowly changing across periods. Propertyism remains incomplete because it adduces no reason why this should happen. Hence, notwithstanding its superiority over monetarism and Walrasianism, propertyism too, as it stands, is not free of logical problems.

The only way that all these problems can be overcome is by conceiving of capitalism as a mode of production that never exists in isolation, that is necessarily linked with the surrounding precapitalist modes, and that continuously keeps itself viable by encroaching on precapitalist markets. The limitation of propertyism is that even though it rejected monetarism for perfectly valid reasons, it remained trapped within the same assumption, of an isolated and closed capitalist economy, that had characterized monetarism. Its rejection of the mainstream view, in short, was not sufficiently radical and thoroughgoing.

To say that the capitalist economy needs to encroach upon precapitalist markets is not to say, as Rosa Luxemburg did, that it needs to "realize" its entire surplus value in every period through sales to the precapitalist sector. Indeed the role of the precapitalist markets does not even have to be quantitatively significant. Much of the time the capitalist economy can grow on its own steam, as long as it can use precapitalist markets as a means of turning itself around whenever it is on a downward movement. And even for this turning around, the quantitative magnitude of sales to the precapitalist markets does not have to be significant. Indeed, strictly speaking, as long as the very availability of precapitalist markets "on tap" can instill among the capitalists sufficient confidence to undertake investment, any downturn can be arrested and even thwarted, without any notable actual encroachment on the precapitalist markets. What is required logically, in other words, is the existence of precapitalist markets that can be encroached upon, not any actual significant encroachment upon such markets. They constitute in short, "reserve markets" on a par with the reserve army of labor. And they do so because goods from the capitalist sector can always displace local production in the precapitalist economy, causing deindustrialization[4] and unemployment there.

Such periodic displacement leaves behind a pauperized mass in the precapitalist economy, which constitutes for the capitalist sector a second, and distantly located reserve army, in addition to what exists within the capitalist sector itself. This distantly located reserve army ensures that the money wage rate of the workers situated in the midst of this reserve army changes only slowly over time.[5] These workers, in short, are price-takers—or, more accurately, their *ex ante* real-wage claims are compressible precisely because they are located in the midst of vast labor reserves. Since the products they produce enter into the wage and raw material bills of the capitalist sector at the core, they play the role of "shock absorbers" of the capitalist system. Because of them, the capitalist economy remains viable both in the sense of always having a level of activity that exceeds the threshold level that provides it with the minimum acceptable rate of profit, and in the sense that its monetary system can be sustained without any fears of accelerating inflation.

The capitalist mode of production, in short, always needs to exist surrounded by precapitalist modes that are not left in their pristine purity but are modified and altered in a manner that makes them serve the needs of capitalism better. The incompleteness of propertyism can be overcome through a cognizance of capitalism as being ensconced always within such a setting.

This perception, though it has some affinity with that of Rosa Luxemburg, differs from hers in crucial ways. First, as already mentioned, it emphasizes the qualitative role of the precapitalist markets more than their quantitative role, and it certainly does not see them as the location for the realization of the entire surplus value of the capitalist sector in every period. Second, it does not see the precapitalist sector as getting assimilated into the capitalist sector and hence vanishing as a distinct species over time; rather, it remains as a ravaged and a degraded economy, the location of a vast pauperized mass of displaced petty producers, a distant labor reserve, which serves the needs of capitalism by ensuring the stability of its monetary system.

Social Relations Underlying Money

Underlying a modern monetary economy, therefore, is a set of social relations that are necessarily unequal and oppressive. The stability of the value of money is based on the persistence of these relations. This does not of course mean that each and every money-using capitalist economy actually has to impose such unequal and oppressive relations upon some particular segment of its precapitalist environment. Typically such capitalist economies are bound together within an overall international monetary system, and the leading capitalist power of the time undertakes the task of imposing the requisite unequal relations upon the "outside" world of precapitalist and semicapitalist economies. The stability of the value of money then gets linked to the stability of the international monetary system, taking the form above all of the persistence of the confidence of the capitalist world's wealth holders in the leading economy's currency as a stable medium for holding wealth.

It is not always obvious that this role of the leading country's currency arises from its ability to sustain a set of unequal and oppressive global relationships. It is sometimes thought that this role arises from the leading currency's being linked to precious metals. But this is erroneous. The link to precious metals itself cannot be sustained in the absence of such relationships. The stability of the international monetary system during the years of the gold standard arose not because of the gold backing of the currencies, including especially of the pound sterling, which was the leading currency of the time; it arose because Britain could impose a set of oppressive and unequal relationships over the large tracts of the globe that constituted her formal and informal empire. The maintenance of the gold link was a signal to wealth holders that these relationships continued. And when these relationships were undermined in the interwar period, even though the pound sterling was formally linked to gold again, this link could not be sustained.

It follows from this that even in the absence of any formal link to precious metals, as long as the leading capitalist power can establish such global relationships, its currency will still be considered "as good as gold"; that is, even a pure dollar standard can constitute the international monetary system as long as the United States can establish the global hegemony required to instill confidence among the capitalist world's wealth holders that its currency is "as good as gold." A precondition for that, however, is that the value of its labor power in terms of its currency must be relatively stable (which rules out significant inflation, let alone accelerating inflation within its own territory); and, related to that, the value of crucial imported inputs that go into the wage bill and materials bill, should also be relatively stable. In fact, as long as this latter condition holds and domestic labor reserves are large enough to prevent any autonomous wage push,[6] inflation can be ruled out as a source of destabilizing its currency's role as a stable wealth-holding medium. The most significant imported input being oil, a dollar standard can work as long as the dollar price of oil is relatively stable. What appears at first sight as a pure dollar standard, on a closer look must therefore be an oil-dollar standard. The post–Bretton Woods monetary system can be characterized not as a dollar standard but more accurately as an oil-dollar standard. The world may have, to all appearances, done away with commodity money with the delinking of dollar from gold. But the crux of the argument of this book is that it can never do so. The value of money, even paper/credit money, arises because of its link to the world of commodities.

The worldwide quest for oil and natural gas that is currently on, led by the United States, is fed not just by the desire to acquire these resources for use. It is fed even more strongly by the need to preserve the oil-dollar standard. Even Alan Greenspan has openly admitted that the invasion of Iraq was for acquiring control over its immense oil reserves; doubtless similar motives underlie the threatened action against Iran. A common perception is that such acquisition of control is needed by the United States and other advanced countries because they are the main consumers of this resource, which is currently under alien ownership. This may be so. But an extremely significant motive that is almost invariably missed is that control over oil is essential for the preservation of the present international monetary system.

This may appear strange at first sight because the very attempt at such control has been accompanied by a massive increase in the dollar price of oil. But that is because the Iraq invasion has not gone according to plan. And in any case a rise in the oil price per se is not destabilizing if it does not trigger persistently higher inflation and if it does not give rise to expectations of persistent increases in the oil price itself or in the general price level in the leading country. Obituaries to the prevailing international monetary system, entailing dollar hegemony, are premature. But while this may be so, there is an important sense in which the capitalist world is more and more beset with difficulties.

Capitalism in Its Maturity

Rosa Luxemburg drew from her analysis the conclusion that the capitalist system was faced with the inevitability of "collapse," when the entire precapitalist sector would be assimilated into the capitalist sector. No such conclusion follows from the argument advanced in this book; and no such conclusion can be validly drawn about capitalism. Contemporary capitalism, however, is faced with serious difficulties, many of which spring from the advance of capitalism itself.

Two consequences of maturity are obvious. First, the weight of the precapitalist sector, and hence of the precapitalist market, declines over time relative to the size of the capitalist sector, so that it is no longer able to play the same role in providing an exogenous stimulus to the capitalist sector as it did earlier. Second, the decline in the share of primary commodity inputs (other than oil) in the gross value of output of the capitalist metropolis, itself a legacy of past squeezes on primary producers, implies that any further squeeze on them becomes increasingly unfruitful. Compression of the *ex ante* claims of such producers, ceases to be a potent weapon for preventing accelerating inflation at the prevailing level of activity.

The first of these problems can be overcome through "demand management" by the state. But with the globalization of finance, not all states can do so, since such state activism will frighten speculators. The government of the leading capitalist country, the United States (whose currency is considered "as good as gold"), can still afford to run a fiscal deficit to stimulate world demand, and a current deficit vis-à-vis its rival capitalist powers to offer them a larger market. It can, in short, act as a surrogate world-state, expanding the level of activity in the world capitalist economy.

There are two obvious obstacles to this. First, the U.S. government, which *can* act as a surrogate world-state, is nonetheless a nation-state. It can scarcely be expected to be altruistic enough to stimulate the level of activity in the capitalist world as a whole, not just within its own borders, while increasing the external indebtedness of its own economy (which such expansionary intervention will entail). Secondly, even at a relatively low level of activity in the capitalist world, the U.S. economy is already becoming more and more indebted. It can scarcely be expected to compound this problem any further for altruistic ends, which implies that the demand stimulus in the capitalist world, and hence the trend rate of growth, will continue to remain low.

The growing U.S. debt, even at the current level of activity, represents a potential threat to its hegemony, and indeed a unique development. The idea of the leading capitalist power also being the most indebted one represents an unprecedented situation in the history of capitalism. To be sure, the leading capitalist power, in order to preserve its leadership role by accommodating the ambitions of its newly industrializing rival powers, has, at a certain stage of its career, necessarily got to run a current account deficit with respect to them. Britain, the leading capitalist power of the time, had to do the same in the late nineteenth and early twentieth centuries, a period of significant diffusion of capitalism. But Britain did not become indebted in the process; on the contrary, it became the most important creditor nation of the world exactly during this very period. The case with the United States today is the exact opposite.

The main reason for the difference is that Britain used her tropical colonies and semicolonies to find markets for its goods, which were increasingly unwanted within the metropolis; and since the primary commodities produced by these colonies and semicolonies were demanded by its newly industrializing rivals, they were made to earn an export surplus vis-à-vis the latter, which not only balanced Britain's current account deficit with them but even provided an extra amount for capital exports to these newly industrializing economies. Britain did not have to pay for this extra amount, since it simply appropriated gratis a part of the surplus value produced in these colonies and semicolonies that financed these capital exports. The United States today lacks such colonies; and as already mentioned, the relative importance in value terms of primary commodity exports to the metropolis has declined so greatly that such an arrangement will no longer work. Political control over oil-rich countries does offer some prospects of successfully resurrecting the old British-style colonial arrangement for settling current accounts without getting indebted. And this, as we have already seen, is exactly what the United States is tempted to acquire.

Thus what lies ahead are a prolonged period of slow growth for the capitalist metropolis, growing indebtedness for the leading capitalist power, and looming uncertainty over the continuation of the oil-dollar standard and the general health of the international monetary system. All this is occurring in the midst of an "opening up" of the third world to the unfettered movement of globalized finance and the unrestricted operations of multinational corporations, and attempts by the leading capitalist power at the political recapture of the oil-rich third-world countries. In the absence of a conscious effort to transcend this situation, it will trap humankind in the vicious grip of a dialectic of imperialist aggrandizement, both engendering and deriving legitimacy from a destructive terrorism as its counterpart. Nobody can seriously believe that this is the final destiny of humankind. To overcome this conjuncture, however, we have to free ourselves first from the blinkers of mainstream economics.

The Value
of Money

1

The Great Divide in Economics

THE CIRCUMSTANCES OF ITS BIRTH have left an indelible imprint on the development of economics as a subject. When Adam Smith wrote *The Wealth of Nations*, his objective was, among other things, to provide the theoretical basis for the removal of the fetters imposed on the emergence of the bourgeois mode of production by the feudal-mercantilist policies of the state. To this end, he showed that a bourgeois civil society, taken as a "complete system" in itself—that is, in isolation both from the state and from its specific surroundings—constituted in its spontaneous operation a "benevolent" and self-acting economic order.[1]

Three elements of this demonstration deserve emphasis. The first is the unit of analysis, namely a bourgeois civil society in isolation. This civil society, to be sure, was not visualized as existing in isolation, that is, without a state, but the state provided only certain minimum prerequisites for the functioning of the civil society, such as law and order; it did not intrude into this functioning, which was seen in its spontaneity. Second, this spontaneous functioning was seen as resulting in the establishment of not only an overall order out of the chaos of myriad individual decisions, but also an order independent of the will and consciousness of the individual participants. This perception echoed the dictum of Hegelian philosophy, which represented a parallel intellectual development to classical political economy,[2] that the "whole" is not merely the sum of the "parts." Third, the "whole," that is, the overall functioning of the system, was seen to be in some sense beneficent, even though the motives underlying the myriad individual actions that went into the fashioning of this "whole" were by no means noble. Smith might have explicitly rejected Mandeville's notion of "private vice, public virtue," but his own perception was not free of its shadow (Dobb 1973, 38).

Liberal economic thought has never really outgrown these basic Smithian birthmarks, no matter how varied in terms of detailed content the alternative theoretical traditions that subsequently made their appearance may have been. Even Marx, the most trenchant critic of bourgeois economic theory in both its classical and its vulgar incarnations,[3] conducted his analysis within these broadly Smithian parameters, with of course one major qualification. He saw the spontaneity of the "self-acting economic order" as productive not of unmitigated beneficence but of class exploitation and class antagonism, which, notwithstanding the enormous development of productive forces it unleashed to start with, would eventually yield stagnation, decay, and social break-down, necessitating its own historical superseding.

We will discuss Marx later. But this Smithian imprint is most clearly visible in what is today the dominant strand of liberal economics, namely Walrasianism, whose raison d'être is to show how a bourgeois civil society considered in isolation reaches an economic equilibrium that is beneficial in some sense for all participants. Indeed, this strand is often explicitly claimed to be the direct descendant of Smithianism.

This claim is questionable. The differences between the Smithian and the Wal-rasian conceptions are enormous; they relate to basic methodological constructs, to categories of analysis, and even to perceptions about the meaning of the term *benefi-cence of the market*. At the methodological level, the Smithian notion of equilibrium (where "natural prices" prevail) as a center of gravity toward which market prices gravitate, is far removed from the Walrasian notion of equilibrium, which is exclu-sively short-run and concerned with market prices alone. Likewise, the difference in the categories of analysis in the two systems is obvious: Smith conducted his analysis in class categories, to which the numerous individual agents belonged, while in the Walrasian system it is individuals as individuals who reign supreme. Above all, how-ever, the Smithian and the Walrasian systems differ on the very criteria for defining the beneficence of the market. Smith sees the beneficence of the market as consisting in its ability to usher in "progress," defined in terms of material production, or "the wealth of nations." (It is for this reason that his emphasis on "increasing returns" is so crucial an ingredient of Smith's thought.) Smith's notion of "progress," in other words, is close to what Marx was later to call "the development of the productive forces." By contrast the beneficence of the market in the Walrasian system is seen to consist in the fact that a competitive equilibrium yields an optimum outcome in Pareto's sense (namely, at this equilibrium no one can become better off without some one else becoming worse off).

This proposition, which is the centerpiece of modern general equilibrium theory, is really not much of an advertisement for the beneficence of the free market. In fact, notwithstanding its mathematical elegance, it is almost a tautology. As long as it is individuals as individuals, always mindful of their self-interest and differentiated from one another only by differences in endowments and tastes, who participate in the mar-ket, and that entirely voluntarily, with complete freedom to withdraw from it if they so desire, without any threat to their survival, it stands to reason that they must be better off through market participation than otherwise. And as long as "competition" ensures that nobody has any control over prices and everybody acts as price taker, it stands to reason that spontaneous price movements, assumed to occur precisely for this very purpose, would eliminate any slack in the system in the sense of unrealized benefits of commerce, thus ensuring that no person in equilibrium can be made better off without someone else becoming worse off. This proposition therefore is not only a rather shallow demonstration of the beneficence of the market, deriving conclusions that are almost assumed, but it can also scarcely stand on a par with Smith's Hegelian proposition that "the whole is not the sum of the parts": the "whole" here is taken to consist almost exclusively of the sum of "parts." (This is even truer, as we will see, of more recent advances such as rational-expectations equilibria.)

Nonetheless, the common strands between Smithianism and Walrasianism, notwithstanding differences in the perception of beneficence, should not be overlooked. An essential characteristic of an equilibrium with beneficent properties must be that it is not demand-constrained, for if it is demand-constrained then the system can be accused of possessing inherent "irrationality" that prevents the full utilization of the productive potential of society, defined not in any absolute sense but even within the given context. In such a case, to call the equilibrium beneficent, no matter how we define the term, would scarcely carry any conviction. Thus, from Smith to modern general equilibrium theory, the beneficent equilibrium that bourgeois civil society, taken in isolation, has been assumed to achieve spontaneously, has been an equilibrium where demand plays no constraining role.

Moreover, the theoretical objective of modern general equilibrium theory is reminiscent of Smithianism: to demonstrate the essential coherence inherent in the economic functioning of the bourgeois civil society. Its universe therefore is the same as that of Smith, namely, the bourgeois civil society taken in isolation, where it shows the spontaneous achievement of an equilibrium imbued with beneficent properties arising inter alia from its being unaffected by demand constraints.

The purpose of this book is to show that any theoretical system that is built around the bourgeois civil society in isolation is fundamentally incomplete. Among such systems, however, which virtually cover the entire corpus of economic theory, a distinction has to be drawn between two strands. The theoretical analysis of one of these strands is fundamentally logically flawed. The other strand overcomes this logical flaw, but it suffers from the contradictions of an incomplete break, in the sense of remaining trapped within the assumption of a closed capitalist system, because of which it, too, remains incomplete. The distinction between these two strands is of great intrinsic importance and should not be lost sight of in the process of developing a general critique of economic theory on account of its looking at capitalism in isolation.

The distinction between these two strands comes out most clearly in their respective theories of the value of money, which accordingly is the central concern of this book. The two strands on the theory of money, and hence by implication on economic theory as a whole, are christened in this book the "monetarist" and the "propertyist" strands.

The Schism in Economics

Economics as a discipline is characterized by several "great divides." The one most commonly identified is the divide between what are, paradoxically, called the classical and the neoclassical traditions, which can, with less ambiguity, be described as the "Ricardo-Marx" and the "Menger-Jevons-Walras" traditions. Among the many and obvious differences between these two traditions, the one that stands out most sharply for a contemporary economist—especially after the labors of Piero Sraffa (1960)—is that income distribution among the two main classes in the former is independently (socially) determined, and the price system is erected on the basis of it. The relative prices between commodities in equilibrium, according to this tradition, is independent of demand, and dependent, solely instead, on the conditions of production and this separately determined distributional parameter. In the Menger-Jevons-Walras—or, more simply, the "marginalist"— tradition, by contrast, all prices, including factor prices (and hence the distribution of income between the two main classes) are determined by demand and supply.

This, to be sure, is a divide of enormous significance. And yet it is quite unsatisfactory to take this as *the* divide, owing to the fact that on both sides of this divide there is a common belief that capitalism, through its internal devices, functions, on average, in the neighborhood of full capacity. Barring Marx, who rejected Say's law explicitly (even though he subscribed to this view of near-full capacity production *on average*), all the other protagonists on either side of this divide were believers in Say's law, that is, in the proposition that aggregate demand cannot be a constraint on output (or, in Say's words, "supply creates its own demand").

This division, in other words, implicitly deprecates the significance of the Keynes-Kalecki revolution, and hence the *theoretical* significance of the demand constraint under capitalism. To be sure, capitalism has not *empirically* been a system that is forever bogged down in a demand constraint of any severity, but then capitalism has never existed in isolation from other surrounding precapitalist and noncapitalist economies, such as is assumed in the theoretical universe constructed by authors on both sides of the divide. This empirical fact cannot justify a depreciation of the theoretical significance of the demand constraint. The legitimacy of this particular "great divide" therefore becomes questionable.

This divide, however, is in conformity with the basic Marxist distinction between the spheres of production and of circulation, and hence between classical political economy, which takes the sphere of production as its point of departure, and so-called vulgar economy, which remains confined to the sphere of circulation. Marx of course subsumed under the latter concept a whole range of relatively minor post-Ricardian writers, and not the authors of the marginalist revolution, among whom Engels referred to Jevons and Menger without, curiously, explicitly labeling them as proponents of vulgar economy.[4] But, strictly speaking, notwithstanding the novelty and the technical sophistication of the marginalists, they would fall under that Marxian rubric.

THE GREAT DIVIDE IN ECONOMICS

Likewise, since the whole question of demand and of "realization" of surplus value (and of social output in general) is a matter pertaining to the sphere of circulation, deprecating the centrality of issues of aggregate demand, as is implied in this particular identification of the "great divide," is a natural part of this basic Marxist position.

Not only is the issue of demand central to capitalism, though it bursts into blinding visibility only sporadically, but this orthodox Marxist interpretation of Marx also does not do justice to Marx himself. Classical capitalism, as Janos Kornai (1979) once remarked, is a "demand-constrained system," while classical socialism (as it then existed) was a "resource-constrained system." The reason why classical capitalism was demand-constrained was discussed with great clarity by none other than Marx himself, who could be considered the pioneer of the Keynes-Kalecki revolution, though he did not carry his ideas in this sphere to their natural, logical conclusion. Putting it differently, Marx authored two great ideas in economics, one concerned with the origin of surplus value, for which he relied very much on Ricardo, and the other concerned with the problem of aggregate demand or the "possibility of generalized overproduction," where he broke sharply with Ricardo. Of the two, he pushed the latter into the background, where it awaited rediscovery by Keynes, Kalecki, and others in the context of the Great Depression; he concentrated instead almost exclusively on the former. He did so, in our view, for reasons having to do with his perception of an imminent proletarian revolution in Europe, for which laying bare the process of exploitation of workers under capitalism was a task of great theoretical urgency, and almost everything else became secondary. But it had the unfortunate effect of submerging a powerful tradition, namely the one that took cognizance of aggregate demand, making it appear to later generations as if it were a preoccupation exclusively of the Keynesians, and preventing an understanding of it in its theoretical totality.

But the effects were even deeper. It is not just that some ideas of Marx were pushed into the background while others got the limelight; since underlying both sets of ideas was a certain unified theoretical system, the pushing into obscurity of one set of ideas meant that this unified theoretical system could never be properly comprehended. The prime example of this is Marx's labor theory of value, which has for long been considered, entirely illegitimately, as being identical with Ricardo's labor theory of value. In short, the pushing into obscurity of one important set of Marx's ideas has meant a lack of understanding of the Marxian system (including its logical problems) in its totality, and hence a misinterpretation of even those components of it which have been in the limelight.

It follows that while the use of the phrase "Ricardo-Marx tradition" is justified to an extent by Marx's own contingent theoretical preoccupations, it prevents a recovery of the other major strand of Marx's thought, which is necessary not merely out of intellectual curiosity or for reasons of hagiography, but for a better understanding, both of the totality of the Marxian system, and of the very real problem of aggregate demand itself. In short, we can identify an alternative "great divide" that exists in economics and has escaped attention till now, a "great divide" between what I would call the "Ricardo-Walras" (monetarist) tradition and the "Marx-Kalecki-Keynes" (propertyist) tradition.

The main reason for discussing "great divides" at all is that they throw light on the present. The "great divide" we focus on at any time is one that is considered most relevant for that time. Given the current sluggishness of the world economy, in contrast to the boom years of the postwar period, the divide between the Ricardo-Walras and the Marx-Kalecki-Keynes traditions, not only *can* but also *should* be considered the "great divide" most relevant for our times. In the present book we focus on *this* "great divide."

The Divide in Terms of the Theory of Money

We have so far talked of the divide in terms of the cognition of the problem of aggregate demand. This, however, is not the basic theoretical difference between the two sides of the divide; it is rather a derivation from the basic theoretical difference, which actually pertains to the theory of the value of money. The monetarist tradition holds that the value of money, like the value of any other commodity, is determined by supply and demand. (Ricardo, who has been included in this tradition, had, to be sure, a more complex theory; but in that theory the short-run value of money in terms of commodities, which is but the reciprocal of the "market price" of commodities in terms of money, was determined by supply and demand.) By contrast, the main feature of the Marx-Kalecki-Keynes tradition is that the value of money in terms of commodities (whether in the short or in the long run) is determined from *outside* the realm of supply and demand, by some exogenous consideration. This tradition considers this "exogenous" determination of the value of money to be a central characteristic of capitalism.

The matter can be looked at somewhat differently. If the excess of demand over supply for any commodity kept *decreasing* as its price fell, then any explanation for the fact of its commanding a positive and finite price in equilibrium, in terms of demand and supply, would be logically untenable. The same holds for money. A demand-supply explanation of the value of money, if it is to explain the fact that money has a positive and finite value in equilibrium, must rule out the possibility of the excess demand for money being an increasing function of its value, that is, a decreasing function of the money price level of commodities. For instance, if money supply is given, then the demand for money must not fall when the money prices of commodities are increasing.

We can go farther. If we are to rule out the possibility of multiple equilibrium values of money, then it must be the case that with given money supply, the demand for money must increase when the money prices of commodities increase.

There is an additional consideration here that is specific to money. In the case of any ordinary nonmoney commodity, to say that, other things remaining the same, its demand increases continuously and monotonically when its relative price falls, may make sense; but not so in the case of money. When the relative price of money falls to zero, that is, when money becomes "worthless," then nobody would demand any of it. Its demand, in other words, must fall to zero when its relative price falls to zero. Hence, for a demand-supply explanation for the value of money (which also explains the fact of money having a positive and finite value) to be logically tenable, two conditions must be satisfied: first, its excess demand must be negatively related to its value; and second, its excess demand must always be such that its value is bounded away from zero. If these two conditions are satisfied and all prices are flexible (which we assume to be the case), then the equilibrium value of money would be determined by demand and supply and would be positive and finite. This is the scenario conjured up by the monetarists. Each of the well-known assumptions in monetarist theory, such as the constancy of the ratio between money income and the demand for money balances — the Cambridge k — or the constancy of the income velocity of circulation of money, is *sufficient* for satisfying both these conditions.[5]

In such a case, since the demand for and supply of money are equal in equilibrium, the demand for and supply of nonmoney commodities taken as a whole must also be equal. The aggregate of nonmoney commodities that is supplied must therefore equal the aggregate that is demanded. Any question of generalized overproduction does not arise. Putting it differently, a deficiency or excess of aggregate demand for nonmoney commodities at any given set of prices must be accompanied by a corresponding excess or deficiency in the demand for money relative to its supply. If the latter is presumed always to be eliminated through a movement of prices, then such price movement ipso facto eliminates the former. The view that the value of money is determined by demand and supply is therefore tantamount to the view that the economy can never be "demand constrained," that whatever is supplied of nonmoney commodities is demanded, and that the economy always functions at "full employment." Monetarism necessarily presumes full employment (or full capacity production, as in Ricardo's case).

By contrast, the other tradition, which I call the Marx-Keynes-Kalecki tradition, believes that the value of money vis-à-vis commodities is not given by their respective demand-supply configurations, but from outside the sphere of demand and supply. This also ensures ipso facto why this value will always be finite and positive. In Marx, who was focusing on commodity money, this value is given by the conditions of production of the money commodity compared to the world of the nonmoney commodities, as captured by the respective amounts of labor directly and indirectly embodied in a unit of each. In Keynes (1949), the value of money in the world of commodities is determined by the fact that the value of one commodity, namely labor (which Marx, more appropriately, calls labor power), in terms of money, is given in any period. This also ensures that the value of money in terms of any or all commodities always remains finite and positive (or, what comes to the same thing, the money price of any and all commodities remains positive and finite), since no commodity can be produced without labor, and the product wage in the case of no commodity can be zero. In Kalecki

(1954) likewise, the value of money in terms of the commodity labor power is given in any period; in addition, since he assumes markup pricing, the value of money in terms of any or all commodities, is also given irrespective of their demand conditions, unlike in Keynes, where demand does affect the product wage.

If the value of money in terms of commodities is not determined by demand and supply in a world with flexible prices, but is fixed in any period in terms of either one or all commodities, then any *ex ante* excess demand for money and *ex ante* excess supply of commodities at "full employment" output cannot obviously be eliminated through price adjustments. Hence the possibility of generalized overproduction emerges, and quantity adjustments inter alia become necessary for ensuring equilibrium between demand and supply. Quite obviously, therefore, locating the determinants of the value of money outside the sphere of demand and supply, immediately gives rise to the possibility of generalized overproduction.

A Closer Look at the Divide

While the link between the belief that the value of money is determined from outside the sphere of demand and supply and the possibility of generalized overproduction is quite clear and has been long recognized, the reason *why* the value of money is seen to be determined from outside the realm of demand and supply by this tradition, is hardly ever appreciated. Wage rigidity in Keynes, for example, is often taken as an *empirical* description of the "real world," whence the claim follows that nothing is wrong with the internal logical structure of monetarism; all that it can be accused of is being out of sync with "reality."

This reading, however, is grossly unfair to Keynes and indeed to this entire tradition. The argument central to this tradition is that a capitalist market economy cannot, logically speaking, function under the assumption of complete price flexibility; inherent to the functioning of a capitalist market economy is an expectation about the value of money that is inelastic with respect to current changes in it. Such an expectation can be entertained by the economic agents only if the determination the value of money is from outside the realm of demand and supply, that is, if the value of money has a degree of invariance with respect to its demand and supply. The dispute between this tradition and monetarism therefore lies not on *empirical questions* but on the *logic of functioning of capitalism*. Let us look at the matter a little more closely.

Any economic agent in a money-using economy is ipso facto holding his or her wealth, no matter for how brief a period, in the form of money. Money necessarily performs the role of a form of wealth in a money-using economy. Even when it functions as a medium of circulation, for the duration that the agent holds M in the C-M-C (commodity-money-commodity) circuit, it is performing a wealth-form role. The moment we recognize this, we must also recognize that the length of time for which M is held in this C-M-C circuit cannot logically be independent of expectations about the future, which means that this length of time cannot be taken to be a constant. Since this length of time is nothing else but a reflection of the ratio of the magnitude of money balance sought to be held by the economic agent to his or her money income, this ratio it follows cannot be taken as constant, in which case, for a given money supply and full employment output, the demand curve for money with respect to its value need not be monotonically downward sloping, and the theory of the determination of the value of money through the interaction of demand and supply ceases to be logically tenable.

Monetarism avoids this problem by assuming constancy in the ratio between the demand for money balance and the money income of an economic agent, or, what effectively comes to the same thing, constancy in the income velocity of circulation of money. This presupposes in effect that money is not a form of wealth. To be sure, monetarism is concerned solely with the role of money as a medium of circulation. But even this role, as just mentioned, presupposes that money must be a form of wealth. To say that monetarism is concerned not with the wealth demand for money but only with the transaction demand (which necessitates the holding of money balances) is to state a widely held view. But this view is partial and inadequate, since there cannot be a transaction demand for money without its being a form of wealth, and hence without there being a wealth demand for it. A hallmark of the Marx-Keynes-Kalecki tradition is the explicit recognition of money as a form of wealth and hence of the wealth demand for money.

If money is a form of wealth, the demand for which is affected by expectations about its value, then it follows that inelastic expectations must prevail if there is to be an equilibrium, which in turn presupposes that there must be some money prices in the economy, pertaining to commodities upon whose prices, in turn, the prices of the entire world of commodities depend, which must be sluggish or rigid. This is nothing else but the determination of the value of money from outside the realm of demand and supply.

A crucial difference, indeed one might even say *the* crucial difference, between monetarism and the propertyist tradition is the latter's recognition of money as a form of wealth, and hence of the fact that it always exists as some one's property; the amount of it held, it follows, is always subject to the wealth holder's choice between different wealth forms. The logical infirmity of monetarism arises from the fact that money cannot be a medium of circulation without being a wealth form: while it invariably sees money in its former garb, it never recognizes money in its latter garb. It is not that monetarists have not been aware of this limitation and have not attempted to correct it; but because this contradiction resides at the very core of monetarism, no attempt, no matter how sophisticated, can overcome it, as we will see. The propertyist tradition sees the "external" determination of the value of money and its capacity to function as property as being intrinsically related.

An Analytical Characterization of Money

We will discuss these two traditions in greater detail. But a preliminary point should be clarified here itself, and that relates to the analytical characterization of money. Marx talked of commodity money, while Keynes talked of fiat money. Keynes himself took money supply as exogenous, while several Keynesians, notably Kaldor, have taken money supply to be endogenous. If these diverse perceptions of money are to be grouped together under one rubric, the propertyist tradition, then the commonness of their perceptions of money must be brought out. This commonness can be captured in the following analytical characterization.

Money is first of all an entity whose excess demand cannot be eliminated through adjustments in its relative value alone. Second, precisely for this reason, the adjustments caused by this excess demand take a form where there is a reduction in the quantity of produced nonmoney commodities, without this reduction being offset by any equivalent increase in the production of money (when money *is* a produced commodity). Putting these two together, we can say that money is that good, the excess demand for which cannot be eliminated through price adjustments alone and gives rise, ceteris paribus, to an excess supply of *all* produced commodities.

A point should be clarified here. Since an excess demand in any market must be matched by an excess supply in some other market, in a world where money is a produced commodity, an excess demand for money must be matched by an excess supply of all nonmoney commodities, but not in an excess supply of all produced commodities, including money. Our characterization therefore must appear prima facie erroneous. But the operative phrase is "gives rise to." While an excess demand for money is necessarily matched by an excess supply only of nonmoney commodities to start with, as adjustments get underway this gets converted to an excess supply of all produced commodities.[6]

The specificity of this characterization can be brought out by contrasting money in this sense with four other concepts. First, it differs from the Ricardian perception of money, since in Ricardo, money being a produced commodity used exclusively as a medium of circulation, an excess demand for it, while it is matched by an excess supply of all nonmoney commodities, does not give rise to an excess supply of all produced commodities (inclusive of the money commodity) as suggested here. Second, it differs from money in the Walrasian world where an excess demand for money, and hence an excess supply of commodities (assuming that all of them are produced commodities), is eliminated through price adjustments alone. Third, while, in a world with produced and nonproduced commodities, any excess demand for a nonproduced commodity, say land, would ipso facto entail an excess supply of the other commodities, including the produced commodities, this would still be eliminated through price changes alone, since neither the wage rate nor any other input price is designated in terms of land (Kaldor 1964; Patnaik 2006). These nonproduced commodities are therefore different from money. (If the wage rate or some input price is designated in terms of land, then in such an economy land acts as money anyway.) Fourth, this definition also captures the difference between money and all other financial assets. An increase in the demand for any financial asset, say bonds or shares, is ipso facto an increase in the demand for capital stock, and hence for producible capital goods. This is not true of money. An increase in the demand for money does not represent, even indirectly, an increase in the demand for any producible nonmoney commodity.

We have so far seen how the analytical characterization proposed above rules out the conception of money in the monetarist tradition; how it captures the conceptions underlying the different authors in the propertyist tradition is a matter that need not detain us here. It will become clear when we discuss the different authors belonging to this tradition. The point to note here is that according to the propertyist tradition, this analytical characterization of money conforms to the basic logical characteristic of money in a money-using market economy.

Part 1

The Infirmity of Monetarism

2

The Monetarist Theory

WHAT EXACTLY CONSTITUTES MONETARISM is a question that needs careful examination. Different writers on the subject emphasize different aspects of monetarism. Among those who are avowedly monetarist there is no homogeneity of views either, with Friedman (1966), for instance, professing to be a Marshallian as against the array of contemporary monetarists all of whom would swear by Walras. And on top of all this, since our characterization of monetarism is an inclusive one, which, departing from the usual dichotomies but with sufficient justification, puts Walras and Ricardo together within this single tradition, a precise delineation of the *differentia specifica* of monetarism becomes important. This cannot consist in the familiar adages, such as, "Monetarism holds that variations in money supply affect only the 'money things' and not the 'real things,'" or, "Monetarism holds the rate of change of money supply as the cause of the rate of change of prices." These statements can at best be consequences of the basic theoretical position of the monetarists, but they do not define that position.

The defining characteristic of monetarism is the proposition that the value of money in the short run is determined by the demand for and the supply of it. This is common to all monetarists by our reckoning, from Ricardo to Walras to the crop of contemporary writers. In fact, the term "short run" is inserted here precisely to permit this wide coverage: while the Walrasian analysis is exclusively confined to the short run anyway (like the Keynesian analysis), Ricardo had a different theory of the value of money in the long run, though he was a monetarist in the short run. Inserting the term "short run" covers them both, though I will frequently use the term "single period" in lieu of it.

To say that the value of money is determined by demand and supply amounts ipso facto to saying that the value of commodities is determined by demand and supply. Monetarism essentially therefore is an assertion of faith in the Walrasian equilibrium. As Hahn (1984) puts it, "The monetarists believe that the real world is characterized by a Walrasian general equilibrium." The Ricardian case, as we will see later, is a specific variation of this. And not too much need be read into Friedman's advocacy of Marshall, since his entire position is based on an unusual and maverick epistemology (on which more later).

The equilibrium is one where the value of money must be positive and finite in terms of all commodities with nonzero money prices. The excess demand for money must be zero when these money prices prevail. The excess demand must therefore be zero for all commodities having nonzero money prices, while for commodities with zero prices the excess demand must be negative—and no commodity can have an infinitely high money price. Such an equilibrium thus precludes the possibility of what is called "technological unemployment" or, sometimes, "Marxian unemployment," that is, unemployment owing to the insufficiency of the means of production, occurring together with a positive wage. It also precludes another kind of unemployment, akin to technological unemployment, that Ricardo emphasized: unemployment owing to the short-run fixity of the wage fund in a situation of a given real wage. (In fact, the nonrecognition of this type of unemployment in the Walrasian system is the basic short-run difference between Ricardo and Walras.) To carry the argument forward, however, I will adopt the Walrasian assumption that there is enough substitutability between inputs in the production process, and enough scope for a reduction in the real wage rate, to rule out technological or Ricardian unemployment.

Assuming for simplicity that there is only one final commodity, so that the marginal product of labor has a clear meaning, it follows that there must be a unique real wage in equilibrium, equal to the marginal product of labor, at which the labor market clears. (We are ignoring here the possibility of labor supply being based on "mistaken" real wage anticipation on the part of the workers.) This real wage must be the outcome of a certain level of money wage and price, at which the money market is in equilibrium. Now, an economically meaningful equilibrium of this sort must be locally stable; otherwise a small deviation from it would give rise to a cumulative movement away from it, or at least a large movement until the economy settles at some new equilibrium (if it exists). It must be the case then that any change in the money wage–money price configuration creates a disturbance in the money market that rectifies this change. The typical manner in which monetarism ensured this is by assuming the aggregate demand for money to be positively related to the aggregate money income. Any change in the money wage rate, then, with price remaining unchanged, would affect the demand for labor in a manner that nullifies such a change. On the other hand, any change in the money wage rate that is accompanied by a pari passu change in price would affect the demand for money in a manner that nullifies such a change. Local stability is thus assured. But, what is more, global stability of the equilibrium is also assured in this case. In other words, if the demand for money is solely a function of money income and is an increasing function, then the equilibrium in this world where there is just one produced commodity, is globally, and hence locally, stable.

The reason for this is simple. The demand for money being an increasing function of money income alone ensures, with a given money supply, a negatively sloping excess demand curve for money with respect to its own value. When the value of money falls, that is, when the commodity price rises, the demand for money, and hence the excess demand for money, increases; likewise, when the value of money rises, the excess demand for money falls. A monotonically downward-sloping excess demand curve of this type ensures a unique equilibrium, if it exists, as well as the local and global stability of that equilibrium.

Looking at the matter formally, when the demand for money is an increasing function of money income alone, we have the satisfaction of the "gross substitute" (GS) assumption, which, in this world, is sufficient for global stability. This assumption, following Mukherji (1990, 71), can be stated as follows:

If p and q are strictly positive prices, and $p \geq q, p \neq q$, then for any j such that $p_j = q_j$, $Z_j(p) > Z_j(q)$, where $Z_j(.)$ refers to the excess demand for j at the price vector $(.)$.

What this means is that in a world of n markets (which includes the money market), if any one price remains unchanged while other prices either increase or remain unchanged (not all can remain unchanged), then the excess demand for that good must increase. In the present case, if the money wage-price configuration (w,p) is greater than configuration (w^*,p^*), then the price vectors can be written as $(1,w,p)$ and $(1,w^*,p^*)$ where 1 is the value of money in terms of itself. To say that the demand for money must be higher at the (w,p) configuration, given the supply of money, amounts therefore to the satisfaction of GS. The monetarist argument that the economy tends to a full employment equilibrium, with the value of money determined by its demand and supply, follows from this implicit assumption that GS is satisfied, which in turn follows from the explicit assumption that the demand for money, and hence its excess demand for a given supply, depends solely on money income and is an increasing function of it.

Monetarist economists traditionally followed two different routes for establishing this functional relationship.[1] One was to say that money was demanded for transaction purposes, that the amount of money demanded depended on the total value of transactions, that the total value of transactions bore a more or less fixed proportion to the value of income transactions, and that the income velocity of circulation of money which depended on "habits and customs," was more or less constant in the short run (though it might be slowly changing over time). It followed, then, that the amount of money demanded in any period would simply depend upon the magnitude of total money income. The second route was the Cambridge route, where the argument did not specifically invoke transaction demand but merely made people's demand for cash balances a constant proportion k of money income, though as a matter of fact k is but the reciprocal of the income velocity.[2]

The first of these routes is questionable, since, strictly speaking, there is no place for a transaction demand for money in a Walrasian equilibrium. In a tatonement process no trade occurs at off-equilibrium prices, and hence the question of a time distance between sale and purchase, which underlies the notion of a transaction demand for money, simply does not arise. Efforts have been made to get around this problem by introducing such a time distance into the Walrasian equilibrium, by assuming, for instance, that the market meets once a week and that the current week's purchases can be financed only with the sale proceeds of the previous week. Thus the transaction demand for money enters the picture disguised as the budget constraint of the economic agent in any particular week. I will examine the validity of this procedure later, but for the time being, since I am sticking to the original Walrasian system (on the basis of which the stability discussion above was carried out), I will ignore this particular route.

The second route is free of this logical problem. Each economic agent, and hence all of them in the aggregate, simply wish to hold an amount of money that is a certain proportion k of their respective money incomes. And if this is the case, the Walrasian equilibrium would be stable, and the monetarist argument would be valid. The question, however, is: why should economic agents wish to hold an amount of money balance that bears a certain fixed ratio to their money income? Why should k, for instance, not depend upon expectations about the future price, rising when the price of the commodity is expected to fall and falling when the price is expected to rise? In other words, the Cambridge equation, while it does make the monetarist perspective logically valid, lacks any rationale whatsoever.

In view of this, attempts have been made by more recent writers in the monetarist tradition to rescue the theory from this unfounded assumption of a constant k and to base the demand for cash balances instead on the outcome of an optimization exercise. These attempts will be reviewed in a later chapter; for the time being, we will consider the implications of the constant k assumption under which the monetarist theory becomes logically unassailable.

The Constant-k Assumption

Let us for simplicity look at a one-good world. With the constant-k assumption, given production function and labor supply as a function of the real wage, expectations about the future cease to matter for the general equilibrium. With a given capital stock, a given production function, and a given labor supply function, the equilibrium real wage gets determined. And given the money stock and k, the money wage rate and price are determined. Expectations about the future may play a role in determining the division of output between consumption and savings, but since money is not a form of holding wealth (otherwise k would not be constant), all "investment-seeking" savings[3] are necessarily invested in equilibrium (that is, held as additional physical capital stock), no matter what the mechanism for ensuring this equality may be.[4] Whether more or less savings occur affects the future, but not the shape of the current equilibrium where all the monetary magnitudes and the real wage and output are uniquely determined, unaffected apparently by expectations.

Since this holds in every period, it follows that for a constant k,

$$m = \pi + n + \beta \tag{2.1}$$

where m is the rate of growth of money supply, π the rate of growth of price, n the rate of growth of the labor force, and β the rate of growth of labor productivity arising from the combined effects of capital deepening and labor-augmenting technological progress. On the steady state where there is no further capital deepening, the rate of inflation simply becomes the difference between the (exogenously given) rate of growth of money supply and the "natural rate of growth" of the economy. This is the form in which we normally recognize monetarism.

Under these assumptions, and also assuming, in the manner of old growth theory, that technological progress is purely labor augmenting (Harrod-neutral) and occurs at a constant exogenous rate, the only role that expectations can play in (2.1) is via the division of current income between consumption and savings, and hence via the pace of capital deepening. Even this meager role, however, is denied to expectations if either one of two extreme assumptions is made about savings behavior. One is the assumption of a constant savings propensity such as Solow (1956) had made (or some alternative version of it), which makes savings independent of expectations; the other is the assumption of rational expectations, where each economic agent decides on his or her savings in any period by carrying out a Ramsay-type optimization exercise. Here the individual agent is taken as a microcosm of society. He or she believes, correctly it is supposed, that every other agent is doing the same and that the aggregate of these optimization exercises is actual social optimization à la Ramsay. Expectations in this case cease to matter, since individual decision making becomes no different de facto from that of a central planner.

What exactly do we mean by "money" in this context and how does it enter the economy? The only "money" in such a world can be that which enters the economy either through domestic commodity-money production, or through commodity money imported from outside, or in the form of non-interest-bearing government debt against purchases by the government.[5] It is the notion of money in the first two senses that figured prominently in Ricardo and Marx, while it is the notion of money in the last sense that figures in current general equilibrium literature following Malinvaud (1977). The process of the entry of money into the economy can be seen as follows: when domestic or foreign gold producers or the government make money available they obtain some commodities in lieu of it. If dM represents the additional money supply and M_0 the initial stock of money in the economy, then we can say that in equilibrium

$$M_0 + dM = k \cdot p \cdot Q^* \tag{2.2}$$

where Q^* is full employment output. In the next period, $M_0 + dM$ will be the initial money stock, which together with the additional money supplied in the next period, will determine, given next period's full employment output, the next period's price level. This is the way that equation (2.1) will hold over time.

Alternatively, we can imagine the supply of money being linked to the purchase of a specified amount of goods, say q^* (which will be particularly true when money is government debt). In such a case we can say that

$$M_0 + p \cdot q^* = k \cdot p \cdot Q^* \tag{2.3}$$

which determines p as long as $q^* / Q^* < k$. Again with $M_0 + pq^*$ being the next period's initial money stock, we get a sequence of equilibria through which (2.1) holds. In fact if q^* / Q^* is a constant, then we can simply substitute k by k', which equals $(k - q^* / Q^*)$ and relate the price prevailing in each period simply to the initial money stock on the assumption of a constant k', that is,

$$M_0 = k' \cdot p \cdot Q^*$$

in which case the rate of growth of money is exogenously given by

$$m = p \cdot q^* / M_0 = p \cdot q^* / k' \cdot p \cdot Q^* = p \cdot (k - k') \cdot Q^* / k' \cdot p \cdot Q^*$$
$$= k / k' - 1 \tag{2.4}$$

The monetarist argument, however, as we will see in a subsequent chapter, is incompatible with "inside money," whether it exists exclusively or in addition to "outside" money. A logically consistent monetarist story thus can be erected on the assumption of a constant k and the exclusive prevalence of "outside" money. In this story, however, expectations play no role whatsoever in determining the single-period equilibrium. The moment we introduce expectations or "inside" money, which necessarily entails inherited payments obligations by private economic agents, the logical structure of monetarism becomes untenable. Since both expectations and inherited payments obligations are symptomatic of a world existing in historical time, the point can be more generally expressed: Monetarist logic fails to hold in historical time. Indeed, all attempts to reconstruct the monetarist argument taking historical time into account, in the context, for example, of a "temporary equilibrium" analysis of the Walrasian system, have been logically flawed. The remaining chapters of this part are devoted to establishing this and thereby leading up to the conclusion that in a world with historical time the value of money cannot be determined by demand and supply; it must be given from "outside" the realm of demand and supply.

Since monetarist theory is derived basically from the Walrasian general equilibrium analysis applied to a world with money, any critique of the Walrasian analysis is ipso facto a critique of monetarism as well.[6] In the remaining chapters in this part, sometimes the Walrasian system in general and at other times the monetarist theory specifically are critiqued. It should be borne in mind that both discussions constitute a critique of monetarism, even though this may not always be explicitly stated. We begin by looking at Walrasian analysis in the context of historical time, especially when payment commitments are inherited.

3

Equilibrium and Historical Time

THE REAL THEORETICAL INNOVATION of the Keynesian revolution, according to Joan Robinson (1966), relates to the treatment of time: the short period of time that was its focus of analysis was located emphatically between a past that was given and unalterable and a future that was unknown. This, she believed, was the *differentia specifica* of the Keynes-Kalecki breakthrough.

Some may question this claim. In comparison with the neoclassical tradition of his day, which tended to deal in terms of logical rather than historical time, this might well have been *the* innovation introduced by Keynes; but, the Walrasian system, as opposed to other neoclassical systems, is certainly capable of being formulated in a manner that does no apparent violence to the concept of historical time. Here, too, we are concerned with a brief chunk of time (the "single period" or "the short period") to which an unalterable past bequeaths a certain set of endowments and tastes, distributed in a particular manner among the economic agents, and a set of techniques of production available to all. Here, too, an unknown future can be made to cast its shadow upon the present in so far as the current period's equilibrium is dependent upon a given set of expectations about the future among the economic agents, the expectations themselves differing among agents. In short, one can think of the Walrasian short-period equilibrium as being a temporary equilibrium dependent upon tastes, technology, the magnitude and distribution of endowments as inherited from the past, and the whole set of expectations among the economic agents about the future.

Temporary Equilibrium

The problem of treating the present as being sandwiched between an unalterable past and an unknown future does not therefore appear to cause any difficulties for the Walrasian analysis, not of course in its original form, or in its Arrow-Debreu version (1954), but in its subsequent reformulations, in which case counting the incorporation of historical time as a virtue, exclusively, of the Keynesian system becomes an act of unfairness to the Walrasian system. Moreover, if the Walrasian system can be reformulated to incorporate historical time, then one would have to concede willy-nilly that the Keynesian equilibrium is really some sort of a "special," or "deviant," or at best "empirically more realistic" (involving rigid wages) case of the Walrasian equilibrium, entailing nothing *theoretically* novel.[1]

This, however, is an erroneous position. It is erroneous not only to see the Keynesian "equilibrium" as a special case of the Walrasian equilibrium, but also to believe that the Walrasian equilibrium can be reformulated (or has been reformulated) to incorporate historical time. The Walrasian temporary equilibrium constitutes at best a partial incorporation of historical time, not a genuine incorporation. This is because, while it can introduce expectations about the future, it cannot deal with payment commitments inherited from the past; indeed, any view that sees markets as "clearing" through price flexibility in any particular period is incompatible with a recognition of the fact that money-payment commitments are carried over from one period to the next, and hence of the fact of inherited payments commitments in the period under discussion.

This point, though obvious, is scarcely recognized in the literature. Consider, for instance, the so-called real-balance effect that has played such an important role in the attempt to revalidate the pre-Keynesian belief in the immanent tendency of a free market economy, with money wage and price flexibility, to reach full employment. The argument is simple: with a given amount of money balance, a fall in money wages and prices increases the amount of real balance with the economic agents. Even if we do not assume any proportionate relationship, of the Cambridge-equation variety, between the demand for money balance and money income (or, what comes to the same thing, between the demand for real balance and real income), as long as the demand for real balance, no matter how complexly determined, does not increase to the same extent as its supply, as is the case when agents are supposed to be behaving optimally under plausible assumptions, there would be an increase in the demand for goods. In short, a reduction in money wages and prices will raise the demand for non-money commodities, resulting in an increase in output and employment. And this process would go on until full employment is reached.[2]

The problems with the real-balance effect (even leaving aside the fact, discussed later, that the very carrying of money balances requires the satisfaction of certain stringent conditions) are well known: it requires that the actions of those who obtain wealth gains from a fall in the money prices of commodities are not nullified by the opposite actions of those who suffer wealth losses by such a fall (which is why there can be no real-balance effect in an inside-money world, where money represents a claim of private economic agents upon one another); its magnitude, and even direction, depends upon the elasticity of wage, price, and employment expectations among economic agents (and even the elasticity condition itself varies, depending upon the *form*, whether money or commodities, in which wealth can be carried from one period to the next); and its operation is determined by the precise nature of the optimizing exercise which the agents are supposed to be carrying out.[3]

In addition to all these factors there is something else that was noted by Kalecki: namely, a fall in commodity prices would threaten firms with bankruptcy, since they have inherited debt commitments (which is *not* the same as the usual statement that debtors lose from price falls). Thus, even if it is the case that such a price fall would lead to a net expansion in consumption demand, if firms become insolvent as a result of it, one can scarcely see it as an "equilibrating" mechanism in the market.

The issue is deeper than merely the real-balance effect; it concerns the theoretical compatibility of a flexible-price equilibrium with inherited payments commitments. The present chapter is devoted to this issue and its implications for monetarism.

Two Concepts of Expectations

At the very outset, it is worth distinguishing between two quite different notions of expectations. I would call them "expectations underlying the equilibrium" and "expectations about the equilibrium." The first is what we have been talking about: in any economy where there are assets promising returns into the future, the current prices of such assets must depend inter alia upon these expected returns, which means that the *current* price vector of *all* the commodities must depend upon the vector of prices *expected* to rule in the future by each of the economic agents.

The second notion arises from the fact that transactions do not actually occur at equilibrium prices. This is particularly true of the labor market, because of which labor supply becomes in effect a function of the real wage that is expected to prevail in equilibrium rather than of any actual real wage.[4] The problem this gives rise to can be seen as follows.

Given the expectations about future periods, which let us assume remain completely invariant with respect to all changes in the current period, if labor supply is taken, as is the usual practice, to be a function of the real wage rate, then there would be a Walrasian temporary equilibrium associated with a unique real wage rate; and with given money supply this would mean a unique money wage rate and a unique vector of prices. But the wage bargain is *not* in real terms, and the equilibrium real wage is a phenomenon that is observable *only* in equilibrium. Workers would determine their labor supply then on the basis of what they *think* the equilibrium real-wage rate to be, that is, on the basis of their expectations *about* the equilibrium. In other words, labor supply, which is in principle a function of the actual real wage rate, becomes in practice a function of the expected real wage. In such a case, however, workers' expectations about the equilibrium (in the sense of where the economy would come to rest) may well affect the position of the equilibrium, that is, the position of the actual state of rest itself.

This point is recognized in the monetarist literature, and it is what permits the monetarists to reconcile their belief in a natural rate of unemployment that must prevail in equilibrium with the observed fact that state intervention *can* reduce the unemployment rate below (what they consider to be) the NRU. The reason the actual rate of unemployment can deviate from the natural rate is that workers' labor supply depends on the expected wage rate which need not equal the actual wage rate; that is, the workers' expectations *about* the equilibrium differs from the actual state of rest of the economy.

But there is a deeper problem here. Consider a situation where their expected real wages are a monotonic function exclusively of the money wages they are offered, and they stop supplying labor below a certain minimum expected real wage; then in the event of the money wage rate corresponding to the Walrasian equilibrium being associated with an expected real wage below this minimum, the Walrasian equilibrium would simply become inaccessible. And at the money wage rate that would prevail at the state of rest of the economy, which would be a non-Walrasian (Keynesian) equilibrium, there would be excess labor supply or involuntary unemployment.

This is by no means the only or the essential characteristic of the Keynesian equilibrium and its difference from the Walrasian equilibrium: our argument is that the differences are far more profound. This illustrates the distinction between "expectations underlying the equilibrium" and "expectations about the equilibrium." Given the former, a Walrasian equilibrium may exist whose configuration depends on those expectations (that is, they *underlie* this equilibrium). But even if it exists it may not be *accessible* because of expectations *about* the equilibrium, in which case the actual equilibrium configuration of the economy, where it would rest, would be quite different from the Walrasian one. Expectations about equilibrium, in other words, may not create problems as far as the existence of a Walrasian equilibrium is concerned, but they do create problems with regard to the accessibility of it. Since our concern in what follows would be with *existence* problems, we shall rule out accessibility problems arising from expectations about equilibrium, by assuming that if a Walrasian equilibrium exists then every economic agent correctly forecasts what the configurations of this (short-period) equilibrium would be, though their expectations about the future, on which this short-period equilibrium is based, may be way off the mark.

Once this assumption is made and we rule out problems arising from expectations about the equilibrium, it may appear that we are back to the point where we started, namely that the Walrasian "temporary" equilibrium can be located within historical time, that the cognition of historical time is not an exclusive contribution of the Keynesian revolution, and that the Keynesian equilibrium is only a special case of the Walrasian equilibrium (shorn of accessibility problems), under the (perhaps more "realistic") assumption of rigid money wages. Such is not the case: the Walrasian equilibrium, in fact, cannot fully cognize historical time.

Walrasian Equilibrium and Historical Time

The Walrasian equilibrium is indeed located in a chunk of time that is sandwiched between an irrevocable past that has bequeathed a legacy and an unknown future about which there can only be expectations. But the legacy it recognizes as being bequeathed is a legacy of endowments, not a legacy of commitments. The distinction may appear at first sight to be a case of overstretching, but it is of crucial importance.[5]

In a monetary economy where the concept of Walrasian equilibrium is based necessarily on the assumption of complete flexibility of all money prices, including the money wage rate, it is clear that the values of the endowments of the agents would keep changing as prices change, and there would be important wealth-redistribution effects across agents. But no matter how these changes occur, and no matter what the wealth redistribution effects, each agent can simply look at his own endowments at the new prices (which he takes as his parameter) and work out his plans. In other words, recognition of the effects of price changes on the endowments of the agents is still perfectly compatible with treating each agent as an atomistic individual. Each works out his plans entirely in isolation on the basis of his endowments and expectations, taking tastes, technology, and of course prices as parameters.[6]

The legacy of payment commitments, however, is an altogether different entity from the legacy of endowments. If some agents are supposed to make available predetermined nominal sums to others, then the latter's demand for commodities depends upon the extent of the former's honoring these commitments. And since this extent in turn depends upon the prices which the former get for the commodities they sell as well as their endowments, it makes the demand of one set of agents dependent inter alia upon the endowments of another set of agents. It is easy to see that a Walrasian equilibrium may not exist at all under these circumstances, or, putting it differently, predetermined payments commitments create serious existence problems for such an equilibrium. Thus, when the concept of historical time encompasses the legacy of predetermined payments commitments, the concept of a Walrasian equilibrium becomes exceedingly problematical.

A Simple Example of Equilibrium

Let us consider a very simple situation. In any period of time there are two overlapping generations, the "young" and the "old." The "young," who are born at the beginning of the period, supply all the labor and obtain wages; the "old," who die at the end of the period, invest their savings accumulated out of their wages earned at the end of the previous period when they were "young," to obtain an amount, principal plus return on it, which they consume. (In keeping with mainstream tradition, we do not talk of workers and capitalists.) All incomes are earned and all consumption and savings are undertaken at the end of the period.

On the production side, we assume that there is one output that is produced with the help of labor and a circulating input (which gets used up in one period itself) consisting of this very good. Since this commodity can be stored for consumption, the rate of return on investment cannot be negative if investment is positive. The production function has all the neoclassical properties.

Firms, which in this context must be worker-managed and whose management therefore must change from one period to the next, possess a stock of money for their transactions. For simplicity we assume that the income velocity of circulation of money is unity, in the sense that each unit of money is used only once in the purchase of the good (which means, however, that it is actually used more than once, since money payments to labor and capital have to be made before any goods are purchased). In other words, the gross value of output is equal to the stock of money in the possession of the firms. With this stock of money, firms pay wages to the young and the principal-plus-interest to the old. This entire sum of money comes back to them in two ways: through the sale of their goods to the young and the old, and through the borrowing of the savings of the young with which they collectively buy inputs from themselves for the next period's production.[7]

Finally, the population is assumed to be stationary.

Let us write down the equations of this system. The young would be maximizing a utility function of the kind (say):

$$U(c_1) + U(c^e_2)$$

subject to

$$(w - p_1 \cdot c_1)(1 + r^e) \geq c^e_2 \cdot p^e_2$$

where subscripts refer to periods (the current being 1), superscript e to "expected," and $w, p, c,$ and r to the money wage rate, commodity price, consumption, and interest rate, respectively.

It follows that for each young person, the level of consumption is given by

$$c_1 = c(w, p_1, r^e, p^e_2) \ldots \tag{i}$$

The production function giving gross output, which is the sum of the net output y and the (circulating) capital K as a function of capital and labor, is:

$$K + y = F(K, L) \ldots F'_k > 0, F'_1 > 0, F''_k < 0, F''_1 < 0 \ldots \tag{ii}$$

In equilibrium we would have:

$$F'_1(L_1) = w / p_1 \ldots \tag{iii}$$

$$F'_k(K_1) = (1 + r_1) \ldots \tag{iv}$$

$$F'_k(K_1) \cdot K_1 + F'_1(L_1) \cdot L_1 = K_1 + y \ldots \tag{v}$$

and hence total consumption of the young will be

$$C_1 = c_1 \cdot L_1 \ldots \tag{vi}$$

It follows that capital stock for the next period will be

$$L_1 \cdot (w / p_1 - c_1) = K_2 \ldots \tag{vii}$$

Total consumption in the economy as a whole of course would be:

$$C = C_1 + K_1 (1 + r) \ldots \tag{viii}$$

Finally, monetary equilibrium would entail:

$$M^* = p_1 \cdot (K_1 + y) \ldots \tag{ix}$$

Given the technology as summed up in the production function, the preferences as summed up in the utility function, the expectations regarding the next period's interest rate and price, the initial money stock and the endowments of capital and labor at the beginning of this period, we have equations (i), (iii), (iv), (v), (vi), (vii), (viii) and (ix) determining the equilibrium values of w, p_1, c_1, C_1, C, r_1, K_2, and y.

This, of course, is the temporary equilibrium, where the equilibrium values are determined inter alia by expectations about the future. Let us, in addition, however, assume static expectations:

$$r^e = r \ldots \tag{x}$$

and

$$p_2^e = p_1 \ldots \tag{xi}$$

With static expectations it can be shown that there exists a stationary equilibrium, such that every period is an exact replica of the preceding one.[8] This equilibrium is characterized by a particular K / L (let us call it k^*), whose determination can be seen as follows.

Since the optimal level of consumption for the young, who are the only ones to have a choice in the matter, would be such as would equate the actual consumption in the current period with the expected consumption in the next period, the savings per young population person in any period, which is the same (owing to the stagnant population assumption) as the capital stock per worker in the next period—$(K / L)_2$ or k_2—would be such that

$$w - k_2 \cdot p_1 = p_2 \cdot k_2 (1 + r).$$

If we put the stationarity condition that $k_2 = k_1$ (and drop subscripts), then the preceding equation can be expressed as

$$w / p_1 - k = k \cdot f'(k) \ldots \tag{i$'$}$$

Since both the LHS and the RHS are functions of k, there is some particular k for which this equality is satisfied, which is our k^*. If the economy starts with a capital-labor ratio of k^*, then it would continue to have the same capital-labor ratio under static expectations and would continue to be on the stationary equilibrium. Putting it differently, we can say that, given the production function (ii), (i$'$), (iii) . . . (xi) determine our set of variables, such that the satisfaction of the following equation

$$M^* = p_1 \cdot K_1 (1 + r) + w \cdot L_1$$

entails the automatic satisfaction of the equation

$$M^* = p_2 \cdot K_2 (1 + r) + w \cdot L_2$$

The money stock, in other words, is adequate for circulating the produced commodities in this stationary equilibrium in every period. If the economy happens to be at such an equilibrium then the fact that there are payments commitments inherited from the past, namely to the old, makes no difference as long as the money stock remains unchanged.

Let us assume that the economy happens to be at this stationary equilibrium (this is just an assumption and we are not claiming any stability property for this stationary equilibrium).[9] It would follow that the consumption per capita would be identical for any member of the population between the two periods. What the economy's being on this equilibrium path implies, however, is that if it is on this path, then it would continue to be on this path. And this remains true even if the payment to the old at the end of the period constitutes an inherited payments commitment. But, as we shall see, if the money stock changes slightly, then, with this inherited payment commitment, a different Walrasian equilibrium would not exist for exactly the same system.

Existence Problems

The firms *ex hypothesi* have inherited a payment commitment to the old at the end of the current period, which equals

$$\{K_1 \cdot (1 + r) \cdot p_0\}$$

where

$$(1 + r) = \delta F / \delta K \text{ at } K_1, L_1$$

and

$$p_1 = M^* / F(K_1, L_1).$$

But suppose owing to unforeseen circumstances the actual money stock turns out to be M^{**}, which equals $\lambda \cdot M^*$ with $\lambda < 1$. Then it is clear that meeting this commitment rules out any Walrasian equilibrium, that is, the existence of a Walrasian equilibrium is incompatible with the honoring of such an outstanding commitment. The reason is as follows.

$$[\{M^{**} - K_1(1 + r) \cdot p_0\} / L_1] / [M^{**} / F(K_1, L_1)] < F'_1(K_1, L_1)$$

The first term on the LHS in square brackets is the money wage rate that can be paid to the workers after meeting the inherited payments obligations from the reduced money stock; the second term is the equilibrium money price that would prevail if all markets cleared. The LHS therefore refers to the real wage rate that would prevail if all markets cleared; the RHS refers to the marginal productivity of labor at full employment. The two cannot be equal. With $\lambda < 1$, LHS < RHS; with $\lambda > 1$, LHS > RHS. The problem, it is clear, would not arise if the second term within the first set of square brackets (in the numerator of the LHS) either did not exist or had p_1 instead of p_0 in it, that is, if either there were no inherited payments commitments whatsoever or such commitments were not fixed *monetary* commitments. But if there are fixed monetary commitments, then a change in the money stock rules out the existence of a Walrasian equilibrium.

Since we have discussed the matter till now in the context of a stationary equilibrium, it may appear as if the problem we are discussing arises only within such a context. This, however, is not the case. In a world such as the one we have sketched here, the equilibrium in any single period in the presence of inherited payments commitments (whether this equilibrium belongs to a sequence of stationary equilibria or not is immaterial) requires the satisfaction of the following three conditions:

$$M = p_1 \cdot F(K_1, L_1) \dots \tag{xii}$$

$$w / p_1 = \delta F / \delta L \text{ at } K_1, L_1 \ldots \tag{xiii}$$

and

$$p_1 \cdot F(K_1, L_1) = K_1 \cdot (1 + r_1) \cdot p_0 + w \cdot L_1 \ldots \tag{xiv}$$

where p_0 is given. If these three conditions are satisfied for $M = M^*$, then they cannot be satisfied for $M = M^{**}$ as well. Or, putting the matter differently, there is a unique level of money stock, in this case M^*, which simply equals $p_0 \cdot F(K_1, L_1)$, which is compatible with the existence of a Walrasian equilibrium in period 1. If the money stock happens to be different from this, and causes prices to be different from p_0, that is, different from what was expected when these commitments were entered into, then a Walrasian equilibrium in which payment commitments are honored ceases to exist.

Notice that the expectations we are talking about refer to the current period, and not to the future. The latter determines what the capital stock for the next period will be, while it is the unrealized expectations for the current period that prevent the existence of a Walrasian equilibrium in the presence of a legacy of payments commitments. It follows that our assumption of *static expectations* is not the cause of the problem. Even if we assume rational expectations (that is, perfect foresight based on all hitherto available information), the same problem would still arise. No matter how expectations are formed about the future, whether there is any learning process, as long as commitments are entered into on the basis of these expectations, and these are not realized because of unforeseen changes in the money stock, a Walrasian equilibrium cannot exist if these commitments are honored. Of course, the nature of the equilibrium that would actually be established in such a situation would depend upon our specifications, that is, would require separate investigation. But it would be a non-Walrasian equilibrium.

The Background to Commitments

While the foregoing may be readily agreed with, two questions would be raised against it: first, why should there be unforeseen changes in the money stock? Or, putting it differently, while unforeseen changes in the money stock may create problems such as we have mentioned, are there any systemic reasons for believing that such changes would in fact occur?

The reason for skepticism on this score lies perhaps in the fact that we have been talking about changes in the absolute level of the money stock. As a matter of fact, if we are talking about a growing economy, as we should be, then it is not changes in the absolute level of the money stock that become relevant, but changes in the rate of growth of money stock. And such changes do occur for entirely plausible reasons. Let us, for simplicity, postulate a steadily growing economy, just as we had postulated a stationary state earlier in this chapter as the context for our argument. The income velocity of circulation of money and the price level are assumed, as earlier, to remain unchanged, that is, the money stock grows at the same steady rate as output.

This money stock, let us assume, is of the outside-money variety.[10] Additional money comes into the system at the end of every period through the sale, against such money, of a part of output which is deducted from the profits paid to the old. In other words, the rate of profit earned by the old $r = F'_K(K) \cdot \mu - 1$, where $\mu < 1$. With population growing at some rate n, we can imagine the economy growing at this rate along a steady-state path, with money stock too growing at this same rate and μ having a constant value. Now, if suddenly in one particular period the growth of outside money falls short of the steady-state growth rate, for whatever reason, then exactly the same problem as mentioned before would occur: there would be no Walrasian equilibrium compatible with meeting the fixed monetary payment commitments. In other words, an absolute fall (or rise) in money stock is not necessary for the argument; any variation in its rate of growth would be quite enough to negate the existence a Walrasian equilibrium in the face of fixed-payments commitments.[11]

The basic point of the argument, however, lies elsewhere, unconnected per se with whether the economy is a growing or a stationary one. It has to do with the proposition that while in the face of inherited payments commitments there is only one particular level of money stock at which a single period equilibrium can be achieved satisfying the equations (xii) to (xiv), all of which must hold in equilibrium, there is no earthly reason why exactly that particular level of money stock should prevail in the economy. It follows that a single-period Walrasian equilibrium can exist only by accident in an economy with inherited payments commitments and an exogenously given (arbitrary) level of money stock.

The second and more important question is: Why should there at all be any payment commitments fixed in advance? Individual old persons can base their savings decisions on the expected interest rate and prices (no matter how these expectations are formed), and if the actual and the expected variables differ, they may gain or lose; where does the question of advance payment commitments arise? Or, putting it differently, is there anything superior in the system of advance payment commitments such that it would be adopted rather than leaving decisions to the expectations of individual savers?

The answer to this question lies in the fact that firms are in a better position to predict than individual savers. One should distinguish here between two different concepts. One is the objective probability distribution of the outcomes, by way of returns, that an investment project yields; the other is the probability distribution of outcomes as they appear to the predictor. The statement that firms are in a better position to predict than individual savers amounts to saying that in the case of firms the latter probability distribution better approximates the former. To say this is not saying much: it only conforms to the commonsense observation that while individuals do not go around building predictive models, feeding in masses of data and using computers for

making predictions, firms do all these very things. They make it their business to predict professionally, unlike individuals.

Of course, the poor prediction by individuals may take either one of the two
forms: individuals may be sanguine about the risks associated with a project; that is,
the standard deviation of their subjective probability distribution (which is a measure of risk) may be lower than of the objective one. Or they may exaggerate risks,
swayed by stories of past bankruptcies and failures. Even assuming that firms and all
individuals have the same best guess, it follows that there would certainly be some
individuals in whose case the perceived risk from a project would be greater than for
the firm. If they are risk-averse (which we assume they are), then they would demand
a higher risk premium as compensation, that is, the certainty-equivalent rate of return
with which they would be satisfied would be lower than the certainty-equivalent rate
of return which firms themselves expect to earn, even in the event of the best-guess
return of both being identical.

True, this would not necessarily be the case for all individuals. But all that is logically needed for the argument here is that this should be the case for *some* individuals.
Firms would always have an incentive to offer certainty-equivalent rates of return to
these individuals, instead of leaving things entirely to their expectations; that is, firms
would like to make advance payment commitments. And once they do so, the implications for the existence of a Walrasian equilibrium are what we have seen.

This fact is of particular significance for the existence of inside money. In the universe described above, the old, instead of lending directly to firms, may prefer to put
their savings in banks in the form of deposits which fetch them a zero or small rate of
return, but which reduce their risks greatly. The banks in turn, as financial intermediaries, would use these deposits for giving loans to firms. In such a situation, a part, at least,
of the money stock consists of inside money. But corresponding to this inside-money
stock there is a fixed payments obligation on the part of the firms exactly as in the above
model. If the stock of outside money declines for some reason (or, more realistically, its
rate of growth slows down) then, exactly as in this model, the economy cannot get to a
new Walrasian equilibrium while meeting the inherited payments obligations.

Finally, let us take the case of a world where there is only inside money. Since
such money necessarily entails fixed payment obligations, it follows that in any single
period there would be a unique level of money stock that is compatible with the existence of a Walrasian equilibrium. There is no reason, except by accident, why precisely
that particular level of the money stock should obtain in the economy. A single-period
Walrasian equilibrium, then, can exist only by accident. True, if the economy is already
on a stationary or steady-growth path, then a simple rule of money supply growth
would ensure the existence of a sequence of Walrasian equilibria. But there is no reason why the economy should be on such a path to start with. And even if it is on such
a path, any displacement of money supply from the equilibrium level in any period
would create a situation, as we have seen, where a Walrasian equilibrium would cease
to exist.

An important conclusion emerges from this: Monetarism is logically incompatible with inside money. Even in an outside-money world, we have seen, the problem of existence of a Walrasian equilibrium would arise in the presence of inherited payments commitments. But an inside-money world necessarily entails such commitments.

The conclusion that monetarism logically precludes inside money goes against a famous proposition of Gurley and Shaw (1960), which, while arguing the logical invalidity of monetarism in a world with a combination of inside and outside money, found it logically tenable if either inside *or* outside money exclusively prevailed. But the Gurley-Shaw result is not derived in the context of a single-period temporary equilibrium, where the context itself dictates that only certain things can be changed but not others. In such a world the conditions for the validity of monetarism, and indeed of the Walrasian analysis generally, become far more stringent.

Concluding Observations

Let us go back to the comment of Joan Robinson with which we started. She was perfectly correct in her assessment that the Keynes-Kalecki treatment of historical time was fundamentally different from the Walrasian one. The problem with her comment, however, is that it was insufficiently explicit on the nature of the difference in the treatment of historical time between Keynes, Kalecki, and, one should add, Marx on one hand and Walras on the other. There is, in other words, a crucial difference between the two, but this difference is not of the bald kind where historical time is handled by one but not the other. The difference relates to the fact that the legacy of past payment commitments, and not just the endowments bequeathed from the past, can be handled by one but not by the other. Just as the recognition of the significance of inherited payment commitments makes the Walrasian equilibrium problematical, the lack of recognition of this would make any understanding of Marx and of Keynes and Kalecki well-nigh impossible.

4

The Modus Operandi of Monetarist Theory

IT WAS SUGGESTED IN CHAPTER 2 that monetarist theory must be distinguished from what is commonly understood as monetarism. The latter term is commonly associated with the proposition that the level of money income is determined by the quantity of money in the economy, or, alternatively, that the rate of growth of money income depends essentially on the rate of growth of money supply (the rate of growth of the income velocity of circulation of money being either zero or exogenously determined). But monetarist theory is more complex. It consists in the belief, first, that the world is characterized by a Walrasian equilibrium in which the money market behaves and clears like any other market, that is, the demand for money is inversely related to its price; and second, that the price of money can be perfectly adequately represented as being the obverse of the prices in terms of money of only the "output goods" and labor. The money market then clears at that general price level of output goods and labor at which the demand for money is equal to its given supply. Since the labor market, too, clears in a Walrasian equilibrium, the equilibrium real wage would have to be such as to ensure full employment, in which case the money price of labor and the prices of output goods must have a determinate relationship. The demand for money then can be said to depend on the price of money, which is the obverse of the prices of output goods alone.

The fact that in any equilibrium, no matter what conception of equilibrium we have, the demand for money would equal its supply is obvious. In Keynes, for example, it is the interest rate, or rather a combination of money income and interest rate, that equilibrates money supply with money demand. The *differentia specifica* of monetarism consists in the belief that, as in the case of any other commodity, it is the price of money that equilibrates its demand with its supply, and that this price depends on the money prices of output goods.

Looking at it differently, the monetarist doctrine answers a specific question: Why does money have a finite positive value? It does so by saying that as the value of money approaches zero, there would be excess demand for money, and at zero value of output goods there would be excess supply of money.[1] Let us examine this answer.

The Demand for Money Balances

Paradoxically, on the question of why exactly the excess demand for money should behave this way, or on the general question of the nature of the demand for money, monetarism does not have a satisfactory answer. This may appear to be a strange assertion at first sight, given that Friedman has called the quantity theory essentially a theory of the demand for money. But Friedman is not a Walrasian. His allegiance is to Marshall, and his particular defense of monetarism is based on methodological premises which are his own and not necessarily shared by monetarists in general. For instance, his view that the validity of a scientific theory is established by its ability to make empirically correct predictions exonerates him from the obligation of building a rigorous theoretical support for his monetarism, even though this particular piece of empiricist epistemology would have very few takers even among the monetarists. Once one abandons this epistemology, however, the obligation to build a rigorous theoretical structure becomes pressing, and the theoretical structure that the monetarists adduce in support of their doctrine is the Walrasian one.[2] Within the Walrasian structure, however, an explanation of the demand for money is problematical.

As mentioned earlier, there are two different versions of monetarism, each looking at the demand for money in a different way. The Cambridge version talks of the demand for money balances, while the alternative version, which strictly speaking is not compatible with a Walrasian equilibrium with tatonement, talks of the demand for money as arising from its role as a medium of circulation of the produced goods and services. We can, following Keynes (1979), call these the cash-balance approach and the cash-transactions approach, respectively. In the present chapter we look only at the first approach.

The simplest exposition of the monetarist theory based on the cash-balance approach is the pre-Keynesian Cambridge theory with a constant k, which we examined in chapter 2. The problem with this Cambridge approach, however, consists in the fact that there is no reason whatsoever why k should be a constant; on the contrary, by its very nature, k cannot be independent of expectations. Several attempts have indeed been made to specify a "real balance" effect, which can serve as a modus operandi for monetarist theory, even while incorporating expectations into the specification. Paradoxically, however, while every effort based on such incorporation is logically flawed, the more robust versions of the modus operandi of the theory are those, like the Cambridge version, that do not invoke expectations. In short, while not incorporating expectations can produce a monetarist theory that is not logically flawed but is obviously devoid of realism, incorporating expectations, while making the theory less unreal, results in its being logically flawed.

Patinkin (1965) was a pioneer in the attempt to move away from the simple Cambridge version. If a real balance effect had to operate on commodities' demand, then the magnitude of real balance in any economic agent's possession had to figure in his or her budget constraint, on the basis of which the agent could decide on the optimal bundle of commodities to be purchased. An increase in the magnitude of real balance in the agent's possession, brought about through, for instance, a reduction in the price level in the economy for a given money stock, would then play the role of relaxing the agent's budget constraint and enlarging the demand for goods and services. Patinkin was concerned not merely with analyzing whether money wage and price flexibility could yield a Walrasian equilibrium with full employment, as the monetarists had been arguing, but also with the circumstances under which money would be "neutral," as the pre-Keynesian Cambridge monetarism had claimed.[3] This "neutrality," whereby an increase in the supply of money is supposed to increase money income in the same proportion or the rate of growth of money supply equals the rate of growth of money income, follows simply from the assumption of a constant k. It is also the central core of monetarism as it is commonly perceived. Patinkin's object was to examine the conditions under which this "neutrality" would be preserved if we reconstruct monetarism on a different basis, incorporating expectations and moving away from the assumption of a constant k.

A formidable array of assumptions, it turned out, was required for preserving the "neutrality" of money. A crucial one among these was the assumption that commodity price expectations must be unit-elastic. The reason for this assumption is the following: since all markets must clear in a Walrasian general equilibrium including the labor market, and since this requires a specific real wage, it follows that equilibrium is compatible with only a specific configuration of relative prices (including the price of labor). Movements in money supply then must not be able to affect the relative prices, but must exclusively affect the overall price level. In the simple world where there is only one commodity and labor, money supply must affect only the *absolute* money prices of commodities and labor, that is, only the exchange ratio between money on the one hand and commodities including labor on the other, but not the relative prices in the nonmoney world.

This much is clear. But neutrality goes a step further. It postulates that the absolute money prices must move in the same proportion as money supply. Now, let us suppose that commodity price expectations are not unit-elastic, but are instead *inelastic*; then any change in the overall level of current money wages and prices would cause a change in the *ratio* between the current and the expected levels of wages and prices. This fact is bound to affect the value of k; likewise, when commodity price expectations are *elastic*, any change in commodity prices would affect the value of k. If we are to get the result that k must remain unchanged, then a necessary condition must be that expectations are unit-elastic.

I will show later that in a world where price expectations are unit-elastic, then, within the cash-balance approach, there would be no finite positive value of money.

But Patinkin's argument was not marred by this problem alone. There were in addition two obvious problems. The first was the fact that in a world with inside money, the argument about the real-balance effect became invalid (Johnson 1958). The second was the fact that the impact of the real-balance effect appeared to depend upon the time period of our analysis, whether the income in question was daily, or weekly, or monthly, or annual income. This follows from the fact that money balance is a stock while money income is a flow; hence the magnitude of price change required to bring about a real balance effect of the appropriate order of magnitude would be different depending upon the time period of analysis. But it lends a methodological infirmity to the entire exercise.

Subsequent formulations on the real balance effect have tended to steer clear of the Patinkin version. Malinvaud (1977) for example, who, while developing a non-Walrasian general equilibrium framework with fixed prices and rationing, believes that flexible prices would take the economy to a Walrasian equilibrium and full employment, invokes the real-balance effect as one element of the modus operandi for this market-clearing outcome. He postulates that a consumer, who initially possesses m_0 amount of cash balance, wishes to maximize a utility function whose arguments are consumption and the terminal real balance. The consumer's problem then becomes

$$\text{Max } u\left(c, m_1 / p^e_1\right)$$

subject to the constraint

$$\left(w_0 \cdot e + m_0\right) \geq p_0 \cdot c + m_1$$

where c denotes consumption, e the degree of employment, w the money wage rate, and p the price. Superscript e refers to the expected value, and subscripts refer to periods (the current period being 0). It is obvious that starting from any consumer equilibrium, if there is a reduction in w because of the existence of unemployment, then an equiproportional reduction in p will ceteris paribus increase c (which is assumed not to be an inferior good), no matter what the elasticity of price expectation may be (as long as it is nonnegative). The real balance effect is thus apparently validated.

The problem with the Malinvaud argument is that it already assumes what is to be proven. If terminal balances are made an argument in the utility function itself, instead of being the outcome of intertemporal optimization, and if they are made substitutes for consumption, then obviously any increase in the current real balance, which in the absence of an increase in the current consumption and in the presence of a nonnegative elasticity of price expectation, would lead to an increase in terminal real balance, must entail some increase in consumption. The whole point, however, is to see whether this would happen through optimizing behavior under plausible assumptions; it cannot just be directly assumed, as Malinvaud does (though of course his theoretical objective is different).

The Malinvaud argument, moreover, while it establishes the real balance effect and with it the modus operandi of attaining a Walrasian equilibrium, does not establish the "neutrality of money" and hence the commonly perceived propositions of monetarism.

Thus, if the validity of the modus operandi of the monetarist theory is sought to be established by fiat, whether by assuming a Cambridge-constant k, or by postulating terminal balances as an argument in the utility function on a par with consumption, then the short-period argument is carried through. But expectations do not play any role, which is unreal: in Malinvaud's case, for instance, there can scarcely be any doubt that the utility from the terminal balances would depend upon the expected wage, the expected employment, and the expected cost of living in the future, so that assuming an unchanging "marginal utility" schedule from terminal balances is an illegitimate closing of eyes to expectations. On the other hand, when expectations are introduced, as in Patinkin, we have problems. Some of these have been mentioned. But there is an even more basic one to which we now turn, namely, money would not have a positive and finite price vis-à-vis the produced goods unless there are inelastic price expectations for commodities.

The Role of Inelastic Price Expectations

This point may at first sight appear to be the same as the one made by Grandmont (1982), who argued that unless money is expected to have a positive value in the next period, no matter what its current value happens to be, it would not have a positive value in the current period itself. In such a case since all holdings of money and of money-denominated assets would have zero value, they would not constitute wealth. No cash balances would be held in the first place, on the basis of which we could postulate a real-balance effect.

The sense of his argument (not the precise details) is as follows. Consider an overlapping-generations model in which the young and the old have the same real income in each period, and each has, in addition, a certain money stock. The old consume everything they have (there are no bequests); the consumption of the young is determined through an optimization exercise, the optimand being the sum of the utilities in the two periods. Let us assume for convenience static expectations, zero time-preference, and identical utility functions in the two periods with consumption as the argument. Let us also assume that there are A young and B old persons. If each young person has m_y amount of money stock, then his or her demand for money, through the optimization exercise, is $m_y / 2$. For each old person, who has m_o amount of money stock, the demand for money is nil. Hence the total demand for money is $A \cdot m_y / 2$, while the total supply is greater at $(A \cdot m_y + B \cdot m_o)$. Under static expectations this excess supply will never be eliminated, and the value of money will fall to zero. The only way that this downward slide can be prevented, and an equilibrium ensured at a positive value of money, is if people expect this value to be positive in the next period, even if it is zero in the current one. As the value of money plummets downward, the expectation that it would increase in the next period, can alone induce greater demand for money and eventually eliminate excess supply.

Grandmont himself has drawn attention to the fact that his condition for money to have a positive value (in a world in which the demand for it in the form of cash balances is the only demand for it) has a resemblance to the assumption of inelastic commodity price expectations. But even though we too are talking about the essentiality of the assumption of inelastic price expectations, and hence coming to the same eventual conclusion as Grandmont, our theoretical proposition is different from Grandmont's. What we are arguing is that in the absence of inelastic price expectations the value of money would be either zero or infinity, while Grandmont is arguing that in the absence of inelastic expectations the value of money would necessarily be zero. The absence of inelastic expectations, in other words, gives rise, according to Grandmont, to an ineluctable state of excess supply of money, but, according to us, to an ineluctable state of either excess supply of money or excess demand for money. The reason for this difference between Grandmont's and our positions will be discussed later; but this difference itself must be noted for the present.

To clarify our argument, let us take a simple universe where production takes place without any capital, where each individual lives for two periods, but where the individual can work with no loss of efficiency in both periods. Each individual plans to bequeath to his children at the time of his death an amount of wealth that is some proportion b of his or her initial wealth. Money is the only form in which wealth can be held and there is no transaction demand for money. We start the period with a certain stock of money distributed among the individuals in some manner. In addition each individual earns a certain income from work during the period. The decision to be made by each individual in the first period is: how much to consume and how much wealth to carry over into the second period? And, this decision is made by maximizing, subject to a budget constraint given by the incomes of the two periods and $(1- b)$ times the initial wealth, a utility function that merely adds together the current period's and the next period's (expected) utilities, each period's utility being a function of the period's consumption. Finally, since our aim is to show the necessity of inelastic price expectations, we start by making the contrary assumption, namely that individuals have static price expectations.

With static price expectations and equal work efficiency on the part of the individual in both periods, the expected prices and income in the second period are exactly the same as the actuals of the current period. It can be easily seen that the optimal strategy for the young in such a case would be to carry into the next period an amount of wealth equal to $m^1_0 (1 + b) / 2$, where superscript 1 denotes the initial wealth of the young (assumed for convenience to be identical for all young).[4] Each old person, on the other hand, would plan to carry over into the next period only bm^0_0 of wealth, where superscript 0 denotes the initial wealth of the old (also assumed to be identical for all old). If there are A young persons and B old persons, then the total demand for money would be $A \cdot m^1_0 (1 + b) / 2 + B \cdot m^0_0 \cdot b$, while the total stock of money in the economy is $A \cdot m^1_0 + B \cdot m^0_0$.

It follows that there would be excess demand for money if $b > 1$, excess supply of money if $b < 1$, and an exact balance between demand and supply only if $b = 1$. But the crucial point is this: This situation of excess supply or excess demand would continue even in the face of adjustments in the price of money, owing to the assumption of static expectations. In other words, the assumption of static expectations precludes, even in this simple model, an equilibrium with a finite positive value of money (except in the borderline case of $b = 1$, and here the equilibrium value of money would not be unique); the value of money would be driven either toward zero or toward infinity, depending on whether b falls short of or exceeds 1.

What is true of static expectations is also true, more generally, of unit-elastic expectations. What unit-elastic expectations entail is constancy in the ratio between the current and the expected prices. Given this ratio the individuals may decide to carry such magnitudes of wealth into the next period that the total demand for money exceeds or falls short of the total supply; but if it does so then changes in the value of money would again fail to bring the two into equality, because any such change would leave the ratio between the current and the expected prices unchanged, and it is this ratio which is crucial in the decision about the magnitude of wealth holding to be carried into the next period and hence for the total demand for money. In other words, variations in this ratio are essential for equilibrating the money market in a world where only money balances are demanded. And variations in this ratio (of an equilibrating kind) can come about only if price expectations are inelastic.

The reason for this can be seen as follows. Suppose at some initial set of commodity prices, the total demand for cash balances to be carried over to the next period falls short of their supply. The value of money relative to commodities will fall, that is, the money prices of commodities will rise. With inelastic expectations, the ratio of the expected commodity prices to their current prices will fall, which will induce a postponement of consumption from the current to the next period, and hence a larger demand for cash balances for carrying over into the next period. Inelastic expectations therefore, by making the demand curve for cash balances downward-sloping, play an equilibrating role.

It follows from the foregoing that the version of quantity theory that relies on the cash-balance approach is internally inconsistent. For the dichotomy between the real and the monetary sectors to be valid, which is an essential requisite for monetarism, unit-elastic price expectations must obtain. On the other hand, the equilibrating mechanism that brings the demand for money into equality with its supply breaks down unless there are inelastic commodity-price expectations.

This is the conclusion of Grandmont as well, but it should be clear by now why our argument is different from Grandmont's. His is an overlapping generation model in which each individual plans to bequeath zero wealth to children, that is, $b = 0$ in our terminology.[5] This is why he argues that in the absence of inelastic price expectations, there would always be an ineluctable excess supply of money. But to talk of wealth without talking of its being passed on to progeny is almost a contradiction in terms. And since the discussion is about money as a form of wealth, the introduction of wealth that is not passed on and the derivation of an ineluctable excess supply of money on this basis, may invite the charge that an easy option is being taken, that a theory is being critiqued by setting up a caricature of it. Our argument is meant to avoid this charge.

Having shown the need for inelastic price expectations, or, more specifically, for the assumption that, no matter what its current value, money is always expected to have a positive value in the next period, Grandmont goes on to justify this assumption on the grounds that in the formation of expectations the past also enters together with the present and that money has always had a positive value in the past. This, however, amounts to stating that money has a value because it has had a value in the past. Since a positive value of money today arises because money is expected to have a positive value, and since this expectation in turn derives from its having had a positive value in the past, the basic question of why money has a positive value at all remains unanswered. In other words, Grandmont's justification of the assumption required for a positive value of money today simply would not do; it leaves the value of money "hanging by its own bootstraps," to use Dennis Robertson's (1940) famous phrase.

Looking at the matter differently, the "cash balance" version of monetarism has *two* distinct problems specific to it: the first is its internal inconsistency arising from the fact that it requires for its validity the simultaneous fulfillment of the assumptions of both unit-elastic and inelastic expectations. Second, to assume inelastic expectations, which is essential for the theory, we need an anchorage for the value of money. Such an anchorage can arise only if the value of money is determined by something more substantial than mere expectations. But this version of monetarism has no such substantial explanation to offer.

5

The Cash Transactions Approach to Monetarism

THE CASH BALANCE APPROACH to monetarism is not logically sustainable. Once we stop making unreal and logically untenable assumptions about a constant (Cambridge) k, or about real balances per se providing a certain utility to the consumer, on a par with consumption, whose magnitude moreover is independent of expectations about the future, there is no way that we can build a consistent monetarist story on the basis of the cash balance approach. A positive and finite value of money can be explained in an equilibrium situation on the basis of this approach only if there are inelastic price expectations. But inelastic price expectations raise two problems: first, they preclude "neutrality of money," a necessary condition for which is unit elastic price expectations; but this neutrality, or the dichotomy between the real and the monetary sectors that holds that changes in money supply affect only the "money things" and not the "real things," is a basic component of Monetarism. Second, the existence of inelastic price expectations itself cannot be explained in a logically satisfactory manner within the Walrasian world. Simply invoking past experience, the fact that money has always had a certain finite value, to explain inelastic price expectations, amounts to arguing in circles, as in Robertson's famous "bootstraps" argument. It begs the question why there were inelastic price expectations in the past, and so on in an infinite regress. On the other hand, if inelastic price expectations are explained by the real-life existence of certain prices that are rigid or at least slow to change, that is, by the real-life existence of an element of fix-price, then this becomes incompatible with a Walrasian world that assumes completely flexible prices.

Such logical contradictions, it will be argued later, do not characterize the Keynesian or the Marxian systems. Fix-price being a part of the Keynesian (and the Marxian) story, what is considered in mainstream literature as the weakness of the Keynesian approach, namely its supposition of fix-price, is precisely its strength, in the sense that inelastic price expectations within this system can be logically explained by the existence of such fix-price. But there is no room for fix-price within the Walrasian story; and if real balances cannot logically be held without inelastic price expectations, for which there is no occasion within a flex-price story, then not only this version of monetarism, but, more generally, this version of the Walrasian equilibrium, has to be abandoned for a world with money.

There is, however, an alternative version, which we called the cash transactions approach, that can be invoked to support the monetarist argument. This is the more common version. It traces the demand for money to the need for settling transactions in a monetary economy. The purpose of this chapter is to examine the logical validity of a monetarist theory erected on the basis of the cash transactions approach.

This version has serious logical problems, too. For a start, as mentioned earlier, it is not clear how the concept of a transactions demand for money can be integrated into the framework of a Walrasian equilibrium. In a tatonement world there is no scope for a separate transaction demand for money: such a transactions demand requires a time lag between sales and purchases, but in a tatonement world there is no such time lag, since all transactions occur at the same instant.

Of course, an alternative route can be followed: the money stock available with an individual can be brought in as one of the arguments of his or her demand function. But if it does not have any sui generis role in the demand function, which is an overriding one in comparison to the role of other endowments, then there is no sense to be made of the concept of a transactions demand for money even when we approach it by this route.

Patinkin, as we have seen, had made the magnitude of real balances influence the demand for commodities, but the transactions-demand version cannot just repeat the same procedure. If it did, then not only would the overriding role which it ascribes to money stock, which constitutes its specificity, have disappeared, but it also would not even be an alternative theory (and would be subject to the same problems that were discussed in the last chapter).

The best-known attempt made in the literature to incorporate the essential features of the transactions demand for money into the context of a Walrasian equilibrium follows the lead of Clower (1967). The idea is to introduce lags such that the inherited money stock determines today's budget constraint, while today's commodity endowments, once they are sold (that is, converted into money), determine tomorrow's inherited money stock and hence tomorrow's budget constraint. The money holdings in this manner then *do* play an overriding role different from the endowments of other commodities. Of late, Hool (1979) has developed a story along these lines.

The Clower approach does successfully reconcile the existence of a transactions demand for money with the context of a Walrasian equilibrium, and in this way does seem to provide monetarism with a theoretical basis. Obviously, as long as *any* transactions occur at all, commodity prices cannot be infinity, that is, the value of money cannot be zero, since the inherited money stock of a finite quantity constitutes the budget constraint. Likewise, the value of money cannot be infinity, that is, commodity prices cannot be zero, since in such a case the budget constraint would not have been binding, an impossibility when individuals are maximizing utility subject to a budget constraint. It appears then that the introduction of a transactions demand for money in the form of a budget constraint overcomes the theoretical problems of monetarism and ensures that money has a finite and positive value in equilibrium.[1]

But the Clower solution is a purely *formal one* and lacks any *theoretical* justification. By postulating a constant time lag between the realization of sale proceeds and their expenditure, it generates a demand for money all right and links it to the value of transactions, but the whole exercise amounts to an ex cathedra pronouncement that provides an artificial solution without justifying it, without explaining for instance *why* there should be a constant time lag between the realization and expenditure of sale proceeds. Putting it differently, our question to monetarism merely gets shifted from "Why should money have a positive, finite value in equilibrium if its value is determined by demand and supply?" to "Why should there be a constant time lag between the realization of sale proceeds and the expenditure of these proceeds?" without getting answered.

Protagonists of this approach may base their case on the argument that some time lag must elapse between the accrual and the expenditure of proceeds, that everything cannot happen at the same instant. But this self-evident proposition does not support the protagonists' case. We are not talking about *some* lag, but a *constant* lag, for if the lag is not constant but depends upon other variables then the transactions demand for money ceases to have a stable relationship with the value of commodity transactions, in which case, as we will see, the value of money in equilibrium need not be positive and finite. And a *constant* lag can be taken neither as an institutional datum imposed by the external environment upon the individual, nor a result of individual maximizing behavior. By postulating a constant time lag, therefore, the theory is not only arbitrarily restricting the scope for individual maximizing behavior whose universality of operation in all possible spheres it otherwise stoutly upholds (thus contradicting itself), but it is also providing a contrived solution to the question of the value of money.

Once we break out of the rigid assumption of a constant time lag, it is clear that commodity prices would not have a finite upper bound. The higher the level of commodity prices, the more the individuals would fall back upon the proceeds of their *current* sales for financing their purchases, that is, the shorter would be the average time lag between the realization and the expenditure of proceeds. Or looking at the matter from the other end, the shorter the time lag the higher the level of commodity prices that can be sustained, and as the lag becomes infinitesimally short, commodity prices would approach infinity. To say this is not the same as asserting that commodity prices would reach infinity; it merely amounts to stating that the theory's explanation for finite positive value of money would have lost its basis if the lag were variable.

Individual maximizing behavior, moreover, would eliminate the constancy of the lag for at least two reasons: first, if there is a positive rate of time preference on the part of individuals (which theories belonging to this tradition often otherwise assume), then their utility-maximizing behavior would dictate a shortening of the lag since the

lag in itself is not productive of utility. In other words, a positive rate of time preference would be incompatible with *any* time lag between the accrual and the expenditure of proceeds, let alone a constant time lag. Even if we start from a situation where
for some reason expenditure in the current period is financed exclusively from the
proceeds of the previous period, a positive rate of time preference would ensure that
the current period's proceeds are not all held over for the next period. The average
time lag between the accrual and the expenditure of the proceeds then would keep
shortening until it becomes infinitesimally small.

The second reason has to do with expectations. For greater clarity with regard to
this point, let us assume that the first reason mentioned above does not operate; that
is, the rate of time preference is zero. Let us also assume that expectations are held
with certainty and that the carrying cost of commodities from one period to the next
is zero. (These assumptions are for simplicity and dropping them does not affect the
argument.)

Suppose, to start with, that the expenditure in the current period *is* financed exclusively from the proceeds of the previous period. Now, if individuals expect that commodity prices in the next period are going to be higher than in the current period, then
they would prefer to carry commodities rather than money into the next period. Of
course, they may not actually (that is, *ex post*) carry greater commodity stocks into the
next period, if their optimal consumption profile remains unaltered, but it is the desire
to carry commodity stocks that matters. Because of this, there would be a rise in the
current period's price, even with an unchanged stock of money available for expenditure. The reason is that there would in effect have been a shortening of the average
period of time for which the proceeds are held in money form.

Now, if the rise in the current price leaves the expected price for the next period
unchanged, that is, the elasticity of price expectations is zero, then this rise is bounded.
In the present case, the current price will merely equal the expected price (since we are
assuming that expectations are held with certainty and that carrying costs are zero).
Even so, however, the price rise may continue even with a given stock of money over a
succession of periods. This would happen, for instance, if the fact of the current period's
price being higher than had been originally expected, while not affecting the expected
price for the next period, causes an upward revision in the next period of the expected
price for the subsequent period; that is, expectations are formed according to the rule:

$$p^e_{(t+2)} / p^e_{(t+1)} = p_t / p^e_t$$

The matter can be seen as follows. Let us assume, with Hicks, that the market meets
once a week. On the day it meets, all participants have an expectation of the price
that would prevail on the next market day, a week hence, just as they have come to
the market with an expectation about today's price, which was formed last week. This
expected price for the next market day, relative to the price today, is such that every
one carries the money, obtained from the sale proceeds today, into the next market

day. In fact, let us assume, to start with, that $p^e_{(t+1)} = p_t = p^e_t$. Now, suppose there is for some reason an increase in the expected price for the market day a week hence. This would give rise to a desire to carry some commodity stocks into the next market day, and hence push up today's price. But this would not affect the expected price for the next market day, so that today's price again equals the (higher) expected price for a week hence but exceeds the originally expected price for today. This increase in today's price will remain in the memories of the participants, and when they meet next week, their expected price for the subsequent market day would be revised upward. In this way the price rise will continue even with a given stock of money. The velocity of circulation of money will rise indefinitely.

The particular expectation-formation rule given here is merely illustrative. But if we have expectation-formation rules of this sort, then over a sequence of periods the demand for money as a ratio of the value of transactions would keep dwindling, which is the same as saying that the constant time-lag assumption would have broken down completely. Likewise, in the opposite case the time lag between the accrual and the expenditure of proceeds would lengthen. In either case the constancy of the lag would no longer prevail even if one started with a constant lag. It follows that the attempt to provide a foundation for monetarist theory by introducing a constant time lag between the accrual and the expenditure of proceeds and taking the lagged proceeds as the budget constraint for the individual within the framework of a Walrasian equilibrium is intellectually unsatisfactory.[2] The internal inconsistency of the monetarist theoretical framework remains unresolved.

An Alternative Approach to the Transactions Demand for Money

The transactions demand for money, it may be argued however, is a reality, whether or not it makes sense in the context of a Walrasian equilibrium. Even though the monetarist story is told in the context of such an equilibrium, to claim, because this story is inconsistent, that the value of money cannot be determined by demand and supply, appears illegitimate. Let us therefore take an alternative approach, which has nothing to do with a Walrasian equilibrium but that permits a coherent story about the transactions demand for money, and see if with this approach we can explain a finite and positive value of money in the absence of inelastic price expectations. This approach is derived from Kaldor (1945), though it is not identical with what Kaldor had actually said. It also broadly corresponds to the approach of Kalecki (1954).

Kaldor's argument went as follows: money has a convenience yield, in the sense that all economic agents find it convenient to hold a certain amount of money relative to the money value of their transactions (M / pT) over a certain period (which we assume to be identical with the money value of their commodity transactions).

The lower is this ratio the greater is the marginal convenience yield of money. Like-wise, economic agents hold commodity stocks for convenience; the lower is the ratio of such physical stocks to the volume of their commodity transactions (C / T), the greater is the marginal convenience yield of commodity stocks. On the basis of this one can argue that since in equilibrium the rates of return must be equal between holding money and holding commodities, we must have

$$f(M / pT) = F(C / T) + \{(dp / dt) / p\}^e - c - r \ldots \tag{i}$$

where f and F denote marginal convenience yields on money and commodities respec-tively, with $f' < 0$ and $F' < 0$, c is the marginal carrying cost on commodities, and r is the marginal risk premium associated with the holding of commodity stocks. This risk premium arises because the expected rate of return on holding commodity stocks, which includes the expected money price appreciation of these stocks, has a prob-ability distribution (derived from the probability distribution of expected prices); this entails a risk, against which a risk-averse individual would like to be compensated. Even assuming static price expectations, for any given volume of commodity transac-tions and of commodity stocks, there would be a certain value of the RHS and hence a certain demand function for money with respect to the price level. Given the stock of money supply, there would therefore be a unique price level that would ensure equi-librium in the money market. It follows that if the stock of money, the stock of com-modities, and the volume of commodity transactions over a certain period are given, then there would be an equilibrium price level of commodities.

Of course, a question may be raised about the "optimality" of the stock of com-modities that the economic agents have, relative to the volume of commodity transac-tions. Or, putting it differently, it may be argued that the RHS itself must always have a *particular* value, corresponding to the "optimum" level of commodity stocks relative to the volume of commodity transactions. While this does not affect our argument (in equilibrium again there would be a unique price level corresponding to the stock of money supply), the determination of this optimum is possible only if some rate of return, or some other analogue of the interest rate, is already given to the economic agents from outside. Rather than assuming such an exogenously given interest rate, we simply assume something that is logically equivalent, namely that the commodity stocks which the agents carry, like their money stocks, are given in any period, as is the volume of commodity transactions.

It may be thought that assuming the volume of commodity transactions to be given is unrealistic, since, if there is nothing sacrosanct about the magnitude of the initial commodity stocks relative to the volume of *ex ante* transactions, then economic agents could well decide to decrease or increase their commodity stocks through larger or smaller sales, so that the *ex post* volume of transactions could well be different from the *ex ante* volume. But the argument presented earlier remains valid, if the assumption is

made that whenever economic agents wish to decrease (increase) their initial commodity stocks, they do so in order to have some increase (decrease) in their money
stocks. With this assumption which is not too demanding, with given levels of commodity and money stocks, and with a given *ex ante* volume of transactions, it follows
that money can have a finite and positive value in equilibrium even when price expectations are not inelastic.[3]

Let us restate this argument. If economic agents hold both money stocks and commodity stocks, then their rates of return must be equal in equilibrium. For money, this
rate of return is nothing else but its marginal convenience yield; for commodity stocks
however this rate of return is the excess of the sum of the marginal convenience yield
on commodities and the expected rate of their price appreciation, over the sum of the
marginal carrying cost and the marginal risk premium, that is, the RHS of (i), which
in Kaldor's terminology is the "own rate of money interest" on commodities. If the
magnitude of commodity stocks relative to the total volume of commodity transactions is given, and so is the expected price appreciation on commodity stocks (which
we have assumed to be zero), then the "own rate of money interest" of commodity
stocks is given, to which the marginal convenience yield of money must be equal
in equilibrium. Since with a given money supply and a given volume of commodity
transactions, the marginal convenience yield of money is positively related to the price
level of commodities, this fixes the price level of commodities.

Even this argument in defense of monetarism is a flawed one. It presumes that
money holding is linked only to the magnitude of money use, and that commodity
stocks are linked only to the magnitude of commodity use. It misses the substitutability between money and commodity stocks. Money can be used not only for monetary
transactions, but also in lieu of commodity stocks. Businesses may for instance economize on their commodity stock holding and hold additional money stocks instead, if
they feel that the latter can be converted easily into commodities whenever required.
Of course money stocks are not a perfect substitute for commodity stocks. There are
certain advantages of holding commodity stocks because of which they are actually
held; but money, too, can certainly be held as command over commodities and commodity stocks procured with it if need be. In talking of the yield of money, therefore,
we must be conscious of both these aspects: its yield as money, and its yield as a possible substitute for commodity stocks.

Let us take the total money stock M as consisting notionally of two components:
M_0, which is held for managing monetary transactions with convenience, and $M - M_0$,
which is held in lieu of commodity stocks.[4] In equilibrium, the rates of return on these
two components of money must be equal at the margin. In addition, since commodity
stocks must also be held (which we assume they always would be), the rates of return
on *all three* must be equal at the margin. In other words, we must have

$$f(M_0 / pT) = F\{(M - M_0) / pT\} - \rho = F(C / T) + \{(dp / dt) / p\}^e - c - r \qquad \text{(ii)}$$

where the first term, the same as in (i) (except that M_0 is substituted for M), denotes the marginal convenience yield of money stock for meeting monetary transactions; the first term in the middle expression (between the two equals signs) is the marginal convenience yield of commodity stocks in equilibrium (even though the actual stocks are held in the form of money and not commodities); the second term ρ in this expression denotes the "cost" of holding money in lieu of commodities; and the last expression, after the second equality, is the same as in (i), that is, the "own rate of money interest" of the commodity stocks *actually held*.

Since $M - M_0$ is held in lieu of commodities, in addition to C amount of commodities, it follows that, at the margin, whether we increase $(M - M_0) / p$ or C or both, we should get the same marginal convenience yield. Hence the following equality must hold:

$$F\{(M - M_0) / pT\} = F(C / T) = F[\{(M - M_0) / p + C\} / T] = y \text{ (say)} \dots \quad \text{(iii)}$$

Now, the term ρ, which we have called the cost of holding money in lieu of commodities, consists of two parts: the inconvenience of having actually to buy commodities with money when the need arises, and the possible risks arising from the fact that the commodities may not be available at the right time. Both this inconvenience and the possible risk associated with holding money in lieu of commodities, compared to holding commodities directly, may be taken, as a first approximation, to be a constant. (This is not too far-fetched if we assume agents to be price takers in which case the perceived risks are small.)

Let us again assume static expectations. We can then rewrite (ii) in view of (iii) as:

$$f(M_0 / pT) = y - \rho = y - c - r \dots \quad \text{(iv)}$$

It follows from (iv) that in equilibrium

$$\rho = c + r \dots \quad \text{(v)}$$

But, unlike ρ which is a constant, $(c + r)$ is a function of C / T. It is reasonable to assume that $(c + r)$ is an increasing function of (C / T), especially since marginal carrying costs tend to increase significantly with the magnitude of commodity stocks.

Let us, to start with, assume that the economy is at an equilibrium where (iv) is satisfied. Now suppose there is a chance increase in the price level above the equilibrium p. This would lead to an increase in f, that is, in the marginal convenience yield of money. With ρ constant, this would push up y. But since $c + r$ must remain unchanged in any new equilibrium, because of (v), C / T must also remain unchanged. We therefore will have a new equilibrium where some money stock, hitherto held in lieu of commodities, will be shifted for transaction purposes, but the magnitude of commodity stocks will not change. In other words, a rise in p increases M_0 only at the expense of $(M - M_0)$ but does not alter the magnitude of commodity stocks held. Since the excess demand for commodities (and money) does not change, the increase in price remains. There is no tendency for the price to come back to the original equilibrium level. Exactly the same happens when there is a chance lowering of price. It follows that we do not have a unique equilibrium price; any price is an equilibrium price even though the level of money stock and the volume of turnover are given.

So far we have assumed static expectations. But exactly the same result holds for the more general case of unit elastic expectations. Since unit elastic expectations imply a constant ratio between the current and the expected prices, the assumption of unit elastic, as distinct from static, expectations, merely means the addition of a constant term to the extreme RHS of (iv) and its subtraction from the RHS of (v), which leaves the argument entirely unchanged. It can also be seen that elastic price expectations will mean that a movement away from any initial equilibrium position will give rise to a cumulative movement in the same direction. It is only in the case of inelastic expectations that a movement away from an initial equilibrium position brings the economy back to the same initial position.

To see these last two points, let us denote $(dp / dt)^e / p$ by x. Then, (iv) and (v) can be rewritten as

$$f(M_0 / pT) = y - \rho = y - c - r + x \ldots \tag{iv$'$}$$

and

$$\rho = c + r - x \ldots \tag{v$'$}$$

Now, in the case of elastic expectations, a chance increase in price, raises x even as it raises y. Hence $(c + r)$ must increase, and this can happen only through an increase in C / T. It follows that a chance increase in price, starting from an equilibrium position, increases the excess demand for commodities, which raises the price level further, and so on. In the case of inelastic expectations, a chance increase in price, by lowering x, also acts in the direction of lowering $(c + r)$, which can happen only through a lowering of C / T. Hence a chance increase in price reduces excess demand for commodities, and restores the original equilibrium.

It may be thought that our conclusion about the necessity of inelastic price expectations in this case, which has till now assumed a constant ρ, will get invalidated if we make a more plausible assumption about the behavior of ρ. This, however, is not the case. On the contrary, a more plausible assumption about the behavior of ρ will only compound the problem further. Since ρ denotes the cost of holding money in lieu of commodities, compared to the direct holding of commodities, a more plausible alternative to the assumption of a constant ρ is the assumption that ρ is an increasing function of the ratio between $(M - M_0) / p$ and C, that is, the more the amount of money held in lieu of commodities, relative to the amount of commodities actually held, the greater is the perceived cost of holding money in lieu of commodities. In such a case, however, it can be checked that there would be instability of equilibrium, in the sense of any initial movement away from it giving rise to a cumulative movement away from it, even with static (or unit-elastic) price expectations unlike in the preceding case, where ρ is a constant. The problem, therefore, becomes even worse.

It follows that even with a Kaldor-type approach to the transactions demand for money, we cannot explain the existence of a positive and finite value of money without the assumption of inelastic price expectations.

Payments Commitments and Monetarism

So far we have not introduced payments commitments, which figured in chapter 3 and, it was argued, created problems for the existence of a Walrasian equilibrium. Even in the absence of payments commitments, however, we have argued that there are serious logical problems with the monetarist theory, problems arising from the side of the demand for money. If the demand for money is interpreted as a transactions demand for money bearing a stable relation with the value of transactions in equilibrium it is irreconcilable with the Walrasian context as well as being incapable of yielding the presumed stable relation. If, on the other hand, the demand for money is interpreted as a demand for cash balances, then in the absence of inelastic commodity-price expectations there is no reason to believe that money would have a positive finite equilibrium value. But inelastic expectations not only go against the assumption of unit-elastic expectations, which is essential for another chunk of what is commonly perceived as monetarist theory, namely the "neutrality of money" and the consequent dichotomy between the money and the real sectors, but are also themselves inexplicable unless there is some other independent anchorage to the value of money, in which case monetarism itself becomes irrelevant. In short, even without introducing payments commitments, we have argued that monetarist theory is internally inconsistent.

The introduction of payments commitments only compounds the problem of inconsistency. To see this clearly, let us deliberately abstract from the problems arising on the side of the demand for money, which we have been discussing until now. Let us deliberately assume, as we did in chapter 3, that the demand for money has a unique relationship with the money value of the GDP. Even then, a problem would arise if we assume fixed payments commitments, as we did in chapter 3. The argument of chapter 3 stated that if payments commitments are entered into on the basis of some expectations that do not get realized, but these commitments are honored, then a Walrasian equilibrium may not exist at all. This argument can be stated with respect to monetarism as follows. If the quantity of money suddenly happens to change, then monetarism claims that all money variables would change pari passu while the real variables would remain unaltered in the new Walrasian equilibrium. But if there are fixed payments obligations that are honored, then it turns out that far from this neat dichotomy getting established between two Walrasian equilibria, a new Walrasian equilibrium may not exist at all. Thus, even if a Walrasian equilibrium perchance had been established, a change in money stock would move the economy out of this equilibrium without necessarily taking it to another equilibrium.

The introduction of payments commitments thus gives rise to two separate kinds of problems in addition to the problems discussed in earlier sections. First, given the payments commitments the stock of money may be such that a Walrasian equilibrium does not exist at all, in which case of course the basic monetarist theory is negated. Second, even if the stock of money does happen to be such that a Walrasian equilibrium exists, a change in this stock would once again put a question mark on the existence of a new Walrasian equilibrium so that the monetarist assertions (i) that a new equilibrium necessarily exists, (ii) that the economy would converge to it, and (iii) that in this new equilibrium the money variables would have changed pari passu with the quantity of money, while the real variables would have remained unchanged, appears without any sound foundations whatsoever.

Concluding Observations

Let us pull together the threads of the argument not only of this chapter but also of the preceding three chapters, even though this will necessarily involve some repetition. What we have been examining over these four chapters is the prevalent notion of equilibrium in mainstream economics, namely the Walrasian equilibrium and the monetary theory associated with it. This notion of equilibrium assumes a legacy of endowments, of commodities and money, for the individual economic agents, each of which also has a set of expectations about the future. On the basis of these endowments and expectations, given the technological possibilities and the tastes of the individuals, the hedonistic agents act in such a manner that, as long as prices are allowed to move freely up or down, a temporary equilibrium, it is claimed, is established where all markets clear. In this equilibrium, it is further claimed, in common-parlance monetarism at any rate, that changes in money stock have no effects upon the real variables compared across equilibria.

This view of equilibrium has been critiqued extensively on account of its being unrealistic, that is, on account of the fact that its assumptions are at variance with the empirical reality to an unacceptable degree. It can also be criticized (and I will do so in passing later) on the grounds that the universe it gives stylized expression to is not one involving capitalist production. Our discussion has not been concerned with either of these issues. It has been concerned with something altogether different, namely, this entire perception is also shot through with logical contradictions. And these can be listed as follows.

First, if there are fixed payments commitments, as there are bound to be, then a Walrasian equilibrium may not exist at all. Second, for that very reason, a change in money stock, far from yielding, through a comparison across equilibria, the same real variables, may in fact altogether deny the economy a new equilibrium even if perchance there was an equilibrium to start with. Third, even if there are no payments commitments, and hence no danger to the existence of an equilibrium from this source, a Walrasian equilibrium with a finite positive value of money would not exist unless we assume inelastic commodity price expectations, and this we can legitimately assume only if the value of money is determined in a manner that contradicts this equilibrium itself, that is, independently of demand and supply. Fourth, even if we do assume inelastic price expectations and keep our minds closed on the subject of why this should be so, even then the inelasticity of price expectations would violate a common postulate of monetarism, which states that changes in money stock have no effects on the real variables, and that, barring exogenous changes (in habits and customs), they have an equiproportional effect on money income. While this monetarist postulate requires unit-elastic price expectations, the modus operandi of monetarist theory requires inelastic price expectations.

Of late, not satisfied with the concept of a temporary equilibrium, some authors have put forward the concept of a rational-expectations equilibrium based on the presumption that each agent has perfect foresight up to a random error. This acquisition of perfect foresight is supposed to come about through a learning process. This view, too, is shot through with logical contradictions, which we examine in the next chapter.

Let us anticipate that discussion and mention some of these logical contradictions here itself: first, in so far as there are inherited payments commitments an unforeseen change in money stock may well prevent the existence of a new Walrasian equilibrium, even assuming that the economy started from one. Second, in such an eventuality the economy would settle in some (unspecified) non-Walrasian equilibrium, and if this happens then the so-called learning process that provides the basis of rational expectations is undermined: people cannot learn more and more about an equilibrium that does not get established, because given the parameter values it does not exist. And if the economy is in a sequence of non-Walrasian equilibria, then, as Harrod's (1939) famous "warranted growth" discussion shows, no amount of learning on the part of individuals can overcome the tendency toward cumulative instability of the system. There is in other words an alienation of the individual, a fundamental distinction between micro and macro terrains that no learning process can overcome even in principle as long as we are in the realm of non-Walrasian equilibria. Third, the concept of a rational expectations equilibrium not only obliterates this distinction, since it does not accept the possibility *ever* of a non-Walrasian equilibrium, but also has to obliterate (for its own consistency) the distinction between the individual as a maximizer of his or her individual interest and the individual as a microcosm of society pursuing social interests through individual actions in the belief that the individual interests too are best served through this pursuit. Such a belief would be palpably unfounded, in the sense that even if perchance an economy was placed on the growth path visualized by rational-expectations theory, each maximizing individual would find it in his or her own interest to deviate from it; and since such deviations would take the economy away from this path, any argument that in the long run the individuals would repent their folly in having deviated from this path, and learn not to do so, becomes entirely irrelevant.

In short, no matter how we see this theory, no matter which version of it we examine, there are fundamental logical problems with it. Economics as a discipline would have been ill founded if this theory, no matter how celebrated by the mainstream tradition, was all that there was to it. Fortunately, there is an alternative theoretical tradition, which, outside of the charmed circle of mainstream theorists, has been far more influential, even though its specificity as a tradition has never been properly discussed. We turn to this in the next part of this book. But before that, we will devote the next three chapters to a critique of certain other aspects of mainstream economic theory.

6

An Excursus on
Rational-Expectation Equilibria

THE ASSUMPTION OF RATIONAL EXPECTATIONS has been much in vogue of late. Expectations can, of course, be assumed to be "rational" about any economic variable, but what has been striking about the recent intellectual fashion is the assumption that expectations about the state of the economy are rational, which amounts to saying that economic agents have perfect foresight about the states of the economy on future dates (subject however to random error, and except insofar as completely novel circumstances, which have not been experienced in the past, and hence about which nothing has been learned, do not arise). The coming into vogue of rational expectations is associated not only with the development of a powerful critique of state intervention, which is seen inevitably and exclusively as price-destabilizing without even the saving grace of any transitional effect by way of output and employment augmentation, but also with a defense of the free-market system. This is because to assume rational expectations about the state of the economy is necessarily tantamount to an absolute denial of any involuntary unemployment (even of a temporary kind) owing to demand deficiency, an absolute denial of the possibility of any macroeconomics as a sui generis subject, and an absolute insistence that all macroeconomics is a mere extension and aggregation of phenomena arising from rational, that is, optimizing microeconomic behavior.

If demand deficiency existed, then the economy could in principle settle at any level of aggregate output, as Keynes argued. Or, putting it differently, the Keynesian system is associated with the possibility of multiple equilibria, the number of such equilibria being in principle infinite. To assume rational expectations in such a world would be absurd. Underlying the rational expectations assumption, therefore, is a denial of involuntary unemployment. And since involuntary unemployment constitutes in a sense the most glaring example of market failure, the denial of any possibility of involuntary unemployment amounts ideologically to a defense of the free market system. This defense, however, is based curiously on premises that are diametrically opposite to those that were in vogue in the 1930s.

Divergent Ideological Defenses of the Free Market

When Oskar Lange (1938) made his famous rebuttal of Ludwig von Mises's argument (Hayek 1935) that rational calculations were impossible in a socialist economy owing to the absence of a market for factors of production that were (at least the nonhuman ones) under the ownership and at the disposal of the state, Friedrich von Hayek fell back on a "second line of defense."[1] This was to interpret von Mises's denial as applying not to the theoretical *possibility* of rational calculations in a socialist economy, but to its practical *feasibility*. Hayek referred to the "thousands of equations" involved in any hypothetical solution of the problem as suggested by Lange for such an economy. The virtue of the free market in his view lay in the fact that nobody had to solve thousands of equations; the market did it for them while everybody merely acted as a price taker and worked out his or her optimal responses to the prevailing prices. By contrast, socialism was considered unworkable because in lieu of the market it is the central planner who would have to solve thousands of equations, which was "not a possible solution" (in the sense of feasibility). Even Pigou (1937, 118–119) was of the view that while the practical task of securing a rational allocation of resources under socialism was solvable *in principle*, it is "extraordinarily difficult… . Except in a world of supermen, many and grave lapses are certain to occur."

By contrast, what the rational-expectations assumption, applied to the state of the economy as a whole, implies is that every economic agent in a free market system habitually solves these thousands of equations.[2] The practical ability that Hayek was not willing to grant to the central planner in a socialist economy, the rational-expectations assumption not only grants to every economic agent but even insists that he or she makes habitual use of it. What is more, the virtue of the free market system on this view arises precisely because everyone solves these thousands of equations and thereby comes to predict the correct equilibrium outcome. We thus have a complete inversion of the premises on which the superiority of the free market is established: from the argument that "the market is good because nobody has to solve these thousands of equations" we now have the argument that "the market is good because everybody solves these thousands of equations." Of course, one could simply follow Hayek's lead and debunk rational expectations on grounds of practical feasibility. But there are in addition serious logical problems with the concept, in particular when applied to the state of the economy as a whole.

Some Implications of Rational Expectations

In the previous chapter we drew a distinction between expectations underlying the equilibrium and expectations about the equilibrium, a distinction corresponding to what one might call expectations about what is going to happen in the coming period or periods and expectations about the nature of the equilibrium in the current period itself. The first question that arises is: To what do rational expectations refer? The answer is: Both.

One may be tempted to believe that the domain of rational expectations can be broken up, that a situation can be imagined where every economic agent correctly predicts the equilibrium of the current period on the basis of knowledge of every economic agent's expectations about the next period, even though these expectations themselves are divergent and therefore not rational. Such a belief, however, is erroneous. In order to know every economic agent's expectations about the future in the absence of clairvoyance, one must know his or her expectation-formation rule. For correctly predicting the equilibrium of the current period, therefore, every economic agent, apart from knowing many other things, must know the expectation-formation rule of every economic agent. But this is knowledge that no amount of "learning" can help one to acquire. It is logically impossible to infer in the case of any agent the expectation-formation rule from his or her observed behavior over a sequence of periods, no matter how long, because, first, one cannot infer from observed behavior a unique set of expectations, and second, one cannot infer from a known set of expectations a unique expectation-formation rule. It follows that the only situation where rational expectations would prevail about the current period's equilibrium, which itself is based on expectations about the future, is if there are rational expectations about this future itself. The domain of rational expectations therefore cannot be broken up, and rational expectations must necessarily refer both to expectations about the equilibrium as well as to expectations underlying the equilibrium.

Rational expectations about the equilibrium in the current period therefore are logically predicated upon rational expectations about the whole sequence of future periods. But since what happens in the future is dependent upon what happens in the current period itself (for instance, the savings of the current period determine what the capital stock for the next period would be, and so on), this is tantamount, in the context of a worldview that sees macro phenomena as an aggregation of individual micro-level optimization, to saying that every individual in every period is on an infinite-horizon optimal path. Society seen as an aggregation of individuals is also on an infinite-horizon optimal path of the Ramsay variety.[3]

In short, rational expectations, applied to the state of the economy as a whole, are bound up with the notion of a rational expectation equilibrium path, or a sequence of rational expectation equilibria, which for each economic agent, and hence, by implication, for society as a whole seen as an aggregation of individuals, constitute an optimal path in the Ramsay sense. And this precisely is what makes rational expectations even marginally tenable: we are not talking about perfect foresight, up to a random error, of any odd sequence of states of the economy, but of a sequence that corresponds to a social optimum. And such a sequence is something about which it is presumably less weird to assume that individual economic agents can have more or less correct foresight.

Individual and Society in Rational-Expectations Theory

Underlying this whole conception, however, is a very specific view of the individual and society, namely that the individual is a microcosm of society, that he or she constitutes a miniature replica of society; or that society is simply an individual blown up n times, that the difference between the two is merely quantitative and not qualitative. This is more than merely an individualistic notion of society. After all, the Paretian notion of what constitutes social improvement is also based on an evaluation of what happens to the welfare of *individuals*, but the Paretian view of society is altogether different from this. In other words an individualistic notion of society, as opposed to a view of society as an indecomposable (Hegelian) entity, has been quite pervasive in economics. But the rational expectations perception is altogether different: it sees society not just as an aggregation of diverse individuals, with problems associated with such aggregation as Pareto discussed, but, literally, as a multiplication of similar individuals; it sees the individual not just as a component of society, but as a miniature version of it.

The proponents of the rational expectations approach make no secret of this view of society, which their approach entails, so much so that it may be considered by many to be a waste of time for us to establish this proposition so laboriously. When they postulate that every individual does a Ramsay-type optimization exercise and that all individuals are similar so that all of them together are also implicitly doing a Ramsay-type optimization exercise for society as a whole, what else are they doing but seeing the individual as a miniature replica of society?

The reason we have spent so much time establishing this point, however, lies in the fact that several writers, such as Hahn (1984), have seen this particular postulate as being merely silly, something superimposed on the rational expectations view. They distinguish in other words between "good" rational-expectations theorists (Lucas) and "bad" rational-expectations theorists (the others) and blame the latter for not knowing the elementary point that Ramsay-type optimization can occur only for society as a whole, and not for individuals. What they miss through this assertion is not only the logical necessity of postulating such optimizing behavior for the entire rational-expectations approach, but also a particular view of individual and society that theoretically sustains postulating such behavior. Rational expectations are inseparable from this, regardless of whether Lucas chooses to remain silent on this question.

Inconsistency in the Rational-Expectations View of the Individual

This view of the individual and society, however, is shot through with logical inconsistency. An essential logical requirement for any hedonistic optimization exercise is that the entity that is doing this exercise and the entity that is supposed to be the

beneficiary from it must largely (apart from minor elements of externalities) be identical. When we talk of social optimization, this condition is fulfilled: society, no matter how we define it, remains an inclusive entity, to which the benefits of any social
optimization can be deemed to accrue. When we talk of individual optimization, as in
mainstream economics, this condition is once again satisfied: we take the individual as
a price taker who optimizes entirely in the belief of being the sole beneficiary of it. Putting the matter differently, the logical prerequisite for any self-absorbed optimization
exercise is that its subject and its object must coincide, and this condition is satisfied
in the familiar optimization exercises in economic theory, either by assuming an inclusive subject or by assuming noninterdependence between multiple subjects.

This elementary and essential logical requirement, however, is not satisfied in the
rational expectations view of Ramsay-type optimization. Clearly we are not talking
about explicit social optimization: it is neither the government nor a central planner
nor some other entity representing society which is doing the optimization exercise;
we are really talking about a host of individuals, each doing a Ramsay-type optimization exercise and achieving as a consequence in an overall sense a Ramsay-type social
optimum as well. But since any such optimization exercise necessarily involves a decision about capital accumulation on the part of each individual, and since the pace of
this capital accumulation affects the overall capital-labor ratio and hence the wage rate
that each gets, the assumption of noninterdependence between the multiple subjects
of such exercises clearly becomes invalid. Let us see the consequences of this.

If the assumption of noninterdependence breaks down, then each entity doing an
optimization exercise would look at the effects of his action on others and of others'
actions upon him. This gives rise to problems of multiple equilibrium possibilities
(different equilibrium states depending upon different assumptions each makes about
the behavior of others), to free riding problems and the divergence between the social
optimum and the equilibrium state arrived at through individual optimization, and
in general to an invalidation of the view that the individual is a microcosm of society.
The logical inconsistency of the rational-expectations view of the individual therefore
consists in the fact that it assumes the individual to be simultaneously a hedonist opti-
mizer (in line with all mainstream theorizing) as well as a miniature version of society.
An individual cannot be both at the same time.

In fact, Hahn is perfectly right in asserting that it is silly to believe that a Ramsay-
type social optimum results from an aggregation of individual decision making. The
silliness arises precisely from the fact that the assumption of subject-object correspondence breaks down in this case, which is why social optimization is a sui generis
exercise. There are powerful but more mundane empirical objections as well, such as
the fact that society has infinite life while individuals do not. But even if we close our
eyes to all these obvious objections to the rational-expectations view, the basic logical
problem with it would still remain.

To see all this clearly, consider a society where the population is constant, and
where all individuals are identical in all respects including their utility functions (and

hence in their conception of the "bliss" level of utility). Each of them also has an infinite time-horizon (alternatively, we can take some poetic license and assume them to be infinitely long-lived). We can imagine that the level of savings, which, since we are going along with the rational-expectations view and ignoring aggregate-demand problems, is the same as the level of investment (let us ignore depreciation in all this discussion), is optimally determined in either of two ways.

We can imagine the social consumption fund being equally distributed among all individuals, in which case corresponding to any particular amount of this fund there is a unique but identical level of individual utility that we can identify as social utility. There would also be a unique "bliss" level of social utility,[4] and we can set up the optimal savings problem as:

Minimize

$$_0\int^\infty \{B - U(C_t)\}\, dt$$

where $C_t = L \cdot [f(k_t) - (dk/dt)_t]$ and the various symbols have their usual meanings (e.g., k denoting K/L).

Alternatively, since all individuals are identical, we can imagine each to be pursuing an *individual* optimization exercise (and their being identical would ensure that each would be getting the same amount of consumption). This latter optimization exercise can be taken to be exactly the same as the former except for the trivial variation that the former has the multiplicative term L in it, which the latter would not have. This is because in the former we are defining social utility, though it is taken to be identical with individual utility, over the entire social consumption fund as opposed to the per capita consumption level; if we defined the social utility function with per capita consumption as the argument, then the two minimands would be absolutely identical. In any case, when individual optimization is of this type, we would be justified in saying that the result of such *individual* optimization is the achievement of a *socially* optimal path. But such a framing of the individual optimization exercise would be a legitimate one only if the assumption of noninterdependence between individuals is justified. Let us see why.

The Euler equation giving the first order condition for this optimization exercise, as is well known, yields:

$$- (dU'/dt)/U' = f'(k) \ldots \qquad (I)$$

which is nothing else but saying that the marginal product of capital at any point along the optimal path is equal to the implicit interest rate given by the rate of fall of marginal utility at that point.

We can interpret this condition in the following manner. Suppose at time t an individual decides to reduce consumption by an infinitesimal amount dc and to devote this for investment. Along the optimal path he or she should not become better off by doing so, and this condition ensures that this is so. The loss in utility from reducing consumption is given by $U'(c(t)) \cdot dc$. On the other hand, the gain in utility from the additional investment is given by $U'(c(t + dt)) \cdot d(dk / dt) \cdot \{1 + f'(k)\}$. These two should be equal along the optimal path, so that (dropping for simplicity any explicit mention of the argument of the utility function)

$$U'(t) \cdot dc = U'(t + dt) \cdot dc \cdot \{1 + f'(k)\} \ldots \tag{II}$$

where we have substituted dc for $d(dk / dt)$ in the RHS because the two are by hypothesis equal.

Since $f'(k)$ is positive, this is possible only if U' is falling through time, as indeed it must be along the optimal path. We can rewrite the equation as:

$$U'(t + dt) - [dU'(t) / dt] \cdot dt = U'(t + dt)\{1 + f'(k)\}$$

If we divide all through by $U'(t + dt)$, then for infinitesimally small dt this comes to

$$-(dU'(t) / dt) / U'(t) = f'(k).$$

In short, the first-order conditions ensure that a small change in the consumption profile along the optimal path does not improve the individual's welfare. But this condition itself is derived by assuming noninterdependence. If there were interdependence, and the individual in question proceeded on the assumption that when he or she reduced consumption nobody else would do so (which is analogous to the standard price-taker assumption), then this path cannot be the optimal path, for the following reason.

Condition (II), from which condition (I) is derived, represents in turn a continuous-time version of the following more elaborate condition expressed in terms of discrete time that sets out clearly the pros and cons of decreasing consumption by an amount dc at time t on the optimal path:

$$U(c(t)) - U(c(t) - dc) = U[c(t + 1) + \{F(K(t + 1) + dK, L) \\ - F(K(t + 1), L)\} + dc] - U(c(t + 1)) \ldots \tag{III}$$

The LHS gives the decrease in utility at time t, and the RHS the increase in utility at $t + 1$. On the RHS the term in square brackets gives the consumption in period $t + 1$ in the new situation, where the middle term (in squiggly brackets) is the increase in output on account of the higher capital stock (owing to the lower consumption in the previous period). The reason for putting the third term ($+ dc$) inside the square brackets is that if we are talking about only a two-period displacement from the optimal path (with all future periods unaffected) then the increase in capital stock in period $t + 1$ has to be negated for the subsequent periods, and hence consumption has to rise by an amount dc, which is equal to the increased capital stock dK in period $t + 1$.

It can be easily checked that (II), and hence (I) can be derived from (III), taking time as continuous rather than discrete as in (III). For our purpose, however, it is (III) on which attention should be focused. The holding of condition (III) would certainly characterize the optimal path for an individual household if the individual households are noninterdependent, that is, the labor available with the household, which is denoted by L, is always confined to working on the capital stock of the household itself. But if this is not the case, that is, individual households do not constitute islands separated from one another, and labor from one household can work on the capital of another provided the wage rate it earns is higher than the marginal product of labor working on its own capital stock (or, what comes to the same thing, the marginal product of labor elsewhere in the economy is higher than within the household), then (III) cannot characterize the optimal path from the individual household's point of view. The individual would be better off breaking the Ramsay rule.

This point can be explained as follows. Suppose the individual, who is on a Ramsay path, decides to consume an additional amount by deducting an infinitesimally small part from his capital stock, which therefore shrinks to $K - dK$. If the same labor as before is applied to the shrunk capital stock, and out of the (lower) output produced, an additional amount dK is invested, apart from the old amount of investment that would have occurred on the Ramsay path anyway, then consumption at this later date would shrink, relative to what it would have been on the Ramsay path, for both these reasons. On the Ramsay path, the loss of utility on account of this shrinking exactly equals the earlier gain on account of the increase in consumption by dK. But if the individual with the lower capital stock (by dK) believes that he can work as a wage laborer with other individuals, and thereby have an income, and hence consumption, larger than what he would have got by working exclusively on his own shrunk capital stock on the Ramsay path, then he would opt out of the Ramsay path, because then the increase in utility by consuming dK would have been larger than the loss of utility on account of the lower consumption, which would be less low than on the Ramsay path. The individual would believe this if he believes that when he drops out of the Ramsay path, others would not. The fact that in such a situation the loss of income, even with a capital stock reduced by dK, is less than on the Ramsay path (when he works exclusively on his own capital stock) is easily demonstrated:

$$F(K - dK, L) = F(K - dK, L - dL) + F'_L (K - dK, L) \cdot dL \text{ (for some arbitrarily small } dL)$$

$$< F(K - dK, L - dL) + F'_L (K, L) \cdot dL \text{ (given the production function)}$$

$$= F(K - dK, L - dL) + w \cdot dL \text{ (owing to the price-taker assumption and the fact that in the economy as a whole } K / L \text{ prevails).}$$

It follows that the individual household would be better off by hiring out some labor than by employing all of it on its own capital, which has now shrunk to $(K - dK)$. Condition (III) therefore cannot define the optimal path from the point of view of the individual in a situation of interdependence, that is, when the individuals are neither islands separated from one another nor always acting in concert (the latter violates the price-taker assumption).

If everybody in other words happened to be on a Ramsay-type optimal path as visualized by rational-expectations theory, then each would find it advantageous to get off the path and consume more than what the Ramsay rule dictates, in the belief that others would be on the path. And since each would behave this way, nobody would be on a Ramsay-type optimal path to start with. And if nobody is on a Ramsay-type optimal path, then not only does a rational-expectations equilibrium, which postulates everybody's being on such a path, become invalid, but, what is more, even the assumption of rational expectations makes no sense (since, as discussed earlier, no amount of learning can give anyone a clue to the expectations-formation rule of anyone else).

There are only two circumstances under which the rational-expectations view would make sense. The first, as was mentioned before, is if each individual constitutes a minieconomy, an island separated from all other islands (that is, other individuals constituting similar minieconomies). This, together with the assumption of identical individuals (which means each has the same amount of labor and capital stock), would make the rational-expectations perception of each individual being a minireplica of society come true, but such a society would, by assumption, have no wage labor and no (labor-hiring) firms, that is, no capitalism. Even the rational-expectations theorists are hardly likely to deny the existence of firms and of wage labor and to establish their argument by referring exclusively to an artisan economy. This escape route is thus of little relevance.

The second circumstance is where individuals act in a manner that approximates the cooperative solution. This case, though it goes against the price-taker assumption, may be sought to be justified by the argument that individuals as individuals may "learn" to adopt the cooperative solution even when there is no explicit collusion between them. For instance, even though it pays each individual to opt out of the Ramsay path, on the assumption that others would continue to be on it, when all happen to be on it to start with, the fact that all would behave in this manner would make everyone worse off compared to the situation where each had adopted the cooperative solution. Therefore, it may be argued, individuals would spontaneously adopt the cooperative solution, in the sense of each being on the Ramsay path without resorting to any free riding (that is, increasing consumption in the belief that others would continue to be on the Ramsay path).

This, however, is totally unrealistic, apart from violating the basic tenet of mainstream economics that a competitive economy is characterized by price-taking behavior. Unless there is *explicit* collusion, with penalties for anyone violating the behavior rule appropriate for the collusive solution, a collusive solution would never be spontaneously arrived at by individuals acting in isolation. The point can be illustrated with reference to the famous case of the Harrodian knife-edge instability. Everybody may know that curtailing investment in a situation where the actual rate of growth falls below the warranted rate would only make matters worse in the aggregate; but anybody who did not curtail investment on this reasoning when the actual rate fell below the warranted rate, that is, anyone who decided to blaze an enlightened trail, would be even worse off than if he or she had curtailed investment. In short, individuals, as individuals, can never be expected to arrive at the cooperative solution spontaneously.

The Problem Looked at Differently

Before proceeding with this discussion, let us present the logical contradiction inherent in rational-expectation equilibria in a different way. The bliss we have been talking about can be of two kinds: a situation where the marginal product of capital is positive but the marginal utility from consumption is zero for each individual, which is what Ramsay had visualized; or a situation where the marginal utility from consumption is positive but the marginal product of capital is zero, which is what Schumpeter (1961) had called the "capital saturation point." Either case represents a state where further capital accumulation is pointless, and the entire output should be devoted to consumption. The second is the more pertinent case for two reasons: first, it can be adapted to the case of population growth (in which case the marginal product of capital is equated to the rate of population growth in the limit, to give highest level of sustainable per capita consumption along what is called the "golden-rule path," which is a generalization of the "capital saturation point"); second, it refers to the properties of the production rather than of the consumption function, and the latter are intrinsically more shaky; for these reasons Koopmans (1965) had taken the golden-rule path as the goal of the optimizing exercise. While sticking to the stationary population assumption, let us take our bliss to be referring to the capital-saturation point.

Now, at this limit point, since the marginal product of capital is zero, the rate of profit must be zero. The entire output therefore consists of the wage bill; or, the wage rate equals the per capita output. In a world where each individual is a price taker, each individual will believe that he or she will get the same wage rate in the market as the per capita output obtained while working with his or her own capital stock. Each price-taking individual therefore would believe, quite correctly, that he or she would be better off consuming his or her capital stock and offering himself or herself for wage labor on the market. Since each believes this and acts accordingly, production becomes impossible at this limit point. This is not a problem that would arise in a centrally planned economy, since the decision to dispose of the capital stock is not in the hands of individuals. But to pretend that a decentralized market economy can spontaneously mimic the optimal path of a centrally planned economy is a gross and serious error.

The matter can be seen formally as follows. The solution to any Ramsay-type optimization problem gives us first-order conditions from which the optimal path is worked out by putting in two bits of information: one relates to the initial state, and the other relates to the terminal state which in an infinite-horizon model is replaced by the "transversality condition." The transversality condition corresponding to the optimization problem presented in the previous section is given by

$$(K_t - K^*) \cdot u'(c_t) = 0 \ldots (T)$$

$$\text{Lim } t \to \infty$$

where lowercase letters denote per capita variables and K^* refers to the social-capital stock associated with the capital saturation point. Since $u'(c)$ does not tend to zero as t tends to infinity (we are taking bliss to be synonymous with the capital-saturation point), it follows that in the limit the level of capital stock must tend to K^*. But maintaining a level of capital stock K^* when the rate of profit on it is zero is incompatible with individual rationality, and hence impossible in a capitalist economy characterized by distinct noncollusive households, though perfectly possible in a planned economy. Hence the rational-expectations equilibrium, which is based on the assumption that each household is on such a path is logically untenable.

It follows from this that even if the population was increasing, so that the limit was not the capital-saturation point but the golden-rule k (Koopmans 1965), it would still be the case that the socially optimal path could not be reached spontaneously through decentralized decision making by a host of price-taking individuals; on the contrary, decentralized decision making by price-taking individuals would necessarily result in free riding, which would logically undermine the rational expectations equilibrium.

Of course, the problem we have highlighted may cease to matter if there were a positive rate of time preference, which is why all arguments about the equivalence between the planned outcome and the decentralized market outcome assume a positive rate of time preference (Blanchard and Fisher 1992). The conditions required for this result are several: first, each individual must have a positive rate of time preference; second, this must be constant (otherwise income distribution would come into play); third, it must be the same across all individuals; and fourth, this uniform rate of individual time preference must be the same as the social rate of time preference. Whether individuals have a positive rate of time preference at all has been a matter of much debate. Indeed, no less a person than Schumpeter, whom nobody can accuse of being unsympathetic toward capitalism, has argued quite forcefully (Schumpeter 1961) that a positive rate of time preference, far from being an innate feature of individual preference, is itself a reflection of the fact that a positive rate of interest exists in the real world and that the innate feature of individual preference is actually a zero rate of time preference.

We do not have to go into these questions here. The basic point is that a result that may hold under very stringent assumptions has been passed off in the literature as if it is the general case. While in an exceptional case it may be that identical individuals undertaking optimizing behavior may spontaneously mimic the plan outcome under Ramsay-type social optimizing, this has been taken to be the general case, and a whole elaborate structure of rational-expectations equilibrium has been erected on this extremely flimsy foundation.

The Market and the Cooperative Solution

For a moment, let us set aside this basic logical problem with rational-expectations theory by attributing to it the unambiguous view that individuals spontaneously arrive at cooperative solutions. In what follows we refer exclusively to this particular interpretation of the "rational expectations view." The question then arises: Can "atomistic" individuals arrive at a cooperative solution *spontaneously*, that is, without any explicit attempt at cooperation? The belief that individuals spontaneously transcend the limits of mundane individualism and arrive at cooperative solutions is interestingly enough paralleled by the Keynesian belief in state intervention. What is common to both perceptions is the conviction of the necessity of the transcendence of mundane individualism.[5] But while Keynesianism believes that this can come about only through the instrumentality of the state, since individuals themselves operating in the market cannot arrive at cooperative solutions, the rational-expectations view may be interpreted as asserting the very opposite, by celebrating the efficacy of the market as opposed to that of state intervention.

This raises important issues about the theory of the state implicit in the rational-expectations view. If individuals functioning in the market can spontaneously arrive at cooperative solutions by transcending mundane individualism, why can individuals functioning in civil society not likewise arrive at cooperative solutions which, from the liberal standpoint that all rational-expectations theorists would claim to share, should then entail that there would be no need for a state whatsoever? In this sense, Keynesianism at least has the virtue of consistency: its theory of the state and its theory of the functioning of the market hold together. The same cannot be said however of rational-expectations theory.

At first sight, the rational-expectations view about individuals transcending mundane individualism to arrive at a cooperative solution may appear reminiscent of the socialist position. This, however, is incorrect. There are two fundamental but related differences between how socialist theory views cooperative association and how rational-expectations theory views this phenomenon. Central to socialist theory is the perception that as individuals come together to cooperate they transcend not only mundane individualism but also, to an extent, individualism per se. The institutional expression of this cooperation becomes, in other words, an irreducible conglomerate agent whose behavior has to be analyzed sui generis. Rational-expectations theory, on the other hand, is anchored in individualism. Central to it is the perception that individuals, even as they transcend mundane individualism to arrive at the cooperative solution, remain within the confines of individualism. There is no qualitative change in them. This is also the basic difference between the game-theoretic notion of coalitions and the Marxist notion of such collectives as trade unions and classes (though the latter has deeper implications).

The second difference follows from this: The arrival at a cooperative solution in socialist theory is made possible through some actual agency going beyond the market rather than through implicit collusion by individuals in the market. Cooperative solutions, in other words, require an actual cooperative, the relationship among whose members is direct and not mediated through the market. The rational-expectations view, by contrast, takes the market as the central phenomenon and postulates a cooperative solution through implicit collusion among individuals in the market.

The problem with this latter view, as mentioned earlier, is obvious. Even if we accept for a moment the fact that individuals do transcend mundane individualism and, if placed on a socially optimal path would not deviate from it in pursuit of free riding, it is a far cry from this to assert that on their own they would grope their way to such a path. In other words, there is a fundamental difference between not deviating from a path if one happens to be there and getting to it if one does not happen to be on it. The acceptance of the first does not entail that of the second. On the contrary, there is absolutely no mechanism to carry an economy governed by individual hedonistic decision making onto a socially optimal path. The reason for this is the following.

Individual optimizing behavior must be predicated upon some assumption about what other people are doing. When the economy is off the socially optimal path, no individual would assume that the others would be following the Ramsay rule. In such a situation even if the individual in question has transcended mundane individualism, that is, if others were following the Ramsay rule, then he or she would do so rather than go free riding, whereas since others are not following this rule, he or she as an optimizing individual would have no reason for doing so either. It follows that when the economy is off the optimal path, the vector of individual investment decisions arrived at through individual optimizing behavior would not only be very different from what should prevail on the optimal path, but would also have no reason for converging to the latter either. The assertion that the socially optimal path is reached through the decision-making process of a group of hedonistic individuals whose relations are mediated entirely through the market, an assertion central to rational-expectations theory, is thus without any foundations.

There are two possible circumstances in which an economy that is off the socially optimal path can transit to it. First, if every individual behaves as if he or she constitutes a minieconomy and starts following the Ramsay rule even when others are not doing so, and even though it is inoptimal from his or her point of view to do so (as indeed it must be when others are not doing so). The second is when individuals get together in an explicit collusion and simply realize the cooperative solution. The first of these involves the transcendence (or at any rate an abridgement) of individualism altogether; the second of these involves the transcendence of the market itself. And either of these requires what I have called "cooperative rationality,"[6] for implicit collusion brought about on the basis of individual rationality (even of nonmundane individual rationality) is not enough. The logical contradiction of the rational-expectations theory consists in the fact that it requires for its validity the assumption of cooperative rationality while it is wedded to methodological individualism and the celebration of the market, which together preclude cooperative rationality.

Concluding Observations

In an earlier chapter we saw that in a world with inherited payments commitments a Walrasian equilibrium may not exist at all, in the sense that with an arbitrarily given money stock in any particular period the mere flexibility of money wages and prices would not necessarily ensure that all markets clear. If a Walrasian equilibrium does not exist, then the very basis of the rational expectations theory as a theory of the functioning of the economy as a whole disappears. This, namely the nature of the equilibrium in the presence of inherited payments commitments, is one central issue that the present book is concerned with.

A second set of objections to rational-expectations theory as a macroeconomic theory focuses on its total unrealism, which, as we mentioned earlier, would have been repugnant to von Hayek himself no matter how sympathetic he would have been to its celebration of the virtues of the free market.

In this chapter we have been concerned exclusively with a third set of objections to rational-expectations theory that involve its logical consistency. The fact that we have concentrated on this third set of objections should not be taken to imply that we exonerate the theory of the charge of failing on the first two objections.

7

An Excursus on
Methodological Individualism

THE ARGUMENTS PRESENTED IN the preceding chapters entail a fundamental critique of methodological individualism, a critique that is best made explicit instead of having to be inferred from arguments relating to other themes. The purpose of this chapter is to do so.

Methodological individualism encompasses at least three crucial elements: ontological individualism, that is, an acceptance of the individual as the preeminent existent category in society; epistemological individualism, that is, an acceptance of the individual as the preeminent analytical category in social theory; and (perhaps implicit in the first two elements but worth emphasizing separately) an acceptance of the view that what happens in society confirms the coincidence between the intentions behind individual actions and the outcomes of these actions. Much of the critique of methodological individualism has concentrated on the first of these elements, and derivatively therefore upon the second; that is, upon arguments such as that the individual represents an abstraction, or that the individual is socially determined and constituted and so on. These are powerful arguments and raise deep issues. This chapter will explore the third element, not only because it has been less discussed, at any rate in the context of methodological individualism, but also because it provides the basis for an internal logical critique of methodological individualism, which is the preferred level of discourse of this book.

Intentions and Outcomes of Individual Actions

Even if we accept that the individual is the most significant existent social category, methodological individualism, which aggregates individual actions to arrive at social phenomena, would be legitimate only if this aggregation is legitimate. If each and every individual decides to save ten percent more but the aggregate consequence of these decisions is to keep total savings unchanged, or if each and every worker offers labor power at 10 percent less in money wages in order to overcome unemployment but the aggregate consequence is to leave unemployment unchanged, then starting from individual motivations and individual decisions ceases to be of any help in explaining social phenomena. An unbridgeable chasm opens up between the aggregation of individual actions looked at from the point of view of intentions and the aggregate consequence of these actions. A mysterious element interposes itself between the intentions in their totality and the outcome in its totality. In such a situation, it is this element that demands center stage in analysis; the analysis of individual motivations and actions then becomes altogether secondary. Methodological individualism then, in a strict sense, that is, unless used merely to flesh out an analysis centering on this mysterious element (in which case we would hardly be justified in calling it methodological individualism at all), becomes a real obstacle to understanding. In short, even if we accept that the individual is the preeminent social category, the legitimacy of methodological individualism cannot be accepted unless the third condition mentioned above about the coincidence between the intentions and outcome of individual actions is satisfied.

Marx clearly underscored the fact that there are two distinct (though of course connected) issues, one relating to the identity of the central social category (which has a direct bearing therefore upon the identity of the central analytical category in social analysis), and the other relating to the noncoincidence in the aggregate between the intentions underlying individual actions and the outcome of such actions. Social classes, in his perception, constituted the central social category, and also the central analytical category in social analysis. But the existence or the preeminence of classes did not mean that the individual was a mere artificial construct. On the contrary, an exchange economy is characterized by transactions between apparently independent and apparently symmetrically placed individual owners of commodities. Class is not a visible entity; it merely underlies, in the pristine state of capitalism at any rate, a world in which individuals play out their (class) roles as individuals. What is more, however, even after associations have appeared under capitalism and have supplanted individual decision making in many spheres, a whole range of decisions still continues to be taken by individual agents, the most significant of which are the investment decisions. Individual actions have to be located therefore within an analysis in which classes occupy a central role. But, Marx argued, the hallmark of the system was that in the aggregate the intentions behind and the outcome of individual actions did not coincide, resulting in anarchy.

Anarchy in this sense is to be distinguished from several other phenomena that are related to it but whose presence would be readily conceded by almost everybody. One would be micro-level deviations from equilibrium, of the too-many-shirts-but-too-few-shoes kind, which may be caused by lags in adjustment or random factors or whatever. The other is macro-level ebb and flow of a regular cyclical kind, which represent in a sense a temporal counterpart of this first phenomenon. The hallmark of both these phenomena consists in the fact that the equilibrium (founded upon methodological individualism) is seen as a tendency, as an average state of affairs toward which the system is always tending without necessarily reaching it. The frustration of individual intentions caused by *such* deviations from "equilibrium," however, would scarcely pose a problem for methodological individualism. The problem would arise only when the frustration of individual intentions is rooted in systemic factors that militate against the very notion of such an "equilibrium."

Of course, in several places in Marx's own writings as well as those of later Marxists, the term *anarchy* is used exclusively in the weak sense, that is, in the sense of being confined to such deviations from equilibrium (of the Marxian kind), the impression given being that an equilibrium establishes itself only as an average of more or less regular deviations. True, the equilibrium being talked about is not one founded upon methodological individualism, since it is characterized by an industrial reserve army, whose existence sustains the process of appropriation of surplus value and militates against seeing the world as the conjoint outcome of a series of individual optimizing decisions. But while this fact undermines methodological individualism, the objection is still of the first kind, relating to the identity of the central social category. The fact of anarchy, if it is only of this weak kind, arouses no serious additional objections. But, as we will see in subsequent chapters, the whole thrust of Marx's argument points toward anarchy of the strong kind; that is, logically implicit in his argument is anarchy of the strong kind, whether he himself consistently recognized it (which, incidentally, is one reason why the Marxian conception of crisis is not synonymous with a mere cyclical trough). And this kind of anarchy destroys the basis for methodological individualism.

The conception of equilibrium, which sustains and is in turn sustained by methodological individualism, is of course the Walrasian conception. It not only posits the centrality of the individual as a social category, and hence as the legitimate focus of any social analysis, but also asserts the coincidence between the intentions behind and the outcome of individual actions, both in the micro sense and in the macro sense. In other words, in its perception, individuals, whether seen in their individuality or in the aggregate, are never frustrated.

Indeed, one can go further. Without a Walrasian equilibrium, methodological individualism will have no *locus standi*, since all the characteristics that must be associated with an equilibrium founded upon methodological individualism can be found *only* in the Walrasian equilibrium. To be sure, this last proposition would be readily questioned, and indeed some writers have been trying to write more realistic stories, of a non-Walrasian kind, without jettisoning methodological individualism. We will turn to these attempts later in this chapter, but let us continue with our argument for the present.

It follows from what has just been said that if the Walrasian picture is at palpable variance with the observed world, then in the process methodological individualism loses its legitimacy. We have been arguing so far that the Walrasian conception is undermined by the cognizance of historical time, characterized for instance by the fact of inherited payments commitments. And since this fact constitutes a real-life phenomenon, the Walrasian conception *is* at palpable variance with the real world. Methodological individualism then cannot retain its legitimacy.

The Classics and the Concept of Anarchy

It is a commonplace observation that the classical economists Adam Smith and David Ricardo operated in terms of aggregate categories such as landlords, laborers, owners of stock, and the like rather than of individuals. Their approach cannot therefore in any sense be subsumed under methodological individualism. True, Smith is often considered a progenitor of the Walrasian equilibrium and even a prescient observer of its optimality property ("individual avarice leading to social good"), but even though there is a strand in Smith's writing that looks at individual interactions in the market, his individuals, despite sharing many common traits, bear the imprint of their class positions. In other words Smith's individuals are not a uniform or symmetrically placed bunch. Their appearance in Smith's analysis cannot stamp the analysis as *individualistic* in any sense.

The same is true even more emphatically of Ricardo. Individual motivations, individual optimizing, and decision making at the level of individual agents is absent from his analysis beyond the obvious assumption that, ceteris paribus, workers would move from low-wage employment to high-wage employment, capital would move from low-profit-rate activities to high-profit-rate activities, and likewise landlords would lease out land to the one offering the higher rent. But individuals are taken in the context of their class positions, and once these minimum assumptions are made, the analysis of value, distribution, and dynamics is made with an inexorable logic using categories where individualistic attributes are marked by their absence.

It is striking, however, that while the classical rejection of methodological individualism is on ontological grounds, the concept of anarchy scarcely figures in the classical writings. This is because the classical system is essentially supply-constrained, Malthus's position on glut, no matter what one thinks of its originality,[1] being intellectually unsatisfactory and unsustainable in the face of Ricardo's argument. In fact the classical value theory presupposes what Marx would have called the absence of a "realization problem." If this problem is absent, then individual market prices can diverge from the equilibrium prices of production, some exceeding and others falling short; but we can still be justified in visualizing the prices of production as the "center of gravity" of the system and carrying out the analysis of the dynamics of the system exclusively in terms of these prices without giving much thought to the market prices. But if a realization problem exists, and the system can settle anywhere depending upon the state of aggregate demand, then the entire vector of market prices can deviate from the prices of production for arbitrary lengths of time, in which case carrying out analysis exclusively in terms of the prices of production can be seriously misleading for several purposes. In other words, the classical (and by classical here we essentially mean Ricardian, since Ricardo represented the apogee of the classical system) rejection of a demand constraint, the classical conception of equilibrium prices, the classical *method* of analyzing the dynamics of the system exclusively in terms of these equilibrium prices: all these elements hung together. And in the process the recognition of the possibility of anarchy was precluded.

It can be argued that the job of a pioneer in the analysis of the market system, such as Adam Smith, is to show how the market works and not to highlight market failures. Mystery at that stage surrounds the question of how the market works and not how it fails, since its working itself constitutes the marvel. In ignoring demand-constrained equilibria, then, Smith was merely doing the job of a pioneer. Since Ricardo simply took over from Smith and attempted to find answers to some burning practical questions of his time, he too operated with a system without any demand constraint. What is more, no serious demand constraint appeared as a practical problem until the end of the Napoleonic Wars. When it did appear, it troubled Ricardo greatly. In short, the classical ignoring of the demand constraint can be attributed to its own early appearance both in the history of theory as well as in the history of capitalism.

Keynesianism and Anarchy

With Keynesianism, we have the very opposite situation: It accepts, though in a slapdash manner, the primacy of the individual in an ontological and epistemological sense but highlights anarchy. In fact, Keynes's "paradox of thrift" can be taken as the classic example of noncoincidence between individual intentions and the outcome of individual actions. Since Keynesianism focused upon demand-constrained systems, and since the concept of anarchy was central to demand-constrained systems (for otherwise there would not be a demand constraint), anarchy constituted the core of Keynesian analysis.

The further extension of Keynesian analysis by his followers brought out the anarchy of the capitalist system with even greater clarity. Thus Harrod's dynamics produced an even more striking result on the noncoincidence between the intention behind and the outcome of action by individuals in the aggregate. An initial reduction in the level of capacity utilization faced by the capitalists makes each of them cut back on investment decisions in order to improve capacity utilization, but the overall result of their action is a further reduction in capacity utilization for all of them. Harrod's famous proposition about the instability of the warranted growth path amounted therefore to an emphatic rejection of methodological individualism. Individual motivations and decisions, such as for instance the capitalists' desire to improve capacity utilization by cutting back on investment, would enter as building blocks for analysis, but do not constitute the totality of analysis. On the contrary, the core of analysis is constituted by that extra element, that mysterious "other thing," which frustrates individual intentions.

Notwithstanding his emphasis on anarchy (though he never used this word), Keynes carried out his analysis starting from the individual. Partly this was a habit of thought for him, a component of his Marshallian legacy that he could not get rid of. Partly, however, he does not seem to have been overmuch concerned with what starting point he adopted. Throughout the *General Theory* Keynes keeps talking about categories such as capitalists, workers, rentiers, and the like, but when it comes to analysis he recognizes only individuals, as when he talks of a marginal propensity to consume that is prima facie independent of income distribution between classes.

Similar practical considerations made him attribute hedonism to individuals rather than any belief that individuals, even under capitalism, did make careful calculations before deciding on their optimum course of action. On the contrary, in one of his famous passages elsewhere, Keynes (1951, 312) questioned the realism of the concept of the maximizing individual: "It is not a correct deduction from the Principles of Economics that enlightened self-interest always operates in the public interest. Nor is it true that self-interest is generally enlightened; more often individuals acting separately to promote their own ends are too ignorant or too weak to attain even these. Experience does not show that individuals when they make up a social unit are always less clear-sighted than when they act separately." Keynes talks here of individuals being only "too ignorant or too weak"; this was written in 1926, long before the *General Theory*, which is why he did not talk of the frustration of individual intentions arising from systemic causes. It is clear nonetheless that taking the hedonist individual as his starting point was for Keynes a matter of practical convenience rather than of firm conviction.

But one crucial element of the Keynesian theoretical system was justified by invoking a supraindividual agent, namely the short-period rigidity of money wages, which Keynes attributed to the presence of trade unions.[2] Whether rigid money wages are responsible for involuntary unemployment is beside the point here (we will come back to it later); but the Keynesian system needs money wages to be determined somehow, and Keynes's explanation gives no role to *individual* behavior. Keynes thus not only undermined methodological individualism through his overall emphasis on anarchy, but he even went beyond it in his theoretical schema notwithstanding his general acceptance, for practical reasons, of the maximizing individual as an ontological starting point.

Individualism and Non-Walrasian Equilibrium

In recent years, several writers have tried to reconcile individualism with the existence of Keynesian or unemployment equilibria. Persuaded on one hand that involuntary unemployment is a fact of life, so that the possible existence of unemployment equilibria has to be theoretically demonstrated, and on the other hand that the individual still represents the best starting point for economic analysis, these authors seek to explain money-wage rigidity through individual behavior, something that Keynes, as we just saw, did not do.

The argument is that the labor market is different from other markets (Solow 1990). This market represents a social institution where individual sellers cannot act in a manner that shows unconcern for the reaction of other sellers, not reaction in the sense of economic retaliation as in an oligopolistic market, but reaction in the more basic sense of social reaction. The fact that money wages are rigid, and it is such rigid money wages that are supposed to give rise to involuntary unemployment, is explained not with reference to supraindividual agents such as trade unions but on the basis of individual behavior itself, the argument being that no individual worker, even if unemployed, would undercut wages since this would invite adverse reaction from other workers to which he is not indifferent. Hence in a world peopled exclusively by individuals involuntary unemployment can still exist because money-wage flexibility, which according to these authors would have got rid of such unemployment, is precluded by the fact of social interaction among these individuals.

Even if we go along with this argument and accept that unemployment equilibrium is a result exclusively of money wage rigidity, this argument still does not amount to a restoration of methodological individualism for at least two reasons. First, insofar as we are talking of an *unemployment equilibrium*, no matter whether the labor-market behavior that sustains it is compatible with individualism, the problem of the noncoincidence between the intentions behind and the outcome of individual actions surfaces once again. The focus of analysis then must move away from the individual and into that mysterious element that underlies this noncoincidence. We can, in short, have individuals as the sole actors in the play, and yet the play would not be in the genre of methodological individualism.

Second, in discussing the social compulsions on the individual, we have already implicitly brought in the larger entity, whether we call it a "class" or merely a "group," to which the individual belongs. We have once again therefore moved away from methodological individualism even while retaining the individual as the main actor in the play. Putting it differently, the individual who constitutes the starting point for methodological individualism is a hedonistic individual who maximizes an objective function defined over things, subject to certain constraints that also relate to the individual's command over resources defined in terms of things. The individual in methodological individualism reigns in isolated splendor over a universe peopled with things. Even if the individual has to reckon with other individuals' reactions, as in oligopoly theory for instance, that reaction is mediated through things (Lange 1963). Direct sensitivity on the part of any individual to the reactions of other individuals on account of their social intercourse and not on account of what these reactions do to the world of things over which the individual presides is precluded by methodological individualism, because such sensitivity already points towards social categories beyond the individual. There are, after all, several analytical systems, and associated with them several philosophical systems, that take the individual as the starting point

(Sartrean existentialism is one of them)—but not all of them can be subsumed under methodological individualism.

Methodological individualism, then, remains tied to the concept of a Walrasian equilibrium, and the untenability of this latter concept as a significant explanatory factor for the real world correspondingly undermines methodological individualism as well. The weakness of the one reflects the weakness of the other.

8

An Excursus on Walrasian Equilibrium and Capitalist Production

THE ARGUMENT SO FAR HAS SOUGHT to establish the following: First, the historicity of time, which manifests itself in terms of inherited commitments from the past and uncertain expectations about the future, makes the Walrasian equilibrium an untenable stylization of the economic universe; second, the introduction of money further accentuates the logical problems associated with this concept of equilibrium, so that the view that the value of money is determined, like that of any other commodity, by its demand and supply, is untenable; third, the concept of a rational expectation equilibrium is afflicted, in addition, by a logically contradictory view of the "individual"; and fourth, if the Walrasian view is flawed, then methodological individualism ceases to be relevant for this reason alone, quite apart from the usual objections to it on ontological grounds.

In addition to these objections arising from the logical problems implicit in its handling of time, as we will see here, there is a further problem with the Walrasian stylization: Its concept of equilibrium is incompatible with capitalist production.

The Cooperative Nature of Production

All production is social, not just in the sense that people live in societies and produce for one another, but also in the sense that the mode of organization of production is not a matter of individual volition. The individual is neither the subject nor the object of production. No doubt, mainstream economics textbooks often begin their exposition by referring to Robinson Crusoe's economy, but that is seriously misleading. As Marx remarked long before Crusoe's economy became fashionable among economists, "The solitary and isolated hunter or fisherman, who serves Adam Smith or Ricardo as a starting point, is one of the unimaginative fantasies of eighteenth-century romances à la Robinson Crusoe" (1971, 188).

An economy of subsistence producers, it may be thought, represents an approximation to Crusoe's economy, but even subsistence producers have to produce for their feudal lords, so that they are not the objects of their own production; and even in the most pristine subsistence economy there is some exchange, which may be different from commodity production (such as in the *jajmani* system of rural India) but entails a degree of social cooperation that nullifies the notion of a solitary individual subject of production. Besides, quite independent of these excursuses into history, there can scarcely be any doubt that under capitalism, at any rate, production is palpably social, that the individual is neither the subject nor the object of production, that is, that production is done through the cooperation of many and is meant for the market rather than as use-value for the producers individually, or even collectively.

All production occurs within a context of specific rules regarding the appropriation of products, or, putting it differently, certain specific property relations; and, since production is social, these are necessarily social property relations. The implications of this proposition in terms of the different forms in which surplus gets appropriated at different historical stages of social development, which constitute the point of departure for Marxian analysis, need not detain us here. Our concern is with an altogether different implication of the social character of production. This has to do with the fact that production is socially organized.

Any such organization must entail some coordination, and hence some means of disciplining individuals engaged in this coordinated production into fulfilling their assigned roles. This would be true even under precapitalist production. Even in a tribal society engaged in hunting, there has to be coordination between those who drive animals from their hideouts and those whose job it is to kill the animals. If the shooters decide to take a nap while the beaters are at work, then the efforts of the beaters would have been completely in vain. Society therefore has mechanisms for ensuring coordination among individuals engaged in cooperative—socially organized—production.

The typical site of such cooperative production in a modern capitalist society is the factory, and the mechanism that ensures such coordination within the factory is the discipline imposed by the "boss," the capitalist, through his agents. But the mode of imposition of such discipline in a social system where the "whip" is outdated is the "sack." Any individual worker who does not "obey" the discipline of the factory gets the "sack"—is fired, that is—and is replaced by somebody else.

The sack, however, holds absolutely no threats in a world of full employment such as the one that characterizes a Walrasian equilibrium. It follows that if a capitalist economy experienced a Walrasian equilibrium, then its very functioning would become impossible, since the shop-floor discipline necessary for it would get undermined.

The Basis of Discipline Under Capitalism

One of Marx's greatest insights was to recognize that what is purchased in the labor market is not labor service per se but the worker's capacity to work. The worker is paid a wage (whether at the beginning or at the end of the production period is immaterial) in return for his commitment to work at a certain intensity for a certain duration of time with a certain level of skill and dexterity under the direction of the capitalist.

This is not just an empirical fact; without it, capitalist production would be impossible. If workers decided to quit a particular shop floor and migrate to some other factory after working for a certain arbitrary period of time, which is unknown in advance and dependent only on their whims, then even though they would be paid only for the time they worked, the organization of production would become impossible. For any group that migrates in this manner, replacements would not be found in time; machines would lie idle for varying lengths of time during which replacements were being arranged, and production would suffer. And since these replacements themselves may seek to drift away whenever their whims so dictate, the production losses would be altogether exorbitant. (Using the terminology of mainstream economics, some might say that the transaction costs would be prohibitive.) Of course, in a world of full employment where the workers would be more or less sure of obtaining work elsewhere, the tendency to indulge one's whim and migrate whenever one so fancied would be quite strong (even the time taken in job search would not be a daunting factor), but the problem would remain no matter what the level of employment. Capitalist production, in other words, necessarily requires a commitment-based labor contract.

The commitment entailed in such a contract however would have little meaning unless there is a threat of punitive action associated with the act of reneging on it. Such punitive action must be distinguished from the cut in wages that any act of nonfulfillment of commitment may bring forth. If such nonfulfillment were punished only by a wage cut, then the commitment would have little meaning. It becomes a commitment precisely because the punitive action threatened is more than a pari passu wage cut. To give an example, if workers engaged for an eight-hour shift with a certain intensity of work decide to work at half that intensity and express willingness to accept only half the wage rate, the capitalist would scarcely accept the arrangement, since the production losses he would be making would far outweigh the saving on the wage bill. He would therefore bind the workers to a labor contract where reneging on it is made costly to the workers (in addition to the wage loss) through the threat of punitive action. The obvious punitive action is the sack.[1] But the "sack" would not be a punitive action if the economy systematically achieved full employment.[2] Hence, capitalist production is incompatible with a Walrasian equilibrium.

The Role of the Reserve Army of Labor

The argument just presented has to be distinguished from another argument to which it bears a family resemblance. This other argument states that a reserve army of labor is necessary for keeping the distributive conflict in check under capitalism; that is, if a reserve army did not exist, then the workers' bargaining power would be sufficiently strong for them to put in wage claims that would be incompatible with what the capitalists consider an acceptable rate of profit, resulting either in a disruption of accumulation (and hence a recreation of the reserve army) or (if we assume that the reserve army is not spontaneously recreated) in a state of accelerating inflation as the capitalists collude, implicitly or explicitly, to fix prices in an attempt to obtain the acceptable rate.[3] It follows from this view that a capitalist economy can never maintain full employment in the sense of an avoidance of an excess supply of labor at the going real wage while simultaneously maintaining price stability in the sense of an avoidance of accelerating inflation. Marx, in other words, was "the first NAIRU theorist"—that is, the first theorist of the nonaccelerating inflation rate of unemployment.[4]

This argument, no matter how powerful and insightful (which in my view it is), amounts to an extrinsic critique of the Walrasian stylization on the grounds that it does not capture the reality of capitalism. My argument is along somewhat different lines. It states that the Walrasian stylization does not itself have a coherent conception of the reality of capitalism, in particular of capitalist production. It cannot, in other words, tell a consistent story about how exactly production is carried out under capitalist conditions, let alone whether this story is "realistic" or not.

Both arguments are derived from Marx, though this point may be missed by those who tend to interpret Marx's concept of the reserve army almost exclusively as a device for keeping down wages. In fact, Marx thought of the role of the reserve army under capitalism as being a multifarious one. It kept down the wage rate by restricting the bargaining power of the workers, thereby ensuring that the extraction of surplus value continued unabated. But in addition, it was also a disciplining device as far as the workers were concerned, which, as already mentioned, was essential for capitalist production. Finally, Marx also saw the reserve army as something that made investment in new products and new avenues possible: large numbers of workers could be mobilized and thrown into work in particular spheres without disrupting the smooth flow of production elsewhere in the economy.[5]

By contrast, Schumpeter's notion of "circular flow," which corresponded according to him to the Walrasian equilibrium, was characterized by full employment. He used this construct to deny the existence of surplus value as a category under capitalism, but this also made his theory untenable, since he had to assert, contrary to what is directly observed, that the workers lost out during a boom (because of "forced savings" at full employment) and gained during a recession (because of price falls relative to money wages in the neighborhood of full employment).[6] For them, according to Schumpeter's theory, a boom was a time of misery while a recession was an occasion for great happiness. This obviously false result arose because of Schumpeter's insistence that the circular flow was characterized by full employment, a possibility that Marx never entertained.

Of the various roles the reserve army can play under capitalism it is the role of disciplining the workers in the workplace, which we have focused on, since, without it, production itself becomes impossible. The Walrasian equilibrium, which does away with the reserve army, has no alternative coherent story on how this discipline might be exercised.

NAIRU and the "Natural Rate"

To say that capitalist production is incompatible with full employment, and hence a Walrasian equilibrium, is not to subscribe to the concept of a "natural rate of unemployment." The natural rate of unemployment precludes involuntary unemployment, defined simply as an excess supply of labor at the going real-wage rate. The natural rate therefore is full employment. The only unemployment visible when the economy is at the natural rate is either of the voluntary or of the frictional kind (including what is associated with job search), but neither of these entails any excess supply of labor. By contrast the argument presented above states that it is unemployment precisely in the sense of an excess supply of labor at the going real-wage rate, which is essential for the discipline needed for capitalist production.

The nonaccelerating inflation rate of unemployment, which is a more generic term, must be distinguished from the natural rate, which of course is only one particular instance of the NAIRU, but by no means the only one: one can in other words be a perfect believer in the concept of a NAIRU without at all subscribing to the natural rate idea. Since the NAIRU may entail excess supply of labor at the going wage rate, a capitalist economy experiencing such a NAIRU will have the appropriate disciplining device required for production (unlike in the case of the NRU). But, quite apart from the fact that such a NAIRU is incompatible with the Walrasian equilibrium, there is no reason why the economy should at all experience such a NAIRU. Indeed, the NAIRU concept itself has serious problems because of its underlying assumption of uniqueness (which presupposes that an unemployment rate higher than the NAIRU would entail decelerating inflation, which is unrealistic) and because of the claims occasionally made on its behalf that it has stability (which are untenable).[7] The natural rate not only reproduces all these problems but also entails de facto full employment.

The argument that capitalist production is incompatible with full employment is therefore completely different from the natural rate idea. The latter is not concerned with the production aspect, and the discipline necessary for that. And even if the economy were at the natural rate, there would still be the problem of discipline insofar as the latter precludes involuntary unemployment.

Finally, there is nothing cynical about saying that full employment is incompatible with capitalism. On the contrary, the statement only underscores the need for transcending capitalism as a necessary condition for building a humane society. To consider it cynical is implicitly to apotheosize capitalism.[8] Our concern here is not with the question of transcending capitalism, but with more immediate analytical issues. Let us proceed with these.

Part 2

The Superiority of
Propertyism

9

A Critique of Ricardo's Theory of Money

I TALKED IN CHAPTER 1 of a Ricardo-Walras tradition in economics and contrasted it with the Marx-Keynes-Kalecki tradition. This would at first sight appear strange, for the Ricardian notion of equilibrium price is so much at variance with the Walrasian notion that they may almost be said to occupy diametrically opposite poles. But Ricardo's equilibrium price was the "center of gravity" toward which his "market prices" tended to gravitate. And it is these "market prices" that have a family resemblance with the Walrasian equilibrium prices. To be sure, even these two are not identical. In fact, as already mentioned in chapter 2, while the Walrasian equilibrium prices are based on universal market clearing, including of the labor market, in Ricardo the market price of labor is certainly not one that necessarily equates demand with supply. There are therefore important differences even in the short-period conception of price between Ricardo and Walras, but, notwithstanding these, they belong to the same genre when it comes to the short-run value of money, which, according to both theories, is determined by the demand for and the supply of money. And logically entailed in this commonness in the understanding of the value of money is a commonness in the attitude toward Say's law, and the possibility of generalized overproduction, which is why they have been clubbed together as belonging to one tradition.

But Ricardo also had a theory of the equilibrium value of money, toward which the short-run value of money was supposed to gravitate, and which was the obverse of the equilibrium prices of production of nonmoney commodities. But his short-run and long-run theories, one dealing with market prices and the other with equilibrium prices, cannot, without giving rise to logical contradictions, be integrated together into a single whole. This chapter, which is devoted to an examination of Ricardo's theory of money, seeks to establish this point, and hence to argue that the critique of monetarism developed in the first part of this book applies to Ricardo as well.

Because this is not a book on the history of economic thought per se, I will not be concerned with the specific development of Ricardo's ideas on money. My focus will be on the logic of his overall theoretical schema in which money enters as one component. For this purpose I will not even be looking at his overall schema in a textual sense, as he had developed it, but in its most logically tight form, such as can be erected on the basis of both his own original work and that of later writers such as Piero Sraffa (1951, 1960).

Ricardo's Critique of Smith

Ricardo's monetary theory can be best understood when counterposed to some of Smith's ideas. Adam Smith, it may be recalled, had an adding-up theory of natural price according to which the natural price of any commodity was the sum of the natural rates of wages, profit, and rent (each multiplied by the amount of the corresponding input per unit of output). This theory ran contrary to Smith's own ideas about rent and profit being deductions from what would otherwise have accrued to labor (which some have seen as a rudimentary theory of exploitation, though whether it was so is immaterial here).[1] What is more, the adding-up theory entailed a specific theory of money.

To see this, consider the important corollary that Smith derived from his adding-up theory, namely, that when the price of corn rises, all prices rise. The question that naturally arises is: in terms of what?[2] If money is commodity money, then the answer cannot be: in terms of money. For if the price of corn rises in terms of money, and hence the money wage rate rises in order to ensure that the natural rate of wages in real terms remains unchanged, then the rate of profit in the money producing sector must fall and remain permanently below the rate of profit in the production of nonmoney commodities; this, however, runs contrary to the notion of all produced commodities, including obviously the money commodity, earning an equal rate of profit (the "natural rate of profit") in equilibrium.

Smith's argument may be valid in a world of fiat money, which is why it has a modern ring about it, but it is certainly invalid in a world of commodity money such as Smith himself was considering. Indeed in such a world, a rise in money wages must be accompanied by a fall in the rate of profit, in the money-commodity producing sector directly and everywhere else by implication. We get in other words what would nowadays be called a "factor-price frontier," that is, a relationship between the money wage rate (whose movements necessarily entail movements in the same direction as the real wage rate, no matter in terms of which nonmoney commodity it is measured) and the rate of profit, which is downward sloping. The idea of a downward-sloping factor-price frontier is the exact opposite of that of independently arrived-at natural rates of wages, profit, and rent being added up to give the natural price.

Ricardo, in the process of giving this refutation of Smith through developing his own theory of value, of which his theory of money was necessarily a component part, discovered the curious effect that a rise in money wages, could, if the money commodity alone was produced with unassisted labor, result in a fall in the money price of every other commodity. This was a direct refutation of the Smithian proposition that a rise in money wages raises necessarily the money price of every other commodity via the adding up of natural rates. Ricardo's "curious case" therefore constituted a perfect counterexample for Smith's adding-up theory.

Ricardo's theory of the value of money, then, was nothing else but an application of his theory of value. Indeed, the essence of commodity money in this perception is that the value of money is determined exactly in the same way as the value of any other commodity, and Ricardo invested such a theory with the same rigor as he bestowed on his value theory.

Ricardo's Theory of the Value of Money

Adam Smith had drawn the distinction, to which the whole of the classical tradition was to adhere, between market price and natural price, the latter being the "center of gravity" toward which market prices tended to move. This conception was not without its own quota of problems: since the calculation of the natural prices was on the basis of a given output vector, while the movement of market prices toward natural prices presupposed some output adjustment, the particular natural prices calculated on the assumption of given output could be the center of gravity only if some assumption like constant returns to scale was made. Is the classical theory then predicated on the fulfillment of this neoclassical assumption?

While the exact assumption underlying this part of classical theory can be debated at length, it should be remembered that the assumption of constant returns to scale as such, which underlies the production function approach, is unnecessary in this context. All that is needed is a local invariance of production coefficients to changes in output. Assuming such invariance is not synonymous with accepting either constant returns to scale, or the production-function approach as we know it, or even the neoclassical methodology.

This distinction between market price and natural price would be reflected in a parallel distinction between the value of money with given supplies of all money and nonmoney commodities, and the value of money in equilibrium when supply adjustments are possible, or, if one can use suggestive Marshallian terminology, between the short-run and the long-run value of money.

Since, given the wage rate in terms of any commodity (including the money commodity), there is a set of equilibrium prices that equalize the rate of profit across all sectors (including the money sector) for given production conditions, it follows that the equilibrium value of money is determined by these conditions of production and the wage rate. At this value of money, it is the supply of money that adjusts to the demand for it. But in any particular period when supplies are given, the value of money, which is determined by its demand and supply, and corresponds to its market price, would be different from this equilibrium value or natural price.

Ricardo, therefore, was a quantity theorist in the short run when money supply, together with the output vector of other commodities, is given. But he differed from quantity theory in the long run when these supplies could change through the mobility of capital across sectors to bring about an equal rate of profit everywhere. Whether in the short or in the long run, he assumed that the demand for money was exclusively a transaction demand arising from the need to circulate produced commodities; there was never any desire for holding idle money balances.

The matter can be put differently. Ricardo took the quantity equation $MV = PQ$, and assumed that the income velocity of circulation of money V was constant. Likewise he took the total production of money and nonmoney commodities as given, determined by the respective magnitudes of capital stock, or simply "stock" in classical terminology. (The term M in the preceding equation can be taken as the sum of the money commodity produced and the preexisting stock of it.) In the short run, if we use Joan Robinson's language to describe the Ricardian position, the quantity equation has to be "read from the left to the right," that is, the price level of commodities P (and hence, by implication, the value of money) depends on the quantity of money M, with outputs given. In the long run, that is, when the mobility of capital has made market prices reach their center of gravity, the natural prices, the quantity equation has to be "read from the right to the left": it is M (and hence, by implication, Q relative to M) that has to adjust to the independently given P (independently, that is, of the levels of M and Q), which consists of nothing else but the equilibrium prices of production.

Ricardo's theory of the value of money therefore amounted to saying that in equilibrium the value of money is determined by the conditions of production, given the wage rate. But in the short run, that is, when the economy is not in equilibrium (in the sense of natural prices prevailing), the value of money is determined by its supply relative to demand. Money has a positive and finite value because as a produced commodity its supply in the short run is given, and the excess demand for it vanishes only at a certain positive finite value; but in the long run, even when its supply varies, it has a positive finite value, since as a produced commodity it entails a certain labor and material cost and has to fetch a certain rate of profit.

It is obvious that the problems arising from the fact that money also acts as an asset, which we discussed in the context of the Walrasian equilibrium, do not figure here since Ricardo ruled out any demand for money other than for circulating commodities. This assumption constitutes an important cornerstone of Ricardian analysis.

The Demand for Money

Ricardo stated in opposition to Bosanquet: "That commodities would rise or fall in price, in proportion to the increase or diminution of money, I assume as a fact which is incontrovertible."[3] But this would happen only if the entire increase or diminution of money manifests itself as an increase or diminution of money in circulation.

More generally, a rise or fall in prices in proportion to the increase or diminution of money presupposes a constancy of the income velocity of circulation of money, which depends on at least three factors: the ratio of money in circulation to the total stock of money, the ratio of money used in circulating commodities to money used in other transactions, and of course the "habits and customs" prevalent in society, which also affect the income velocity of circulation. If the last of these is taken as unchanging and the second kept out of consideration, since the transactions demand for money for financial and other transactions is not given as much importance by Ricardo, then the assumption of constancy of the income velocity of circulation of money hinges in effect on the constancy of the ratio of money in circulation to the total stock of money. Ricardo's argument rests on his assuming this ratio to be constant.

James Mill put forward the case for this to happen in the following manner: "The same piece of money which is paid in one exchange today, may be paid in another exchange tomorrow. Some of the pieces will be employed in a great many exchanges, some in very few, and some, which happen to be hoarded, in none at all. There will, amid all these varieties, be a certain average number of exchanges, the same which, if all the pieces had performed an equal number, would have been performed by each; that average we may suppose to be any number we please; say, for example, ten... . In whatever degree ... the quantity of money is increased or diminished, other things remaining the same, in that same proportion the value of the whole ... is reciprocally diminished or increased."[4] But Mill's fallacy in this argument, as Marx had pointed out (1971, 181–182), consisted in drawing from the existence of such an average the inference that this average must be constant, which is a complete non sequitur.

Underlying this assumption of the constancy of the ratio of money in circulation to the total stock of money, which is a strong and specific assumption and does not follow, as Mill had suggested, from the mere fact that each unit of the stock of money may be said to circulate on average a certain number of times in any period, is the view that money in effect is used exclusively for circulating commodities. To be sure, the latter is only a sufficient condition in the context under discussion for the constancy of the income velocity of circulation. We can for instance have money being hoarded, but as long as the ratio of the hoarded money to its total stock remains unchanged the income velocity of circulation would still have remained unchanged. But, to say that the hoarded stock of money always bears a constant ratio to its total stock is to deny the sui generis character of hoarding. It amounts in effect therefore to ignoring all other considerations underlying the demand for money apart from the need for it as a circulating medium.

Ricardo on International Currency Equilibrium

Ricardo gave his theory an international dimension in the following way. Money, he argued, must have the same value in all countries, for otherwise it would move from the country where it has a lower value to one where it has a higher value. This is merely the obverse of the statement that the money value of all commodities must be the same everywhere because of trade, which implies in turn that in equilibrium the values of national currencies relative to one another must be such as to ensure purchasing power parity.

Assuming identical income velocity of circulation of money in all countries (an assumption that can be relaxed without damaging the argument), the amount of money that has to be held in each must be proportional in equilibrium to the money value of its output. It follows that in equilibrium there must be not only a unique ratio of exchange rates between countries, but also a unique distribution of the world's money stock between countries.

Now, suppose for some reason the actual distribution of the world's money stock happens to become different from this equilibrium distribution, with a particular country acquiring a larger stock than the equilibrium amount (and some other country being left with a correspondingly smaller stock). Then the country with the larger stock would witness an increase in its price level of commodities (in keeping with Ricardo's acceptance of the quantity theory in the short run). As a result, the country's trade would go into a deficit, which ceteris paribus would have to be settled through an outflow of gold. An equilibrium is therefore is possible only when the actual stock of money corresponds to what is required for circulating the mass of commodities evaluated at their equilibrium value.

Of course, taking the world as a whole the magnitude of gold stock also has to be such that the sum total of commodities at their equilibrium values[5] can be circulated by the sum total of gold stock at the prevailing income velocity of circulation. But this adjustment can always come about through capital flows between the gold-producing sector and the sectors producing other goods, whether within countries or across countries. Such flows, by altering gold production relative to the output of other commodities, will bring about changes in the relative magnitude of gold stock.

The international version of Ricardo's theory, though in conformity with the national version discussed earlier, is nonetheless not identical with the latter, since a belief in the Ricardian theory of equilibrium prices of production is, strictly speaking, not necessary for subscribing to the international version. It is perfectly possible for instance not to accept the idea that in the long run the magnitude of gold production adjusts to the demand for it, and yet feel comfortable with the notion that through commodity and money movements the world's money stock would eventually be distributed in a unique manner across countries corresponding to their respective levels of output value. Even among those who do not believe in the long-run adjustment of money supply to money demand, and yet subscribe to the proposition of a unique distribution of money stock across countries, there can also be divergent opinions about the mode of determination of the money prices underlying this "output value." All that is necessary for the international version to hold is that each commodity must have the same money value everywhere, no matter how this money value is determined.

This money value, in short, need not be determined in the manner visualized by Ricardo. To be sure, the determination of the value of money in the manner visualized by Ricardo is compatible with this international version, but so are other theories that have nothing to do with Ricardo's theory of value.

Indeed, Ricardo's international version is derived from David Hume, who clearly did not have any theory of value akin to Ricardo's, but who was the original proponent of the quantity theory, and who had put forward in 1752 in a volume of essays called *Political Discourses* an almost identical theory. Hume's proposition that "in all neighbouring nations" money must be preserved "nearly proportionable to the art and industry of each nation," even though an exact precursor of Ricardo's similar proposition, was, needless to say, not based on any general theory of value, and hence of the value of money, such as Ricardo later propounded.[6]

Theory of Money and the Possibility of Overproduction

Ricardo's theory of money, as already mentioned, is based on the premise that money is demanded essentially as a medium of circulation of commodities. This precludes any recognition of overproduction crisis on his part. A necessary condition for overproduction (which of course is *ex ante*) of the group of produced commodities, is an *ex ante* excess demand for some nonproduced commodity, at maximal output of the former and at some base relative price between the two. If this *ex ante* excess demand cannot be eliminated through a change in the relative price between the two either because the flexibility of the relative price is effectively restricted or because the excess demand for the nonproduced commodity is insensitive to its relative price, then, since *ex hypothesi* there cannot be any shift of productive resources from the produced to the nonproduced commodity for augmenting the output of the latter at the expense of the former, there would be an overproduction crisis necessitating some other form of adjustment.

Now, in the economic universe of the Ricardian theory where all commodities are produced, capital movements from one sector to another are nonetheless precluded in the short run so that relative outputs cannot be adjusted rapidly enough. In such a world there can in principle therefore be a generalized overproduction of nonmoney produced commodities, if, at the maximal output of such commodities, there is an *ex ante* excess demand for money that cannot be overcome by a mere fall in their money price. But if money is used essentially as a medium of circulation, then in the first place there would not be any *ex ante* excess demand for money if the price level prevailing is such that the money stock equals the transaction demand for it; besides even if there is *ex ante* excess demand for money either because the initial money prices happen to be higher than this level or because of some parametric shift, say in the income velocity of circulation of money, it would automatically be rectified through a fall in the price level.

It is only if some other role of money is taken into account—for instance, as a "store of value," which makes it a form of wealth holding, or as the medium in terms of which debts are incurred and settled—that the possibility of overproduction of produced nonmoney commodities can be cognized. Since Ricardo looked at money essentially as a medium of circulation, it is not surprising that there was no room for an overproduction crisis in his theoretical schema.

Looking at it differently, if the role of money is seen essentially as a medium of circulation (and, as a fallout of this, the income velocity of circulation of money is taken to be constant), then we are in effect back in the world of a constant Cambridge k, as discussed in chapter 2. In such a case the excess demand function for money with respect to its price (drawn on the assumption of the output of nonmoney commodities being at its maximal level) is necessarily downward sloping and must necessarily be zero at some price. Any *ex-ante* excess demand for money therefore, if at all it arises for some reason despite money being only a medium of circulation, can get eliminated through an appropriate variation in the value of money vis-à-vis all nonmoney commodities including labor power.[7] Ricardo's taking money essentially as a medium of circulation (thereby assuming a constant income velocity of circulation of money), and postulating a subsistence real wage (so that money wages change with prices), precludes any possibility of overproduction crises.

The Ricardian system therefore hangs together: his theory of money, his theory of wages, his denial of overproduction, are all interlinked. There are, however, serious logical problems with it.

The Role of Expectations

The basic problem with the Ricardian monetary theory is the following. If there is any divergence between the short-run and the long-run values of money, then the role of expectations must be brought in; but Ricardo never did so. And once expectations are brought in, there has to be some holding of money for reasons other than its use as a means of circulation, or, what comes to the same thing, the income velocity of circulation of money cannot possibly be taken to be constant.

The equilibrium value of money, which acts as the center of gravity toward which the short-run value of money would tend to converge in the absence of fresh disturbances, depends exclusively on the wage rate and the conditions of production, about neither of which is there any mystery. Whenever the current value of money happens to differ from this value, the wealth holders would certainly expect the current value to move toward it.[8]

Let us now look at the implications of this fact for Ricardian theory. Let us confine ourselves to Ricardo's own premises (based on Say's law), namely that the real demand for nonmoney commodities is always equal to their real supply, a proposition that necessarily holds in nominal terms no matter what the prices (whether market or equilibrium prices); and that the excess supply or demand for money, with given output and at equilibrium prices of commodities, can only bring about a deviation of their market prices from their equilibrium prices. In short, all excess demand or supply in the system arises from the money market and not from the commodity market, that is from too much or too little money being supplied to circulate the output of nonmoney commodities at their equilibrium prices.

Let us, for convenience, start from a situation of equilibrium, and assume that suddenly there is a ceteris paribus increase in money supply. Now, money, even when it is commodity money, has very low carrying costs: indeed the commodities typically chosen as money are precisely those, like gold and silver, whose value relative to their volume is extremely high, resulting in low carrying costs. Because of low, almost zero, carrying costs, whenever there is any tendency for the market value of money to fall below its equilibrium value, and hence an expectation of an appreciation in the value of money in future, money will be hoarded, nipping this tendency in the bud. (We are ignoring here issues of risk and uncertainty, since these do not figure in Ricardo either and only complicate the discussion without nullifying the main point being made here.) The actual value of money therefore can never fall below its equilibrium value; any excess supply of money at its equilibrium value will simply be hoarded.

Let us now consider the opposite case. Starting from a situation of equilibrium, let us suppose there is suddenly a ceteris paribus decrease in money supply. Ricardo would argue here that commodity prices would fall, since there would be reduced demand for them at the prevailing equilibrium prices; that is, the value of money will increase. But again, since this would generate an expectation of a decline in the value of money in future, people would try to economize on money holding by purchasing commodities, not necessarily for carrying into the future (since there would be carrying costs) but simply for maintaining their "normal" purchases in the current period itself. In a situation where they have hoarded money from which they can dishoard, they will unambiguously maintain their real demand for nonmoney commodities at the prevailing equilibrium prices despite a reduction in the supply of money, and thereby ensure that the equilibrium prices persist.

Of course, it may be argued that the case of people having hoarded money is a special case and one cannot generalize from it. But once hoarding is theoretically admitted for reasons given in a previous paragraph, dishoarding out of this hoard will always occur. And what is more, as long as some economizing takes place in money holding, for maintaining the level of real demand for nonmoney commodities in the face of falling money supply, then if excess supply and excess demand occur randomly (or cyclically) in the money market, a hoard will keep building up over time until no price deviation from the equilibrium level will occur any more owing to money-market disturbances. This is because of the asymmetry whereby an increase in money supply at equilibrium will entail *no* increase in prices, while a reduction will entail a less than proportional fall (owing to some economizing on money holding). Over time in the latter case, too, the fall will become less and less until it becomes zero. In other words, in the Ricardian system, any *ex ante* tendency for the actual value of money to deviate from its equilibrium value would nullify itself through the hoarding and dishoarding of money, that is, through a change in the income velocity of circulation of the total money stock.

A Critique of Ricardo's Monetary Theory

The argument of the previous section points to a logical flaw in the Ricardian system arising from the fact that deviations of the actual prices of commodities from their equilibrium prices are not supposed to generate any expectations whatsoever. The "natural prices" are the "center of gravity" of the market prices, but even as the latter are forever gravitating toward the former, nobody is supposed to expect them to do so. This is obviously untenable. Expectations must be introduced into the system. Once they are introduced, even when we impose no extraneous assumption on the system and remain faithful to its own structure, Ricardo's short-run monetarist position becomes logically unsustainable.

This is because he assumes a constant income velocity of circulation of the stock of money for explaining deviations of the actual from the equilibrium value of money. But whenever such deviations arise *ex ante*, the role of expectations will be such that the income velocity of circulation not only does not remain constant but also itself adjusts to ensure that the actual and the equilibrium value of money never diverge from one another. Ricardo was a monetarist in the short run and a "propertyist" (believing in the exogenous determination of the value of money outside of the realm of demand and supply) in the long run. I might add, it is logically impossible to be a monetarist in the short run and a "propertyist" in the long run.

The three precise areas where the Ricardian theory gets undermined through the introduction of expectations, whose role is unavoidable within the logic of the system itself (even though Ricardo ignored it), are the following. First, in addition to its role as a circulating medium, money also plays, necessarily, the role of a wealth form or a store of value. There will always be a hoard of money with the people, so that the total money stock is divisible into two parts, one meant for circulating commodities and the other constituting this hoard. Second, changes in the supply of money relative to the equilibrium value of produced nonmoney commodities, which are the only source of macro-level excess demand or excess supply within the Ricardian system and are supposed to affect prices, causing deviations between market and equilibrium prices, do nothing of the sort. On the contrary, changes in the supply of money relative to the equilibrium value of produced nonmoney commodities have no effect on prices, but rather affect the division of the total money stock between the circulating and the hoard components. Third, once we recognize the existence of a hoard, the possibility of overproduction crises opens up. Ricardo assumes, and we have faithfully followed him in this till now, that the only source of macro-level excess demand and supply in the system is the money market. But if money can be held as a form of wealth, so that not all "savings" out of full capacity output need be invested, *ex ante* overproduction becomes a distinct possibility.

All these three points are consciously incorporated into the Marxian system. The next chapter turns to a discussion of the Marxian system, which is of great importance, since Marx sought to combine a rejection of monetarism and of Say's law with a theory of prices of production.

10

Marx on the Value of Money

MARX SHARED WITH RICARDO the idea that money has a positive and finite value, because, being a produced commodity, it requires, directly and indirectly, the expenditure of a positive and finite amount of labor on its production, which can be compared with what is expended upon the production of any other produced commodity.[1] Apart from this basic commonness of perception, which arose from the fact that both saw money as commodity money, he differed from Ricardo on the determination of the value of money both in the short run and in the long run. To say that both saw money as commodity money does not mean that they ignored the existence of paper money, but the paper money they considered was not fiat money: it was supposed to have been linked to gold, whether it was directly convertible to gold or not. There were important differences between Marx and Ricardo on the question of the value of paper money relative to gold, but our concern is with somewhat broader issues. Accordingly, let us assume in this discussion of Marx, as we did for Ricardo, that he is exclusively concerned with money in the form of a money commodity. We now come to their differences.

Marx on the Quantity Theory

Ricardo, we have seen, subscribed to the quantity theory as the short-run determinant of the price level. Marx, however, was completely opposed to the quantity theory. He read the quantity equation consistently "from the right to the left": "the quantity of the circulating medium is determined by the sum of the prices of the commodities circulating and the average velocity of the currency."[2] This "may also be stated as follows: given the sum of the values of commodities, and the average rapidity of their metamorphoses, the quantity of precious metal current as money depends on the value of that precious metal" (1974, 124). The exact equivalence of the two statements follows from the fact that Marx defined prices of commodities as their (labor) values expressed in terms of money. (Even if this particular definition of prices is substituted by one that defines "prices" as prices of production of commodities expressed in terms of money, it would still be true that Marx read the quantity equation "from the right to the left.")

This view (on which more later) that the quantity equation must be read from the right to the left runs directly contrary to the quantity theory. The reason is obvious: the latter view takes the price level of commodities as being determined by the magnitude of money, while the former takes the prices as determined independently. Marx was clear in his criticism: "The erroneous opinion that it is, on the contrary, prices that are determined by the quantity of the circulating medium, and that the latter depends on the quantity of the precious metals in a country; this opinion was based by those who first held it, on the absurd hypothesis that commodities are without a price, and money without a value, when they first enter into circulation, and that, once in circulation, an aliquot part of the medley of commodities is exchanged for an aliquot part of the heap of precious metals" (1974, 124–125). The fact that money has a positive and finite value not because the interaction of demand and supply confers such a value upon it, irrespective of its intrinsic worth as a commodity, but precisely because it has a value as a commodity is articulated here quite unambiguously.

But the question arises: If the value of money is independently determined from the conditions of production in the economy, then how do we get money market equilibrium? And here, Marx, unlike Ricardo, put forward the view, taken from James Steuart and anticipating Keynes, that the total money stock in the economy consisted of two parts: that which was used for the purposes of circulation and that which remained in the form of idle balances, that is, constituted a hoard. Of course, in discussing the motives behind this hoard, Marx did not have the Keynesian speculative motive in mind. Even though his discussion of the motives is scattered through his writings, we can discern at least three elements.

The first element relates to the fact that accumulation that is not immediately converted to productive capital must take the form of money. There are several reasons why unconsumed surplus value is not necessarily immediately converted into elements of constant or variable capital. An obvious one has to do, among other things, with the fact that accumulation must attain a minimum scale before it can be so converted.[3] Besides, the actual conversion to productive capital would also depend upon market conditions. The important point is this: money being the initial form of accumulation, which is then converted to productive capital after a variable time lag, a certain amount of idle money balance would always remain. This is true not only of individuals but also of society as a whole. In other words, even if in the aggregate in every period the entire produced surplus value equals what is added to constant and variable capital, there would still be a certain amount of idle balances held in every period in the society as a whole on account of the lag in capitalizing the surplus value in each case. Second, Marx talks of a "reserve fund" that is held because of the role of money as a means of payment, that is, because of the fact that debts are contracted and repaid in terms of money. To meet contingencies where payments have to be made while receipts are delayed, such a "reserve fund" becomes necessary. And third, money is a "terminal asset." If any accretion to assets occurs, for whatever reason, in the form of money, then it is held as such for some length of time before being converted into some other asset whose holding may be the preferred alternative.

Having postulated a hoard, Marx then suggests that any excess of the supply of money over what is required under "normal" circumstances, that is for circulating the normal capacity output (to be defined later) at equilibrium prices at the average velocity of the circulating medium, equals the size of the hoard. This means that if more money is needed for circulating full-capacity output at equilibrium prices than exists in the sphere of circulation, then the hoard is depleted (and in extreme cases "symbolic money" is produced for augmenting money supply), while if less money is needed then the size of the hoard expands. Under normal circumstances, then, the output level is at normal capacity, the price level is what is warranted by the conditions of production, the magnitude of the circulating medium is what is warranted by these two (together with the average velocity of circulation of this circulating medium), and the magnitude of the hoard is simply equal to the difference between the supply of money (including symbolic money) and what is needed for circulation.

The determination of the price level requires some clarification. Marx's rejection of the Ricardian version of the quantity theory has an important implication. If the quantity of money does not affect the money prices of commodities, even in the short run, then it follows that the money commodity is outside of the equal-rate-of-profit-across-sectors rule. The acceptance of the quantity theory in the short run, in other words, goes together with treating the money commodity as any other commodity. And in this respect Ricardo was being perfectly consistent (even though his over-all position was untenable since there was no cognizance of expectations while discussing the relationship between the short run and the long run). But if the short-run quantity theory is rejected, then it follows that money, despite being commodity money, is *not* like any other commodity when it comes to relative price determination. The exchange ratio between money and the totality of the other commodities is then determined by something outside of, but underlying, the realm of the prices of production. This something, according to Marx, was the ratio between the labor embodied in a unit of money and that embodied in the totality of nonmoney output.[4] Now, even though among the nonmoney commodities there is a transformation of labor values into prices of production, since the sum of values equals the sum of prices (while the money commodity is not affected by this transformation since it is outside of the profit-rate equalization process), it follows that the money value of the total output remains unchanged by the transformation of values into prices. The money prices of particular commodities now equal their prices of production expressed in terms of labor divided by the labor value of a unit of money.

In fact of course it is not even the prices of production but market prices that rule in the short run. What happens to the money value of the total output when market prices prevail? It is important to remember however that the concept of market prices in Marx is not the same as the concept of market prices in Walras, precisely because their understandings of money are so different. To understand Marx's notion of market prices, we must first make a distinction. We must distinguish between a situation in which the aggregate demand and supply are different and one in which, even though the aggregate demand and supply are matched, particular commodities have divergences between their demand and supply. The equality between aggregate demand and supply in turn can be given a precise meaning, namely that the aggregate money expenditure is such as to equal the aggregate value of normal capacity output in terms of money, defined as the total direct and indirect labor embodied in the normal capacity output divided by that embodied in a unit of money.

Now if the equality between aggregate demand and supply, so defined, holds, then it follows that the sum of market prices in terms of money must equal the sum of the prices of production in terms of money and hence the sum of labor values divided by the labor value of money. And if the sum of the market prices is equal to the sum of the prices of production of the output vector, then the demand for the circulating medium would remain unchanged, no matter which set of prices we are talking about. It would thus be the same, even in the short run, as if the output vector was evaluated at the equilibrium prices.[5]

The proposition that the money value of total output is determined by the relative quantities of labor embodied, it may be argued, does not follow from anything that has been said until now. Indeed if money stands outside the profit rate equalization process, then the relative labor embodied rule for fixing the money value of output becomes, in the strict sense, unnecessary. All that is needed logically is a fixity in the exchange ratio between money and commodities in the short run, which rules out the effect of demand and supply as in the quantity theory but entails that under given conditions of production a given quantity of commodities is exchanged for a certain amount of newly produced gold. If this is assured, then the theory remains intact.[6]

We should distinguish therefore between the fixity-of-exchange-ratio postulate, which is all that Marx's monetary theory needs, and the relative-labor-values-determine- this-fixed-exchange-ratio postulate, which is an additional one. The justification for this additional postulate will be discussed in the next chapter: it hinges on the fact that money and the nonmoney commodities are both products of human labor and become commensurable only because of this fact.

Marx's differences from Ricardo thus stand out. To highlight these differences, let us, in Ricardian fashion, abstract deliberately from all problems of deficient or excess aggregate demand (on these more later). In the short run, the prices of commodities are not determined by the quantity of money, as Ricardo believed; rather, it is the quantity of money in circulation that is determined by the value of output. In the long run, on the other hand, the value of money is not determined by the relative prices of production, with the rate of profit being equalized in all sectors, including the money-producing sector as Ricardo believed; rather, money does not enter into this rate of profit equalization process, and it is the labor embodied in a unit of money in comparison with the labor embodied in the totality of the output of nonmoney commodities that determines the value of money in terms of the latter. In fact in Marx this is what determines the value of money both in the short run and in the long run. Thus the value of money in terms of the totality of produced nonmoney commodities is fixed according to Marx for any given set of conditions of production, which is what makes Marx a propertyist.[7]

This fundamental difference between Marx and Ricardo has, strangely, been missed by most writers on the subject. There has of course been very little discussion of Marx's theory of money anyway, despite Marx himself having written copiously, clearly, and unambiguously, on the subject. But even more surprising is the fact that in discussions of Marx's theory of value, this basic difference between Marx and Ricardo, namely that money enters into the equalization-of-the-rate-of-profit process like any other commodity in Ricardo but not in Marx, has been almost completely missed. As a result, what Marx called the process of "transformation of labor values into prices," has been discussed invariably as if the transformation is from labor values to Ricardian prices (where the money commodity has the same rate of profit as elsewhere), and not to Marxian prices (where this is not the case).[8]

Theory of Money and Overproduction Crises

So far I have been talking of "normal" circumstances, referring in particular to the prevalence of normal capacity output. Focusing on this state may give the impression that overproduction crises are being precluded. But such is not the case. The recognition of the existence of idle balances opens up the possibility of overproduction crises. Overproduction in an *ex ante* sense arises when the capitalists do not wish to convert the entire unconsumed surplus value produced during any period into productive capital in the form of produced commodities. But this presupposes that they wish to hold it in some other form, that is in the form of some asset that itself is not a produced commodity. In a world where no such other asset is available, they would willy-nilly have to hold produced commodities and there cannot be any possibility of overproduction crises.

This is the case with Ricardo. Not only is money, the only other possible asset that the capitalists can hold, itself a produced commodity, but it is also held only for purposes of circulation, never as an asset. In Ricardo therefore there is no possibility of overproduction crises. But if money balances are habitually held as a form of wealth (that is, over and above what is required for circulation purposes), then clearly one chink opens up to allow the possibility of overproduction, namely the possibility of overproduction crises for nonmoney commodities.

Of course, when such a possibility arises, that is, when an *ex ante* excess demand for money appears, it still does not entail generalized overproduction for all commodities, money and nonmoney taken together. This is because the *ex ante* excess demand for the money commodity in such a situation counterbalances the *ex ante* excess supply of nonmoney commodities. But if the higher *ex ante* demand for money does not lead to a higher production of the money commodity (both because it is outside the profit-rate-equalization process and hence decisions about the level of its production are based on autonomous considerations, and also because a higher output of it would in any case take time to materialize), then this counterbalancing ceases to matter. A vectorwise decline in overall output becomes possible, through an output decline for nonmoney commodities, without any opposite tendency, in the period under question, for an output increase of the money commodity. And what is more, when such an output decrease occurs in the nonmoney commodities, this fact itself eliminates the excess demand for the money commodity, so that there is no tendency for the latter's output to increase even in the subsequent periods.

To be sure, if relative price variations could eliminate the higher *ex ante* demand for money balances, then again there would be no question of overproduction. But if there are restrictions on relative price variations, then this possibility gets excluded. Thus an *ex ante* excess supply of commodities at "normal" capacity output, which has as its counterpart an *ex ante* excess demand for money balances at the prevailing money price, and which, being incapable of elimination through relative price changes, causes overall output to slip below the "normal" capacity level, now becomes a distinct possibility.

This is not the same as saying that *ex ante* overproduction is *caused by* an *ex ante* excess demand for money balances, since this may suggest that any increase in money supply, no matter how it is brought about, would result in an alleviation of the problem of overproduction. Such a view is erroneous, even though there may be *particular* ways of bringing about an increase in money supply, say through an increase directly in the demand for commodities, that does overcome overproduction. In other words, the existence of idle balances, the *ex ante* demand for which may vary compared to what it would be under "normal" circumstances, makes it *possible* for the *ex ante* demand for the aggregate of commodities to be different from "normal" capacity output at the equilibrium prices of production. But making it possible is not the same as causing it.

Let us look at the matter in a somewhat different way. In Ricardo, we saw, the only way that *ex ante* excess demand or excess supply in the macroeconomic sense could be introduced into the system was from the side of the money market. But if hoards are habitually held, then it becomes possible to have such *ex ante* excess demand or excess supply arising not only from the side of the money market but also from the side of the nonmoney commodity market. The very existence of hoards ensures that when such disturbances arise from the side of the money market, they dissipate themselves without affecting nonmoney output or prices, solely through variations in the size of the hoard. But now that the possibility of disturbances arising from the side of the commodity market opens up, there can be overproduction crises, not only for the nonmoney commodities (offset by an *ex ante* excess demand for money), but also of the *generalized sort* that leads to a vectorwise decline in overall output.

For greater clarity, let us restate the point as follows: let us assume that each unit of the circulating medium is used for only one transaction per unit period. Then if the "normal" capacity output vector during the period is denoted by q^*, the equilibrium price vector by p, the total stock of money in the economy (at the instant that all transactions occur) by M, and the *ex ante* demand for idle balances by D, then Marx's position can be summed up as saying

$D = M - p \cdot q^*$ when q^* is demanded;

$D = M - p \cdot q$ when $q \neq q^*$ is demanded.[9]

What this entails is something quite striking: the view that, since the *ex ante* excess demand for commodities (positive or negative) and the *ex ante* excess demand for money are simply the two sides of the same coin, the effect of any such *ex ante* excess demand must be the same irrespective of where it originates, is wrong. Any *ex ante* excess demand for money originating from the money side is self-liquidating (in the sense that it has no effect either on the prices or on the output of nonmoney commodities); but any *ex ante* excess demand for money arising from the (nonmoney) commodity side is not self-liquidating: it does affect commodity prices and output. This is an asymmetry that is completely foreign to both the Walrasian and the Ricardian approaches, which have this one element in common (which is why both subscribe to Monetarism in their different ways), namely, they treat money and commodities exactly on par. In contrast, Marx treats the two as being fundamentally dissimilar even though money too is a commodity. The question arises: What can be the theoretical basis for such dissimilarity?

From Marx's discussion of the reasons for there being a hoard, it is clear that we can analytically look at it in either one of two possible ways. We can either visualize an equilibrium situation where the marginal rates of return from holding money and holding some alternative real asset (an asset in the form of commodities) are equal (most likely at zero, but that is not germane to the argument), that is, $r_m = r_c$, but $r'_m = 0$ with respect to the quantity of money stock held, while $r'_c < 0$ with respect to the quantity of real asset stock. A change in the *ex ante* excess demand for money in this case arising from the money side, that is, not arising as the mere obverse of a corresponding change on the commodity side, leaves r_m, and hence by implication r_c, unchanged, so that the magnitude of real asset stock held does not change. In other words, any *ex ante* excess demand for money, arising from the money side, has no effect on commodity prices or output. On the other hand, any *ex ante* excess demand for money, arising as the obverse of an *ex ante* excess supply for commodities, does affect commodity prices and output.

The other possible interpretation of the hoard would be in terms of a disequilibrium situation, where the marginal rates of return on holding money and on holding real assets in commodity form are not equal. Wealth in excess of whatever is sought to be held in the form of real assets is simply held transitionally in the form of money. Even here, since the demand for real assets is a function of their expected rate of return (which need not equal to the expected rate of return on money), what affects commodity markets is some change in the *ex ante* excess demand for commodities as such, and not any change in the state of rest arising from a disturbance on the side of money.

On either of these interpretations we can theoretically base an explanation of the asymmetry between the effects of the changes in the *ex ante* excess demand for money arising from the commodity side, and the effects of the changes in the *ex ante* excess demand for money arising from the money side. These changes of course can arise either because of changes in expectations or because of erratic disturbances. But since wealth holders themselves would be conscious of the aforementioned asymmetry, their expectations would be influenced by this consciousness, and hence the same conclusion would hold regarding the asymmetry, no matter *how* the change arose. In other words, what matters is *where* the change in *ex ante* excess demand arises (whether in the commodity or in the money market) and not *how*.[10]

This asymmetry is central to Marx, though it does not exist in Keynes, except in the case of the so-called liquidity trap, which is the Keynesian equivalent of the Marxian hoard. It is not fortuitous that in Keynes, unlike in Marx, a change in *ex ante* excess demand for money, no matter whether it arises from the commodity side or from the money side, has the effect (other than in the liquidity trap) of changing commodity prices and output, a conclusion that has been utilized subsequently for a revival of monetarism (since monetarism, as already mentioned, has a similar conclusion).

To recapitulate, implicit in the Marxian notion of a hoard is not only a rejection of the quantity theory, not only the possibility of a generalized overproduction crisis for all commodities, but a rejection of the view that any change in the state of *ex ante* excess demand in the money market ipso facto has an effect on commodity markets, a view that even Keynes does not reject except in the case of the liquidity trap.[11]

The Reason for Quantity Adjustment

Let us now move on to the next question: Why should an *ex ante* excess supply of commodities not get eliminated through changes in the price level *alone*? Why should it lead to any quantity adjustment at all, that is, to an actual situation of coexistence of idle capital with idle workers?

Before discussing this question, we should first recapitulate the answer to an even more preliminary question: why should the price level change at all when there is an *ex ante* excess supply (positive or negative) of commodities, when it does not in the case of an *ex ante* excess supply of money arising from the money side? The answer is as follows. Assuming "normal capacity output" and given money stock (including newly produced money), an *ex ante* excess supply of money at its equilibrium value is hoarded because any fall in its value sets up expectations of value appreciation, which, at zero carrying cost, makes hoarding profitable. An *ex ante* excess demand likewise leads to dishoarding, since money at the margin has zero returns, while cutting down the demand for commodities (owing to shortage of money) represents a cost. But an *ex ante* excess supply of commodities represents such a desire to restrict demand anyway; hence there is no reason why this should stimulate dishoarding of money instead of a fall in commodity prices. The same is true of an *ex ante* excess demand for commodities. Hence disturbances arising from the commodity market lead to price changes, but those arising from the money market do not. Simply put, the cause of the asymmetry lies in the fact that people always carry a hoard of money, but not a hoard (as distinct from stocks) of commodities.

Now let us take up the original question: Why shouldn't these disturbances affect only prices? The *ex ante* excess supply of commodities arises from the fact that capitalists do not wish to undertake investment equaling the unconsumed surplus value from "normal capacity output." There is no reason why a mere fall in commodity prices would make them invest more. Such a fall, however, would increase the demand for commodities in lieu of money.

But there are two different kinds of substitution of commodities for money between which we should distinguish. There is the substitution among stocks held for "convenience," which would occur with any fall in commodity prices that is expected to reverse itself in the near future. And then there is the large-scale substitution that would occur when the price fall has proceeded sufficiently far, that is, where the expected price appreciation is large enough to offset the carrying and other costs of holding commodities as opposed to money.

The first of these, discussed in chapter 5, is straightforward. Let us look briefly at the second of these. As already mentioned, implicit in the concept of a hoard is the fact that an asset is held that does not earn any rate of return at the margin. Now if commodities are expected to experience a price appreciation, then holding them would be preferable to the holding of money at least on this count. But they would be relatively illiquid, they would involve carrying costs, and price expectations about them would be associated with a degree of uncertainty. If the extent of expected price appreciation is sufficiently large, then the demand for commodities, not for use but for holding, would be large since commodity holdings would replace money holding.

Both these ways assume inelasticity of price expectations, which is not far-fetched. Since the value of money relative to commodities is given by their conditions of production (that is, the relative quantities of labor embodied), it follows that no matter what the current price of commodities in the aggregate, their expected price would be the equilibrium price, in which case any price fall of commodities would boost aggregate demand for them, and if the price falls sufficiently then the problem of *ex ante* excess supply of commodities would be completely overcome.

From this, however, it does not follow that *ex ante* overproduction can be overcome entirely through price adjustment. Indeed any price adjustment, though no doubt helpful in itself, would inevitably be accompanied by output adjustment as well.

This is because of a number of asymmetries, of which Marx noted two in particular. The first arises from the fact that there are inherited payments commitments. If "normal capacity output," whose equilibrium value is, say, 100, can be sold only for 50, then this fact may appear at first sight to be of no consequence: after all, if all prices have been halved then this 50 represents exactly the same real constant capital, the same real variable capital (since money wages too would have been halved to maintain the same level of real wage rate), and the same real surplus value (involving the same command over commodities) that the 100 had represented earlier. If such a price fall in addition increases the demand for commodities, then why should there be any output adjustment at all? The reason is that inherited payment commitments, fixed in money rather than real terms, will be difficult to meet when there is a price fall. Some firms therefore would become financially insolvent and cease production. A price fall would thus be necessarily accompanied by an output contraction as well, so that *ex ante* overproduction would entail idle capital and idle workers relative to the normal situation.

The fact that payment obligations cannot be met, which we have used as the reason for output adjustment, figures clearly in Marx: "It must be added that definite, presupposed, price relations govern the process of reproduction, so that the latter is halted and thrown into confusion by a general drop in prices. This confusion and stagnation paralyses the function of money as a medium of payment, whose development is geared to the development of capital and is based on those presupposed price relations. The chain of payment obligations due at specific dates is broken in a hundred places. The confusion is augmented by the attendant collapse of the credit system . . . to the actual stagnation and disruption of the process of reproduction, and thus to a real falling off in reproduction" (1974b, 254).

The second kind of asymmetry arises from the fact that not all prices move up or down in tandem, as we have been imagining till now. Price falls in particular sectors, if unaccompanied by equivalent falls in the values of their constant and variable capitals, would necessarily entail cutbacks in production. Output adjustment therefore becomes unavoidable for this reason as well.

Marx did not work out the actual contours of an overproduction crisis. While he demonstrated the possibility of an overproduction crisis, showed it as being immanent in the money form, which commodities assume in an exchange economy, took Ricardo to task for denying the possibility of overproduction, and described what such a crisis entailed, he did not analyze disequilibrium behavior. In other words, while he studied the economy in equilibrium and explained why it moved into disequilibrium, he did not study the economy *in* disequilibrium.

Overproduction, of course, means overproduction relative to the normal capacity output. It is time for us now to examine this concept in greater detail.

The Concept of Normal Capacity Output

The idea of quantity adjustment, which necessarily implies that the system is largely a "demand constrained" one, appears to go not only against what is generally taken to be Marx's economics, but also against the entire labor-theory-of-value approach. A common perception of Marx's economics for instance invokes a distinction between "Marxian unemployment" and "Keynesian unemployment." While Marxian unemployment is supposed to refer to a situation where labor demand at full capacity use of the equipment falls short of labor supply, Keynesian unemployment is understood to refer to that unemployment that exists together with unutilized capacity. A demand-constrained system, in short, is invariably associated with Keynes while Marx is invariably seen as dealing with a supply-constrained situation, in which there is unemployment but no unutilized capacity (Goodwin 1967; Patnaik 1998).

To be sure, full capacity output, which is supposed typically to characterize Marxian analysis, is not an easy concept to define. In the range of situations in the real world that the theory is supposed to be dealing with, the aggregate supply schedule never becomes absolutely vertical. Nonetheless one can give a meaning to full capacity output as follows. Full capacity output can be defined as that level of output beyond which the economy cannot produce, because, given the legacy of payments obligations, the level of real wages does not permit it. I will elaborate.

Technological progress typically implies that in any given period of time there is a coexistence of different methods of production, involving different levels of labor productivity for producing the same goods; some of these are in the process of gaining ground, while others are on their way out. Since workers earn the same wage rate under free competition, the capitalists employing these different methods earn different rates of profit, with the average rate of profit for the sphere as a whole, which must be the same for all spheres in equilibrium, being a weighted average of these different rates. But even the capitalists employing the least profitable method have to meet their payment obligations such as amortization of debt.

Let us for simplicity assume a one-good economy where each capitalist uses only one method and the ith method employs l_i numbers of workers per unit of machine to produce $l_i \cdot \beta i$ output. Let the number of ith method machines be K_i (i runs from 1 to n, starting from the most "efficient" machine), the total labor force L, employment E, and the real wage rate w. The payment obligations of the capitalists out of their surplus value that have to be met by all operating (that is, nonbankrupt) firms are fixed in money terms; but let us for simplicity assume, only momentarily in the present context, that they constitute a fixed proportion m, equal for all capitalists, of their real output.[12] We then have:

$$Q = \Sigma_i \, K_i \cdot l_i \cdot \beta_i \ldots i = 1,2,\ldots j. \tag{i}$$

where the jth vintage is the marginal one, that is,

$$\beta_j \geq \{w / (1 - m)\} > \beta_{j+1} \ldots \tag{ii}$$

$$E = \Sigma_i^j K_i \cdot l_i \ldots \tag{iii}$$

$$wE / Q = f(E / L) \ldots f' > 0 \ldots \tag{iv}$$

which makes the wage share a function of the proportion of the reserve army of labor.

These relationships give us E, Q, w, and j; and the Q so determined can be called full capacity output (say Q^*). Even at Q^* (with employment E^*) there is unemployment of $(L - E^*)$ laborers, which can be called "Marxian unemployment" on the standard definition.

Even this standard definition of Marxian unemployment, however, differs from Malinvaud's notion of "classical unemployment," despite the fact that he too is discussing a state of affairs where employment cannot increase because the real wages cannot fall. There are two fundamental differences between the Malinvaud concept and the concept that has just been outlined here.[13] First, in Malinvaud's concept of classical unemployment, it is sellers who are rationed in the labor market and buyers who are rationed in the product market, while here the product market clears. Second, the wage rate prevailing is not the accidental byproduct of a configuration of fix-money wage and fix-price but has an economic foundation, given in (iv), according to which the real wage claim, relative to labor productivity, is dependent on the relative size of the reserve army of labor.[14] In other words, unlike Malinvaud's "rationing equilibrium," where the economy happens to be stuck because the prices in particular markets are not fully flexible, the system (i)–(iv) describes an alternative equilibrium different from the Walrasian one, with an alternative perception of the labor market.

I want to make a different point. The possibility of quantity adjustment suggests that the economy cannot in general be at full capacity output, however defined. And if Marx's analysis is supposed to be centered on full capacity output, then postulating quantity adjustment appears contrary to Marxian analysis.

Likewise, postulating quantity adjustment *appears* to go contrary to the entire labor-theory-of-value approach. Labor values, or prices of production are based on given conditions of production, as summarized in particular production coefficients. If output can vary with demand, for a given capital stock, then the production coefficients too (at least the B matrix, if not the A matrix) become dependent on the level of demand. If a machine worth 1,000 lasts five years, then its annual depreciation is 200. If it produces 400 units of output, then the capital used up per unit output is 0.5. If it produces 200, then the corresponding figure is 1. The labor value of a unit of output then becomes dependent on demand; and so does the price of production (or the Sraffa price). This goes completely against the entire labor-theory-of-value approach, which considers equilibrium relative prices to be independent of demand.

The question naturally arises: if the possibility of quantity adjustment goes against the entire labor-theory-of-value approach and against Marxian analysis as commonly perceived, and yet if Marx theorized about this possibility, then did he just commit an error? In fact he did not. He had a more sophisticated theory than is commonly supposed, which is free of the logical contradictions to which we have just referred. His position is as follows.

Unlike Keynes, whose notion of a period is a segment of real time during which the magnitude of capital stock remains unchanged, Marx's notion of a period refers to a hypothetical entity, the average of the cycle. The production coefficients that underlie the labor values and the prices of production refer to this average. But the actual production coefficients during any period of real time would be different from these because the level of output, being influenced by demand, would vary from one period to the next during the cycle. There is, in other words, no contradiction between the labor-theory-of-value approach and quantity adjustment as long as the former is concerned with the average of cycles in a world of regular cycles. It follows that the benchmark level of capacity utilization is not full capacity utilization as commonly understood or as interpreted here, but some normal capacity utilization that constitutes the average of cycles. The level of unemployment that prevails when this normal capacity output is being produced would then qualify as Marxian unemployment, from which the actual unemployment in any period of real time would diverge.

Marx, in short, visualized quantity adjustments occurring together with price adjustments, owing to changes in the *ex ante* excess demand for commodities. And in doing so he was by no means being logically inconsistent, provided cycles necessarily occurred in a more or less regular fashion.[15] The real critique of Marx's analysis lies not in his postulating quantity adjustment, and hence a demand-constrained system, even while espousing a theory of price determination based on the conditions of production; it lies in the fact that his resolution of the contradiction between the two, through postulating a regular cycle, is not (and can not be) theoretically defended, as we will see in chapter 12, in the context of the closed capitalist economy that formed his unit of analysis.

Concluding Observations

Any belief in the quantity theory, that is, in the view that the price level of commodities is governed by the quantity of money stock in the economy, must presuppose either that all money functions only as medium of circulation or, what virtually comes to the same thing, that money in circulation bears a fixed ratio to the total money stock. But this is logically incompatible with the view that in the long run the value of money vis-à-vis commodities is given by conditions of production. This contradiction, which existed in the writings of Ricardo, who believed both in the theory that long-run prices depended on the conditions of production (given the real wage rate) as well as in the quantity theory of money (admittedly in the short run), does not figure in Marx, who adhered consistently to the theory of a unique exchange rate between money and commodities in equilibrium and rejected the quantity theory of money. In the process, he recognized not only the existence of idle balances, but also the possibility of overproduction crises that the existence of such idle balances necessarily entailed. What Marx does not seem to have paid sufficient attention to is the fact that once we recognize overproduction crises, the concept of normal circumstances, where a certain normal capacity output and prices of production rule, even as averages, loses its meaning in a closed capitalist economy. In other words, once we recognize that the quantity theory becomes untenable, and that overproduction crises are possible where output can well fall below the "normal capacity output," this fact itself puts a question mark over the entire Marxian price theory (developed as it is for a closed capitalist economy).

The next chapter is devoted to an excursus on Marx's theory of value, which, in my view, has been improperly understood. It has been interpreted as being identical with Ricardo's theory, with only an admixture of a Hegel-inspired perception of a "qualitative value problem" (Sweezy 1946), which, moreover, cannot be logically reconciled with the rest of the theory. But since any theory of value is necessarily associated with a theory of money, and since Marx's theory of money, as we have seen, is vastly different from Ricardo's, it stands to reason that his theory of value, too, must be distinguished from that of Ricardo. The next chapter does so in a very preliminary way—preliminary, because the concern of this book is not with value theory in general.

11

An Excursus on Marx's Theory of Value

THERE ARE FEW SUBJECTS in economics that have been discussed so thoroughly as Marx's value theory. An attempt to do so yet again may appear at the very least to be unnecessary, if not a tax on the reader's patience. But the reason for doing so here is, as mentioned earlier, the fact that Marx's value theory, like Marx's monetary theory, has been systematically misunderstood. It has been systematically assumed that in the analytical structure of the theory there is no basic difference between Marx's and Ricardo's views. This is incorrect. Like Marx's monetary theory, Marx's value theory too must be looked at sui generis, not just in its philosophical underpinnings but also in its formal structure. Indeed, precisely because Marx's monetary theory is *different* from Ricardo's, his value theory too, it stands to reason, must necessarily be different from Ricardo's. The purpose of this chapter is to explore this difference briefly.

The Formal Discussion on Marx's Value Theory: An Overview

Marx, as is well known, considered his "prices of production," that is, the equilibrium prices that would rule in a regime of wage- and profit-rate equalization for any given level of the wage rate and the conditions of production, to be "transformed" labor values. Ricardo, too, started with labor values, that is, with the proposition that the exchange ratios between commodities were determined by the relative quantities of direct and indirect labor embodied in them; but then he added a *second* determinant that was relevant for a regime of positive profit rates. While he expressed this second determinant as the change occurring in the wage rate, what he clearly meant was the time pattern of the application of the labor input (and not just its aggregate amount, which the first determinant talked about). Marx was critical of Ricardo's putting the two determinants on par, which he considered to be an example of the latter's jumbling up the spheres of production and of circulation. Instead, he saw labor values as a concept relating to the sphere of production, and hence a concept giving expression to the equalization-of-the-rate-of-surplus-value rule (which in a world of homogeneous labor and free labor mobility is a real phenomenon that must obtain in the sphere of production); the aggregate surplus so extracted (that is, extracted equally from each laborer) is then distributed among capitalists according to a different rule that obtains in the sphere of circulation, namely the equal-rate-of-profit rule. This latter rule yields the prices of production (we assume all along that real wages are given).

But, he argued, because of the fact that when the sum of values equals the sum of prices (a "normalization" rule), the sum of surplus values equals the sum of profits (the aggregate surplus value being what is distributed as profits among capitalists under the equal-rate-of-profit rule), the equilibrium rate of profit in the price system was nothing else but the general rate of profit ($S / (C + V)$) of the value system, and the prices of production were nothing else but "transformed" labor values. The labor values in other words could be visualized as underlying the price system.

It is generally accepted that Marx's formal reasoning was at fault here. Barring the cases of zero rate of profit, and of "equal organic compositions of capital," in which labor values coincide with the prices of production, the only circumstance where, despite their noncoincidence, $S / (C + V)$ calculated in the value-accounting system equals the equilibrium rate of profit of the price system is where the economy's output vector is in von Neumann proportions (that is, its different components are in the same proportion to one another as would obtain if the economy were on the path of the maximal rate of steady growth).[1] In other words, for any *arbitrary* output vector, the equilibrium rate of profit is not equal to $S / (C + V)$, in which case Marx's description of a two-stage process, of extraction of surplus value in the sphere of production and the distribution of the same amount of surplus value through the equal-rate-of-profit rule in the sphere of circulation, lacks any formal validity. One can still believe in this description, but then the value accounting system becomes a mere add-on as far as the determination of the equilibrium prices is concerned, since the latter system can stand entirely on its own without the rigmarole of labor values. Samuelson's (1971) remark that the transformation of labor values into prices consists in writing the value system, then erasing it out and writing the price system, may be a strong way of putting the matter, but it is not without substance. What is more, since, as Sraffa has shown, the equilibrium rate of profit is determined entirely within the "basic" system, that is, entirely within that subset of sectors whose outputs enter, directly or indirectly, into the production of all goods, and is unaffected by the conditions of production of the nonbasic goods, any theory, like Marx's, which makes this rate of profit equal to the general rate of profit ($S / (C + V)$), into whose formation all commodities, whether basic or nonbasic, enter, is not only logically erroneous but also practically misleading.

These well-known results relating to the standard interpretation of Marx's value theory can be presented formally as follows. Denoting the direct labor inputs by the row vector $1'$ and the current input-out matrix by A (we assume a single turnover period for each input),[2] the labor values (row vector v') are given by

$$v' = l' (I - A)^{-1} \dots \tag{i}$$

Assuming that wages and current inputs are advanced at the beginning of the period, and that the wage rate and the rate of profit are equal across sectors, the equilibrium prices are given by $p' = (p'A + wl') (1 + r)$, from which we get:

$$p' = wl' (1 + r)[I - A(1 + r)]^{-1} \dots \tag{ii}$$

For given wages in terms of any numeraire, the rate of profit and the equilibrium prices (in terms of the same numeraire) are determined from (ii). Or, putting it differently, (ii) and (N) completely determine the prices and the rate of profit for given w:

$$p_1 = 1 \dots \tag{N}$$

It can be easily seen that any change in the conditions of production, that is, in the direct labor input or the current inputs, of a nonbasic good has no effect on the rate of profit, thus directly contradicting Marx.

Let us now look at the special cases when Marx's conclusions on the relation between values and prices *are* valid. For doing so, however, we assume that the numeraire chosen for expressing prices and wages is labor time, and that the *wage rate*, expressed as labor time per unit of labor time, is a pure number (Foley 1982). Of course wages are not paid in exchange for labor time; they are paid in exchange for labor power, whose use consists in labor time. But we assume that the parameters affecting the conversion of labor power (a stock) into labor time (a flow), such as the length of the working day and the intensity of work, are given and remain unchanged, in which case we can, without any formal incorrectness, take wages as representing payment for labor time. Let us denote the wage rate, which thus becomes a pure number, by ρ. Marx's contention was that in any economy producing some output vector y, if the sum of values equals the sum of prices then the sum of surplus values for any given ρ equals the sum of profits. This latter condition, it can be easily shown, boils down to $v'Ay = p'Ay$. Marx's assertion therefore can be expressed as

$$\text{when } p'y = [\rho l' (1 + r)][I - A(1 + r)]^{-1} y = v'y = l' (I - A)^{-1} y \dots \tag{iii}$$

$$\text{then } p'Ay = v'Ay \dots \tag{iv}$$

The basic criticism of Marx's theory has been that for any arbitrary ρ, $1'$, A, and y, there is no reason why both (iii) and (iv) should hold. It would, when $\rho = 1$, for then, from (iii) $r = 0$, and $p' = v'$ which ipso facto makes $p'Ay = v'Ay$. Likewise, when l' is the left eigen vector of the A matrix and has a positive Frobenius root μ associated with it, the price vector becomes (from the second term in (iii)) equal to $1' \cdot \rho \,(1+r) \,/\, [1 - \mu \,(1+r)]$, which is a scalar multiple of $1'$. Likewise, the value vector becomes a scalar multiple of $1'$, and if $p'y = v'y$, then it follows that that p' must be the same as v', and hence $p'Ay = v'Ay$. These are the two cases of zero rate of profit and equal organic composition of capital where labor values and equilibrium prices exactly coincide.

But in the case where they do not coincide, that is, where neither of these two conditions holds, (iii) and (iv) would still hold together if the output vector is in von Neumann proportions. If x is the right eigen vector associated with the Frobenius root of the A matrix, then $p'Ax = p' \,\mu x$, and $v'Ax = v' \,\mu x$; since $p'x = v'x$ from (iii), it follows that $p'\mu x = v'\mu x$, that is, (iv) holds. If these exceptional cases are ruled out, then, it is argued, the Marxian assertion that $r = S \,/\, (C+V)$ becomes invalid, and therefore the entire discussion of the value system becomes a mere rigmarole that is logically unnecessary.

There are two separate logical issues here between which we must distinguish: one, whether Marx's specific conclusion about the "transformation of values into prices," namely that the rate of profit remains the same between the two systems, is valid; and two, whether a complete price system can be obtained, from the conditions of production and the specification of a distributional parameter (as Sraffa has done in his validation of the Ricardian system), with no reference whatsoever to any extraneous information or convention. Of course, if the latter is true, then Marx's specific conclusion must be wrong, that is, an affirmative answer to the second question necessarily implies a negative answer to the first (though a negative answer to the second does not necessarily entail an affirmative answer to the first).

Marx's basic assertion was that a complete price system could not be obtained without bringing in labor values, that is, without bringing in extraneous information and conventions of the sort that he derived from his value discussion. This forms the core of the labor theory of value. Whether Marx's specific conclusion about the rate of profit is valid is of secondary importance. The real issue is whether a complete price system can be constructed without bringing in labor values.

If it can be, then the relevance of the labor values is much diminished. It is not enough to show, as Morishima (1973) has done, that a positive rate of profit in the price system is associated only with a positive rate of surplus value in the value system, as proof of the relevance of the value-system, and hence of Marx's value theory. That demonstration establishes at best a certain correspondence between the two systems; it proves nothing about prices being "based" on labor values, in the sense that the determination of prices is impossible without certain extraneous information and conventions such as are derived from Marx's value discussion.

Marx's argument that a complete price system could not be constructed without bringing in labor values was not because of an algebraic error, as has been generally supposed; it was because his economic universe was different from Ricardo's, and within that universe this argument has validity.

An Alternative Interpretation of Marx's Value Theory

In the way that Marx's value theory was presented earlier, which, as already mentioned, is the standard way, money did not enter the picture in any essential manner. With the conditions of production and the real wage rate given, the latter in terms of any particular commodity or a bundle of commodities entering into the wage-rate-and-profit-rate-equalization process, the only problem that remains before one gets a complete characterization of the equilibrium is the choice of a numeraire in terms of which all prices can be expressed. And if this numeraire bears a fixed relationship to money, then we get the equilibrium money prices. But even though prices here are expressed in terms of money, money plays no role in their determination. Even without specifying the value of money in terms of any one or more commodities, we already get the equilibrium rate of profit and the equilibrium prices here, which can be expressed in terms of any commodity. Money in short is just a measure, not a determinant of equilibrium.

Suppose, however, that wages are paid in terms of money, which is what Marx had postulated. This fact, together with the fact that money does not enter the profit-rate-equalization process, implies that the equilibrium relative prices and the equilibrium rate of profit cannot be determined unless the value of money is specified. The value of money is no longer necessary only as a measure of equilibrium prices; the latter cannot be determined without specifying the value of money. This remains true no matter what the production structure happens to be, that is, whether all goods are basic goods (that is, the A matrix is indecomposable), or whether there are some (at least one) basic and some nonbasic goods (that is, the A-matrix is decomposable) or whether there are no basic goods at all (that is, the A-matrix is completely decomposable).

Once we recognize the essentiality of the prior specification of the value of money (in terms of which costs, particularly wage costs, are incurred but which itself is outside the profit-rate-equalization circle) for the determination of the prices of production, it is obvious that the view of the price system as being logically self-contained, with nothing else needed for its determination, under given conditions of production, other than the wage rate, breaks down. This view underlies the Sraffa system, which represents a formalization of Ricardo's, not Marx's, price theory; it also underlies Samuelson's remark that the "transformation of labor values into prices" consists in first writing the value system and then erasing it to write the price system, which implies that the price system stands on its own with no reference to any other logically prior exchange ratio (other than the wage rate). Clearly the grand exchange ratio between money and commodities has to be prior specified. The question arises: What determines this grand exchange ratio?

The specification of this grand exchange ratio, to recapitulate, together with the money wage rate, which is but the exchange ratio between money and labor power, determines, under given conditions of production, the exchange ratio between the various produced commodities. Now, instead of looking at each of these three sets of exchange ratios separately, Marx postulated a comprehensive and overarching theory within which the concrete determination of each can be located, a theory moreover that was in keeping with his historical method. This was his theory of value, which was neither a logically unnecessary bit of Hegelian legacy nor a mere add-on to a hardcore economic structure of price theory. It represented a comprehensive perception on the basis of which a logically necessary specification for the determination of prices could be made. And this comprehensive perception was derived not from any "natural rights doctrine" as is often supposed, nor from any from moral considerations in general, but from a reading of history.

Exchange, Marx argued, began at the borders between tribes, initially as sporadic acts but later as a general phenomenon. Only subsequently did it get generalized to transactions within the tribe itself giving rise to important structural changes. The only basis on which commodities could become commensurable, and on which exchange ratios could be determined once transactions had become somewhat regular was the rule that equal amounts expenditure of labor added equal amounts of value to commodities, or, what comes to the same thing, the relative values of commodities were determined by the relative amounts of labor directly and indirectly embodied in them, a proposition that Ricardo also had accepted as his starting point. The fact that with the emergence of capitalism, and with it the category of the rate of profit, the time pattern of expenditure of labor assumes a significance that it never had earlier, and hence the exchange ratios diverge from relative labor values does not negate their being embedded theoretically and historically within the system of labor values.

Labor values, in fact, constituted an ideal starting point for investigating the sui generis character of capitalism as a mode of production, through an examination of how surplus, which existed in earlier modes of production too, took the form of surplus value and got appropriated even in a world of voluntary exchange. This enabled Marx to make an "exact specification of the institutional datum distinguishing Capitalism from the concept of an exchange economy in general," a fact that contributed to the "superiority of Marxian economics" (Lange 1963, 196, 201; Dobb 1973, 149).

Marx's procedure in his analysis of exchange under capitalism was to take the exchange ratios between nonmoney commodities, brought by capitalists to the sphere of circulation, to be divergent from their relative labor values, but to take the exchange ratio between money and the totality of commodities to conform to the relative labor values.[3] (The third exchange ratio, between money and labor power, of course was determined by a set of complex considerations having to do with the bargaining strength of workers versus the capitalists). This raised no logical problems since the sum of labor values being the same as the sum of prices of production of nonmoney commodities, the deviations of these prices from labor values still left the *aggregate* money value of the nonmoney commodities unchanged.

In taking the exchange ratio between money and the aggregate nonmoney commodities to be equal to their relative labor values, Marx was not necessarily asserting that this is what actually obtained in real life. Monopoly control over the production of the money commodity for example might entail a divergence of this exchange ratio

too from their relative labor values; but any such divergence would then be attribut-
able to the existence of monopoly; the relative labor values would still constitute the
benchmark.

To sum up the argument thus far, the real debate about Marx's claim about the
"transformation of values into prices" is not whether his algebra, postulating two
equalities simultaneously, of the sum of values with the sum of prices and of the sum
of surplus values with the sum of profits, is correct in general; it clearly is not. The
real debate is about what this entails for the value system. If prices of production can
be obtained directly from the conditions of production, given the wage rate, then the
value system appears to have no relevance; but this result is valid only for a world
where the money commodity also enters into the profit-rate-equalization process,
which is a Ricardian, and necessarily a Say's law, world. If we abandon the Ricardian theory of money and take instead the Marxian theory of money, then the problem of the transformation has to be differently interpreted, too. And here it turns out
that with money wages given, the prices of production cannot be determined without
specifying the value of money from the "outside" and Marx did so by invoking the
relative labor values. In short, equilibrium prices cannot be obtained without *logically*
bringing in labor values.

The Case of Nonmarketed Commodities

There is an additional reason why a complete system of relative prices cannot be
obtained merely upon the specification of a distributional parameter alone, without
bringing in an additional criterion of comparison from outside, such as is given by
the labor values. And this has to do with the pervasive existence of "nonmarketed
commodities."

Unfinished goods in different stages of production constitute the prime example of
such nonmarketed commodities. Since they constitute working capital they must have
a value, without which we cannot estimate the value of capital as a whole and hence
cannot calculate the rate of profit. On the other hand, they have a life solely within the
firm itself and are not in general marketed. They are commodities in the sense of having an exchange value, in addition to their use value; but they are not bought and sold
in the market, which is why they may be said to constitute nonmarketed commodities.
The question therefore arises: If they are nonmarketed, then what is the rule governing the determination of their value?

The entire Sraffa system is predicated on the assumption that any commodity,
whether marketed or not, is evaluated in exactly the same manner as any other commodity, that is through the equalization-of-the-rate-of-profit-and-of-the-wage-rate
rule. This amounts to postulating that every activity carried out within a firm must
earn the same rate of profit, which in effect does away with the concept of a firm altogether. The concept of a firm in other words is substituted by an agglomeration of

activities, each earning the same rate of profit. No boundaries can be drawn which show that a specific set of activities belong to a particular irreducible entity called a firm. To put it differently since a firm on this conception can have *any* combination of activities, no sacrosanct meaning can be given to the concept of a firm.

This is not only inaccurate as a picture of the actual state of affairs in a capitalist economy, but also contrary to Marx's perception. In his discussion of John Stuart Mill in *Theories of Surplus Value* (1975, 216–217), Marx has this to say: "Even for the individual capitalist with regard to such complex enterprises which do occur, for example when the capitalist is at the same time engaged in spinning and weaving, making his own bricks etc. . . . what is decisive is the real saving in production costs, through saving of time on transport, savings on buildings, on heating, on power, etc., greater control over the quality of raw materials etc." In other words, the degree of vertical integration is decided upon by considerations independent of whether particular activities in this vertical chain yield the same rate of profit or not. It follows that equal rate of profit across *activities* cannot be a legitimate basis for the determination of prices of production. We have to take firms, typically with a given level of vertical integration in particular spheres as our starting point, in which case the question again arises: How is the value of commodities that are produced for use within the firm itself determined?

An example will make the problem clear. To focus attention upon this particular problem, let us deliberately ignore the problem discussed in the previous section, namely the comparison between commodities and money, and assume instead that all valuation is done and all payments made in a commodity that enters the profit-rate-equalization process. Consider now the following production system:

Sphere A:

100 units of corn + 200 labor produce 500 units of corn

400 units of corn + 500 labor produce 800 units of flour

Sphere B:

150 units of manufactured good + 200 labor produce 500 manufactured good.

This is not a case of joint production, since each activity is a single-product activity. But, let us assume that the firms in Sphere A are all vertically integrated, combining the production of corn and flour in the same proportion as for the economy as a whole, and that corn is a nonmarketed commodity. Assuming real wage to be 0.5 flour, the price equations in this case would be:

$$(500 \cdot p_1 + 350 \cdot p_2)(1+r) = 500 p_1 + 800 \cdot p_2 \tag{i}$$

$$(150 p_3 + 100 p_2)(1+r) = 500 \cdot p_3 \tag{ii}$$

Even if we take flour, which is a marketed commodity, as our numeraire, we still have three unknowns here, r, p_1, and p_3, and only two equations. Notwithstanding the specification of the wage rate and the fact that the numeraire good is part of the profit-rate-equalization process, we still have an underdetermined system. In general whenever we have integrated production, unless some additional rule for the valuation of nonmarketed commodities, is specified, we cannot get a system of prices of production.

Now the obvious additional rule that can be specified is that a unit of (homogeneous) labor adds the same value in the course of production of nonmarketed commodities in every sphere, and that this value bears the same ratio to the wage rate as the average for the economy as a whole.

Let us now integrate this discussion with that of the preceding section. If wages are paid in money, which is outside the profit-rate-equalization process and whose value relative to the world of commodities is determined by the relative quantities of labor embodied, then the specification says that a unit of (homogeneous) labor adds the same amount of money value in the case of nonmarketed commodities as it does in the aggregate.[4]

The amount of money value added per unit of labor, however, differs between the value-accounting and the price-accounting systems, which is but a reflection of the rates of profit being unequal between the two systems. Which of the two different amounts should be taken as underlying price determination? It stands to reason that the value added per unit of labor in the price-accounting system, being the one that is visible when prices of production prevail, should also underlie the pricing behavior of the firms. In other words, the money value added per unit of labor in the value-accounting system does not directly affect price determination. Even so, however, the fact remains that the price-system cannot be determined without a specification of the money value added per unit of labor, i.e. without bringing into the system considerations such as those highlighted by the discussion of labor values.

It can be verified that a complete system of prices of production can be obtained with this specification. In the above example, this means adding extra equations:

$$100 \, p_1 + 100 \, p_2 \cdot \lambda = 500 \cdot p_1 \tag{iii}$$

and

$$(800 \cdot p_2 + 350 \, p_3) \, / \, 450 \, p_2 = \lambda \tag{iv}$$

In general, since an equation such as (iii) will be inserted for every nonmarketed commodity and the λ occurring in such equations will be determined by an equation such as (iv), we will always get a completely determined system once we adopt such a specification. And in the case of money-wage payments there will be an additional equation determining the value of money, corresponding to the additional unknown, namely the value of money, which will be entering the production equations.

It follows that contrary to the usual interpretations of Marx's views on the transformation of values into prices, all of which suggest that the price system is a complete and self-contained system once a distributional parameter is specified, the determination of prices requires certain rules for making commodities and money commensurable and for making marketed and nonmarketed commodities (and hence by implication different nonmarketed commodities themselves, or, what comes to the same thing, the value created by labor in the different spheres of production) commensurable. For all these specifications, Marx took the simple labor-embodied criterion as the grand unifying principle of commensurability, aware that in practice the relative prices would differ from these labor values but emphatic that these divergences will have to be specifically explained, and through such explanations alone the specificity of the case revealed. His algebraic conclusion about the relationship between the value and the price systems is generally not valid,[5] but his main point, that something else underlies the price system, continues to retain its validity, unlike what virtually every interpreter of Marx has argued.

Before we close this discussion, we must take note of three possible objections to what we have said about nonmarketed commodities. First, it may be argued that the problem of underdetermination of the price system would be true, even when there is no joint production, whenever there are integrated firms, all of whose products are marketed, as long as the firm concerns itself only with the overall rate of profit and not with the rate of profit in every activity. Why should one specifically bring in nonmarketed commodities for showing this underdetermination? While this argument is perfectly correct, the existence of nonmarketed commodities is pervasive, even in the case of economies consisting of firms that have only one product to sell. It therefore has a basic *logical* force.

Second, it may be asked: if firms have nonmarketed commodities, then how does capital from outside move into the industry? How, in other words, do we explain the tendency toward an equalization of the rate of profit in such a universe? In the preceding example, if the flour production sector has a higher rate of profit than the average, then how does outside capital move into it if corn, the basic capital input used in this sector, is not even sold in the market? The precise manner of capital movement across sectors of course is a complex issue. But one can visualize the following as one possible scenario. When the rate of profit in the flour sector exceeds the average rate, outside capital will try to buy up firms in this sector, which will raise the value of capital stocks of these firms. Some firms will change hands and some will not. But since the market value of these capital stocks in their totality will exceed their replacement cost at the equilibrium prices (including the prices fixed by convention for the nonmarketed commodities), the firms themselves will try to enlarge their capital stocks. In this manner, supply of this sector's output will increase over a period of time, restoring the equilibrium rate of profit. Thus the existence of nonmarketed commodities as inputs does not create any special problems over and above the usual problem of describing any traverse to an equilibrium position.

Third, if the nonmarketed commodities are not initial-stage commodities, as in the preceding example, but come only later in the production chain (say, like cotton yarn in a textile plant that only sells cloth), then capital entering the sphere has to wait for some time before being able to sell its final good. During this waiting period it has to build up its own stock of goods-in-process, including the internally produced nonmarketed commodities. Should it not then obtain the average rate of profit for this waiting time? Is it not the case then that the Sraffian contention that even nonmarketed commodities must earn the average rate of profit gets validated? If the rate of profit on capital, even for the waiting period, falls short of the average rate, then surely this sector would be abandoned, since it would be better to invest one's money capital in an industry earning the average rate of profit but having a zero gestation lag. In other words, why should any one enter this particular sector if it does not give the average rate of profit during the gestation period itself? And why should anyone stay in this sector if the value of capital stock is less than what it would be if the average rate of profit were earned for the gestation period?

The firm, as we mentioned, is a sui generis concept, not just an arbitrary collage of activities. In a world peopled with firms, mobility of capital does not mean capital rushing around indiscriminately and without any constraints from any one set of activities to another. This may be true under the assumption of "perfect competition," but not in the world that Marx was talking about. The entry of capital into a new sector is not easy even when there are no legal barriers to it. Typically, therefore, it takes the form of sales and acquisition of firms, or of money capital being invested in one sphere rather than in another, that is, within the existing structure of firms with the existing valuation of their capital stocks. And since all capital, given the prevailing criteria of valuation, earns the same rate of profit in equilibrium, there is no reason why these criteria of valuation should be challenged per se. In short, these criteria are prior to the determination of equilibrium.

Summary and Conclusions

The entire discussion of Marx's theory of value to date has never distinguished between the Marxian and the Ricardian value theories. This is because it has never distinguished between the Marxian and the Ricardian monetary theories, notwithstanding the fact that Marx himself wrote copiously on the differences between Ricardo's and his own views on money, and notwithstanding the fact that he persistently attacked Say's law, which Ricardo had accepted; he could have done so only because his theory of money was different from Ricardo's.

Marx's theory of money entails that there must be some determinant of the exchange ratio between money and nonmoney commodities, which must be given prior to the determination of the prices of production of nonmoney commodities: the postulation of a distributional parameter alone is insufficient for the determination of equilibrium relative prices.

Likewise Marx saw the firm as a sui generis entity, not just an arbitrary collage of activities. Every firm has a set of nonmarketed commodities that have a value even when they are produced and used within a vertically integrated firm itself. A rule has to be devised for the valuation of these nonmarketed commodities before any equilibrium prices can be arrived at.

The equilibrium prices, therefore, are formed only on the basis of the prior postulation of some criteria for relative valuation, between money and the nonmoney commodities, and between marketed and nonmarketed commodities. Marx saw labor values as providing the grand unifying criterion on the basis of which the equilibrium prices are formed. He did so because he saw labor values as having a certain historical validity. He did not, of course, claim that labor values obtained in the world, but he saw them as providing the basis for prices that deviated from them but whose deviation itself therefore became a matter for concrete investigation, the ground for concrete analysis.

The fact that his algebraic claim about both the sum of values and the sum of surplus values being identical between the value and price systems was generally not correct, unlike what he thought, does not mean that Marx's theory of value becomes irrelevant. The real argument against Marx's theory of value all along has been not this algebraic proposition, but something else that its nonfulfillment allegedly indicates, namely that the price system can be erected as a complete and self-contained system, upon the specification of a distributional parameter, without needing any other valuation rules. This is the real issue of debate, and on this Marx is correct, not his critics.

12

Marx's Solution to a Dilemma

WE ARGUED EARLIER THAT THE Ricardian theory of value, which takes money as simply another commodity whose relative price vis-à-vis the world of nonmoney commodities is determined exactly like that of any other commodity, necessarily entails (in the short run) a belief in the quantity theory of money. This in turn presumes that the only role of money is that of a circulating medium and thereby precludes any possibility of overproduction crises. The fact that Ricardo believed in Say's law was not a mere coincidence. It was logically entailed in his theory of value. But this theoretical totality, embracing his theories of value, of money and of aggregate demand (which could never be deficient) was logically faulty. It was self-negating in the sense that the assumption needed for its validation was undermined by its own implications: it assumed the absence of idle money balances, but any tendency for the short-run value of money to fall below its long-run value, a possibility that the theory visualized, could not but result in the holding of idle money balances.

Marx rejected the notion of money being simply yet another commodity. He rejected the quantity theory of money in favor of an alternative theory that assumed the perpetual existence of a hoard of money, so that the value of money was not determined, whether in the short or in the long run, by demand and supply. It was given from outside the realm of demand and supply by the conditions of production, which were captured by the relative quantities of labor embodied in a unit of money and a unit of the nonmoney commodity basket. The recognition of idle balances (in the form of a hoard) implied in turn the recognition of the possibility of overproduction.

But a logical problem arose here. If we recognize the possibility of overproduction and quantity adjustment, then the notion of a long-run or "center-of-gravity" equilibrium ceases to have any meaning. Hence a dilemma arises in the context of Marxian economics: either we stick to the notion of a center-of-gravity equilibrium and implicitly accept Say's law and monetarism, or we reject this entire set of equilibrium notions and accept that the economy can settle "anywhere." Marx's solution to this dilemma, and his theoretical device for combining both, the notion of an equilibrium and the possibility of overproduction, within a single comprehensive schema, is discussed in the current chapter.

Marx's solution, to anticipate matters, was unsatisfactory, which is why this dilemma has haunted Marxist economics in later years. It surfaces in the controversy surrounding Rosa Luxemburg's (1963) theory of imperialism. Bukharin's critique (Tarbuck 1972) that Luxemburg, in opposition to Marx, was visualizing the possibility of an isolated capitalist economy's being afflicted by "permanent general overproduction" (which is synonymous with our phrase "the economy settling 'anywhere'") is certainly apposite. His own position however is based on an acceptance of a "center of gravity" equilibrium and hence de facto of Say's law. Thus, Luxemburg and Bukharin may be seen as occupying the two contrasting positions.

The Commonly Held View

Bukharin's position would perhaps be the commonly held one among Marxist economists. They would not only accept his proposition that the compulsion felt by each capitalist to accumulate would result in the realization and capitalization of the entire unconsumed surplus value, thus negating any problem of deficient aggregate demand,[1] but would even see this as being in conformity with Marx's overall historical approach. Let us see why.

Marx's analysis of capitalism, as is well known, was located within an overall historical understanding that distinguished several different "modes of production," such as primitive communism, slavery, feudalism, the Asiatic mode (a variant of feudalism but with sui generis characteristics), and (in some writings) the Germanic mode (Marx 1969a). Capitalism, which had arisen in Western Europe on the ashes of feudalism, was to be superseded by the socialist mode of production, which marked the end of class antagonism. Each mode of production was seen as a self-contained system. It was characterized, after the stage of primitive communism, by antagonistic classes, whose struggle was the instrument of its replacement.

The *Communist Manifesto*, which first put forward the idea of class struggle and class antagonism, mentioned a set of binary opposites: "Freeman and slave, patrician and plebeian, lord and serf, guild-master and journeyman, in a word, oppressor and oppressed." It noted that capitalism had not done away with class antagonism but had simplified it by increasingly polarizing society "into two great hostile camps, into two great classes directly facing each other: Bourgeoisie and Proletariat."[2] Thus, Marx's analysis of the dynamics of the mode of production in general and of capitalism in particular was focused on an isolated, self-contained system characterized by the existence of binary opposites.

Within such a system, class struggle was not the location of the source of change, but was only its instrument. The source of change was the development of the productive forces that came into conflict with the relations of production at a certain stage. The study of a mode of production therefore had to include both its coherence and also the threat to its coherence brought on by the development of the productive forces.

The conceptual apparatus used by Marx for this study was the notion of "equilib-rium." To deny the tendency of the system to settle at an equilibrium, and to assert that because of its being demand-constrained it could settle "anywhere," is to deny the coherence of the system. Problems of aggregate demand therefore must necessarily be relegated to the background, which is also in keeping with the fact that demand influ-ences only the realization process and hence belongs to the sphere of circulation that has only a secondary role compared to the sphere of production.

Within this perception, the threat to the system's coherence, arising from the devel-opment of productive forces, would be generally seen as stemming from the "tendency for the rate of profit to fall." An index of the development of the productive forces is the increase in labor productivity, reflected inter alia in the increasing mass of the means of production used per worker, of which a rise in the "organic composition of capital" (the primary cause of the falling tendency of the rate of profit) is believed to be only a counterpart. Thus, it would be argued, the development of the productive forces threatens the coherence of the system, because such development is associated ceteris paribus with a rise in the organic composition of capital, which sooner or later must give rise to a falling tendency of the rate of profit.

The problem with this commonly held Marxist view, however, is that it does not distinguish between Ricardo and Marx and does not appreciate the specificity of Marx's theory of money. As a result, it does not recognize Marx's absolute opposi-tion to monetarism and to Say's law, which is an integral part of monetarism. It sees the single-period equilibrium in Marx as a de facto full-capacity-use equilibrium. More important, quite apart from not doing justice to Marx's ideas, this view does not do justice to reality itself. The argument that demand plays only a secondary role in explaining the dynamics of capitalism cannot stand scrutiny in the light of post–First World War developments in capitalism. To ignore Marx's writings, which anticipated the problem of deficient aggregate demand well before they came to the fore in the twentieth century and nearly three-quarters of a century before Keynes, and that too in the name of adherence to Marx's approach, can scarcely be justified.

The Nature of the Dilemma

If we take the totality of Marx's theory, both his theory of value and surplus value and his theory of money, then the dilemma facing his theory becomes clear. If the value of money vis-à-vis the world of commodities is given from outside the realm of supply and demand, then there must be not only a hoard of money, but also the possibility of quantity adjustment in the world of commodities.

This becomes clear if we consider a reduction in the demand for commodities at full-capacity use, through a shift from demanding commodities to holding money. It may appear that in such a case commodity prices would fall until inventory holdings out of full capacity output have increased sufficiently to make good the deficiency in the autonomous component of demand (that is, demand other than for additional inventories). It may appear, in other words, that (leaving aside the issue of firms going under, owing to inherited debt commitments), the economy can always maintain full-capacity use, even when there is a decline in the autonomous component of demand, through an appropriate fall in prices and hence an appropriate increase in inventories. This, however, is not true. Firms are always better off carrying unutilized capacity rather than inventories, since the former entails lower carrying costs. They would therefore reduce output below full capacity in the event of a fall in demand, that is, full-capacity output would not be sustained in the event of a reduction in demand, even if the economy happened to be producing it to start with. It follows that since variations in demand for commodities characterize any situation where a hoard of money always exists, the perennial existence of some unutilized capacity too will be a general phenomenon.

Thus, implicit in the view that the value of money is given from outside the realm of supply and demand, is the possibility of quantity adjustment as far as the commodity sectors are concerned. These may be accompanied by some price adjustment as well, as we noted in chapter 10, but the existence of a perennial stock of unutilized capacity is inherent to the theory of "extrinsic determination" of the value of money (since inventories are expensive to carry). The commodity-producing sectors in short must be perennially demand-constrained, a fact that is also recognized in Marx's own writings.

But if output is determined by the strength of demand in any period, then a new and different problem arises. The conditions of production, upon which the determination of labor values and the prices of production depend, and which are summed up as a set of input coefficients, obviously vary according to the degree of capacity utilization. If output in any period is determined by demand, so that the degree of capacity utilization becomes a variable, then the production coefficients would no longer be constant. Then at any level of technology, the labor values and the prices of production would no longer be independent of demand, as they are supposed to be.

To be sure, the production coefficients need not be defined at "full capacity use"; they may be defined for any level of capacity use, and, as suggested in chapter 10, they make sense in the context of Marxist economics, only if defined with respect to some "normal" level of capacity use. But then if output depends on demand, then it can be "anywhere," and not necessarily at the "normal capacity use" level. Thus, while one part of Marx's theory, his monetary theory, entails that output can be anywhere, another part of Marx's theory, his theory of value and prices of production, entails that output must be at some particular ("normal") capacity level. Since output cannot be both anywhere and at some particular level, it follows that the two parts of Marx's theory are pulling in two different directions and are mutually incompatible.

This is the dilemma faced by his theoretical structure. Either he has to abandon his monetary theory and with it the theory of the economy being demand-constrained in equilibrium, and slip into the Ricardian acceptance of monetarism and Say's law, which he himself has explicitly and unambiguously rejected, or he has to abandon his value and price theory and with it the entire analysis of surplus value and the anatomy of the capitalist mode of production.

Together with this there is the larger issue, namely the primacy of the sphere of production. If demand has a role in the determination of output in any period, then the sphere of circulation, where produced commodities are realized, acquires a status that Marxist economics does not generally accord it. Hence if the reconciliation of Marx's theory of money with his theory of value and surplus value poses a problem, then this problem itself is embedded within a larger problem, namely the reconciliation of the theory of the possibility of overproduction (which logically entails the system's being demand-constrained in equilibrium) with the theory of the primacy of the sphere of production.

Marx's Resolution of the Problem

Marx's way out of this dilemma was to postulate, as already discussed in chapter 10, that output is not at full capacity in any period, nor even at some "normal" capacity; it deviates from "normal" capacity output owing to the influence of demand, but this influence itself operates in a random or cyclical manner, so that ceteris paribus "normal capacity output" would be the center of gravity toward which actual output would move. Marx of course expresses it as the "average" output through fluctuations, and there is no reason why an observed average should coincide with the center of gravity. But clearly the average that Marx was talking about was a conceptual and not an actual one, and this conceptual average ceteris paribus should coincide with the center of gravity.

This solution was quite ingenious. It permitted the determination of output by demand in any period. At the same time it postulated that the effect of demand on output, compared to the average situation, was only an evanescent one, confined only to cyclical and random deviations. Looking at it differently, if we define the period not as a hypothetical chunk of actual *historical time* during which the level of capital stock remains unchanged, which is how Keynes had defined it, but as a hypothetical chunk of conceptual historical time that represents the average of a cycle with given technology, then in that period, if there is no positive or negative random deviation of demand from its mean, we must have "normal" capacity utilization. The production coefficients calculated when "normal" capacity utilization prevails constitute the basis for the determination of labor values and of the prices of production. The dynamics of the system can then be analyzed and the implications of technological progress accompanying capital accumulation examined by focusing attention on what happens across "periods" defined in this manner. The effect of variations in demand can then be completely eliminated from the analysis, which can proceed as if we are in a Say's law world, even though output in each chunk of time corresponding to the period defined by Keynes is determined by demand. Demand-determination of output in any period, corresponding to one concept of period, is thus compatible with demand's not determining output in any period, corresponding to another concept of period.

What is logically required for this perception to be a meaningful one, however, is that deviations of demand from the normal level must be cyclical or random and not cumulative. The fact that demand, if it goes on rising, would cease to determine output when capacity constraints are reached, would be readily conceded, so that a cumulative movement of demand upward does not pose any problems for the theory. But it must also be the case that deviations of demand in the downward direction should be self-negating and not cumulative. The Marxist theory of crisis sought to demonstrate this: as crisis pushes an economy in a downward direction (and all crises are associated with a downward deviation of demand from its normal level), it leads at some point to a scrapping of capital stock, which creates the condition for a revival of the economy.

While Marx does not provide any formal demonstration of how the crisis is self-negating, that is, how it creates the conditions for the start of a new boom, one can piece together the following picture from his writings. Any crisis, which, no matter what its origin, shows itself in the form of an (*ex ante*) excess supply of commodities, implies ipso facto an excess of capital as well. It is this jostling between a plethora of capitals giving rise to an *ex ante* excess supply of commodities that brings prices down, lowering the rate of profit, and thereby lowering the rate of accumulation in the form of capital goods further, and accentuating *ex ante* excess supply of commodities even more. This whole downward spiral comes to an end, and indeed can only come to an end, when a sufficient amount of capital has been destroyed during the crisis, removing the earlier plethora of capital that had become an impediment to further investment.

This reasoning, which sees crises as self-negating and hence necessarily transient, though significant, phenomena (in so far as they are manifestations of the contradictions of the system), and therefore argues the legitimacy of the center-of-gravity equilibrium, has logical problems with it. But before looking at these problems let us first attempt to build a formal model of the argument for the sake of greater clarity. Of course, Marx did not have a single model of crisis, and he did not spell out all the complex processes through which a crisis would manifest itself. The model presented here therefore is merely illustrative, designed only to give some precision to our discussion. Even if this model is not accepted as being sufficiently faithful to Marx's ideas, as some no doubt would feel, the arguments that we develop in the context of it would retain their relevance no matter how Marx's theory of crisis is interpreted.

An Illustrative Model of a Crisis

We discuss the dynamics of the system in the familiar manner, in terms of a sequence of single periods within each of which the level of capital stock remains fixed, rising only from one period to the next by the amount of gross investment undertaken during the period, less what is destroyed or retired. . Normally in any such single period the size of the available labor force is assumed to be given. But if we are discussing in the Marxian context, then postulating an exogenously given time profile of labor force cannot be justified. There is no reason why international migration of labor from labor-abundant regions, or, what comes to the same thing, international migration of capital to labor-abundant regions, cannot be used to prevent labor supply from constraining capital accumulation. In what follows we assume that labor supply is adjusted to labor demand in the long run (in the sense that it has the same trend rate of growth as labor demand, whatever the latter's trend rate of growth). This overall long-run balancing does not, of course, preclude variations in the relative size of the reserve army from one single period to the next, which would have the usual effect on the single-period wage share. But for the sake of simplicity, we assume for the present that the wage share is simply a given constant μ.

There is a set of equipment vintages, which last into the infinite future with undiminished efficiency, an identical capital-output ratio for all of them but different capital-labor ratios, and a rule where a new vintage is never found to be idle whenever an old vintage is being used. Denoting total output by O, output-capital ratio by b, the oldest vintage in use in any period by $t - T(t)$, and the equipment on the purchase of which expenditure is incurred in period $t - 1$ and which is added to the capital stock at the beginning of period t by I_{t-1}, we have

$$O\left(t\right) = \Sigma^{t-1}_{t-T(t)-1} b \cdot I\left(\tau\right) \dots \tag{i}$$

The total gross profit accruing to both the entrepreneurs and the rentiers is denoted by P. A fixed proportion c of this, together with the entire wage bill is consumed, so that we have

$$P(t) = I\left(t\right) / \left(1 - c\right) \dots \tag{ii}$$

where I denotes gross investment, and

$$O\left(t\right) = P\left(t\right) / \left(1 - \mu\right) \dots \tag{iii}$$

The gross investment in any period or instant of time is given, in which case these three equations determine the three unknowns O, P, and T. (We assume that the marginal vintage always succeeds in meeting its wage bill and any inherited payments obligations.) The movements of gross investment over time are governed by changes in the rate of profit. As denominator in the calculation of the rate of profit we simply take the total stock of equipment available for use in any period, that is, any equipment that is not scrapped. Availability for use, however, is different from actual use, owing to the fact that the actual use is determined by the level of aggregate demand.

We assume that when the rate of profit remains unchanged, then the capitalists plan to increase investment in the next period over the current period's level in the same ratio that gross investment in the current period bears to current period's capital stock. We thus have

$$I(t+1) - I(t) = I(t) \cdot [I(t) / K(t) + d \cdot \{r(t) - r(t-1)\}] \dots \qquad \text{(iv)}$$

where d is a positive constant, and a definitional equation

$$r = P / K \dots \qquad \text{(v)}$$

The maximum rate of profit r^* that can prevail in such an economy is given by

$$r^* = b \cdot (1 - \mu) \dots \qquad \text{(vi)}$$

The increase in capital stock from one period to the next is given by gross investment less the capital stock scrapped, that is,

$$K(t+1) - K(t) = I(t) - \delta(t) \cdot K(t) \dots \qquad \text{(vii)}$$

where $\delta(t)$ denotes the proportion of available equipment in period t that is scrapped at the end of the period. We assume that the proportion δ of equipment scrapped depends upon the rate of profit in the economy. Obviously, when the rate of profit is high, scrapping will be less, and when the rate of profit drops, the ratio of available equipment scrapped will be high. To establish the nonlinear character of the scrapping function, we assume that

$$\text{For } r > (\text{some}) \; r', \delta = 0, \text{ while for } r \leq r', \delta = 1 - r / r' \dots \qquad \text{(viii)}.$$

This completes the system. The fact that no reference has been made either to the vintage composition of equipment in any period (and its change across periods) or to the rate of growth of labor productivity may appear intriguing to some. But these, which have to be addressed in any meaningful model, have been kept out of the picture because of our assumptions of constant and equal capital-output ratios for all vintages and of a constant wage share for all periods. Our model is only an illustrative one whose object is to highlight certain theoretical points.

It can be seen from this system that there is a maximum rate of growth of capital stock g^* equals; $r^*(1 - c)$, which prevails in the economy when the rate of profit is at its maximum, r^*. Consider an economy where the capital stock has been growing at this maximum rate. If perchance it suddenly slips below this maximum rate, the rate of profit too will come down from r^*, in which case, from the investment function $\Delta I / I$

will fall below I / K, resulting in I / K in period $(t + 1)$ being lower than in period t. The rate of profit, however, is nothing else but $I / K(1 - c)$; hence the rate of profit in $(t + 1)$ will be lower than in t, leading to a still lower rate of accumulation in period $t + 2$, and so on. But once r has fallen to r', scrapping will begin, and since scrapping increases sharply as r falls, the downward movement in I / K, and hence of the rate of profit will come to an end sooner or later, and a new boom will begin. This is seen from the fact that for $r \leq r'$,

$$I(t + 1) / I(t) - K(t + 1) / K(t)$$
$$= [d / (1 - c)][I(t) / K(t) - I(t - 1) / K(t - 1)] + (1 - r / r')$$

so that when the rate of accumulation remains unchanged in the current period compared to the previous one, it increases in the next, giving rise to an upswing that carries the economy to g^*. It follows that the economy oscillates between g^* as an upper bound (when it reaches full capacity) and some lower limit from where it recovers owing to large scale scrapping, exactly the way that Marx had visualized.

It follows then that we can picture a "center of gravity" equilibrium, which, whether or not it constitutes an average state of affairs, in the statistical sense, for the economy through its fluctuations, certainly constitutes a benchmark. Deviations away from it are self-negating even though the negation of deviations in one direction gives rise to deviations in another direction. Can one find fault with this picture, which, whether or not it is faithful to Marx, certainly represents the kind of argument he was advancing?

A Critique of the Marxian Perception of Equilibrium

The Marxian perception of equilibrium as a center of gravity can be summarized as follows. Even though there are overproduction crises, through such crises there is an average (not in the statistical sense) that prevails. It is a center of gravity for the economy, with deviations away from it being self-negating. We can define the conditions of production, on the basis of which the "center of gravity" prices or equilibrium prices (Marx's "prices of production") are determined, as referring to "full capacity use." We can alternatively define the conditions of production on the basis of which the center-of-gravity prices are calculated as referring to this center-of-gravity state of the economy. But the important issue is not the exact state of affairs that constitutes our reference point for defining the equilibrium prices, but the fact that the very existence of a center-of-gravity state of the economy makes the notion of equilibrium prices meaningful.

Marx had no doubt about the existence of such a center-of-gravity state of the economy, because of which he could both recognize overproduction crises and yet commit himself to the labor theory of value with its notion of "given conditions of production." His view of the crisis as being essentially self-negating, indeed as being a mechanism of forcible destruction of capital through which the conditions for the resumption of capital accumulation are recreated, is a part of this perception. In his words: "How is this conflict settled and the conditions restored which correspond to the "sound" operation of capitalist production? The mode of settlement is already indicated in the very emergence of the conflict whose settlement is under discussion. It implies the withdrawal and even the partial destruction of capital amounting to the full value of the additional capital ΔC, or at least a part of it. . . . The loss is by no means equally distributed among individual capitals. But the equilibrium would be restored under all circumstances through the withdrawal or even the destruction of more or less capital" (1974b, 253).

But how exactly does the destruction of capital help a recovery? Marx's answer, which is reflected in our illustrative model, is that it would do so by raising the rate of profit. This would happen because of reduced wages: "The stagnation of production would have laid off a part of the working class and would thereby have placed the employed part in a situation, where it would have to submit to a reduction of wages even below the average" (1974b, 254). But, above all, the rise in the rate of profit through the destruction of capital in a crisis would occur because of the reduction in the size of the denominator over which the rate of profit is calculated: "Ultimately the depreciation of the elements of constant capital would itself tend to raise the rate of profit" (1974b, 255).

Let us look at this mechanism closely. We will discuss wage reduction later; let us first consider capital destruction. Suppose there are three capitals of (output capacity) 100 each, and suppose during the crisis the first two use only 70 each of their capital while the third uses only 60. Now if each of them scrapped only the unused portions of their capitals, then there is no reason why this fact per se should act as a stimulus for accumulation. Whether unused capital is reckoned or not reckoned in the calculation of the rate of profit is a matter relating to nomenclature and cannot possibly have any substantial implications. So, when scrapping is said to stimulate capital accumulation, something else obviously is being referred to, and that is the following.

It is not as if merely unused capitals of all capitalists are scrapped; rather, the weaker capitals go under altogether. In our example, the third capitalist, who is likely to have relatively more obsolete equipment, disappears completely from the scene, so that the 60 being produced by him now can be produced by the first two, who therefore experience full capacity use. The rate of profit of the latter two increases sharply and the jump in their accumulation rate as a consequence is such that the total accumulation by the surviving two after the scrapping is greater than what all three would have undertaken otherwise. In other words, underlying Marx's theory that the crisis, through capital destruction, provides the basis for a new upsurge of accumulation is the view that capital destruction means not just retiring some *unused* equipment, but above all retiring some *used* equipment.

But if used equipment is retired, then the income that was accruing through its use to those working on or owning it no longer accrues to them, and hence their demand must also decline. On the other hand, as our example shows, for capital destruction to raise the rate of profit on the surviving equipment it must be the case that demand does not decline pari passu with capital stock. Is there any mechanism to ensure that capital destruction does not reduce demand pari passu?

In this example, suppose of the output of 60 on the third capital, 30 was the wage bill and 30 profit. Assuming all wages and a fixed proportion c of profits are consumed, workers' consumption would go down by 30 and capitalists' consumption by $c \cdot 30$; and of course investment on this capital would fall to zero when this capital is scrapped. Now, if the savings out of these 30, that is, $(1 - c) \cdot 30$, would have exceeded own investment, that is, would have financed investment elsewhere, which remains unaffected even when these particular savings are no longer available, then capital destruction would *not* have reduced aggregate demand pari passu. But if this firm were itself a deficit firm in the sense that its gross savings were less than its gross investment, then its elimination would reduce aggregate demand to a greater extent than the fall in output through capital destruction. Since it stands to reason that a firm that is about to be eliminated from business is likely to be a deficit firm rather than a surplus one, capital destruction, far from keeping aggregate demand unchanged as Marx assumed, is likely to reduce it to an even greater extent than the output foregone, in which case, capital destruction would lower rather than raise the rate of profit. The proposition that capital destruction in the crisis creates the basis for a new boom then becomes invalid; on the contrary such destruction aggravates the crisis.

Of course, it would be argued that workers' consumption does not fall to zero when they become unemployed, or that capitalists do not cease to consume when the capital under their control is destroyed. In other words we have made certain stark assumptions until now that are invalid, since in real life there is a certain floor to consumption and hence to aggregate demand. This is certainly true. At the same time, we have not yet reckoned with the fact that capital destruction leading to enlarged unemployment would lower the wage rate of even the employed workers to below what it otherwise would have been. And the effect of this would clearly be in the opposite direction to that of the fact that there are floors to consumption.

No doubt, ultimately, if capital destruction goes on and on, a time would come when the fall in aggregate demand would be less than that of output through capital destruction (owing to the existence of these "floors"), at which point the rate of profit would cease to fall any further and would start climbing up. But any economy that has been pushed into such a deep crisis would witness such a significant undermining of the "state of confidence" of the capitalists that a spontaneous resumption of capital accumulation, if at all it occurs and if at all the system is not swamped by political convulsions by then, would be far too protracted an affair. Marx's description of the downturn being self-negating through the crisis that precipitates capital destruction would certainly not be an appropriate description.

Marx's description derives from the assumption that the loss of output entailed in capital destruction is not accompanied by any reduction in demand, as a result of which the output loss on the destroyed capital is made up by output gain on surviving capital leading to a rise in the rate of profit on the latter. This was precisely the assumption made in the illustrative model of the previous section. And it is this assumption (together with the assumption of constant wage share) that gives the Marxian result of a center-of-gravity equilibrium.

Marx's insufficient attention to aggregate demand effects is borne out by his remark that the reduction in wages during the downturn has the effect of increasing the rate of profit. This is certainly true if we ignore demand effects altogether or if these effects are nullified by the availability of external markets. But in a "closed" capitalist economy, such as what Marx postulates, we are not entitled to do either. It follows that Marx's solution to the dilemma discussed earlier, though ingenious, is still unsatisfactory.

Concluding Observations

That Marx's solution is unsatisfactory does not mean that a solution does not exist. Indeed, a solution *must* exist, since both the theoretical structures that Marx erects, namely the theory of surplus value and prices of production on the one hand, and the theory of money and possibility of overproduction on the other, are rooted in the reality of capitalism. The appropriation of surplus value in the realm of production is as much a reality under capitalism as the fact of quantity adjustment and demand-constraint. Marx's deep insight into the functioning of capitalism led to his discovery of both these aspects, but his attempt to combine the two was unsatisfactory. How the two can be combined, that is, how the dilemma facing the Marxian system can be resolved, is a matter we shall take up in the next part of this book.

It is important, however, to be clear on one point: The dilemma we have talked about, or the internal problems we have talked about in the context of Marx's theory, are of a different kind altogether from the problems associated with the Walrasian or the Ricardian systems. The problems with the latter were *logical* problems that undermined the *logical* validity of their theoretical systems. These authors determined the value of money through demand and supply. This would be valid only if money were exclusively a medium of circulation and not a form of holding wealth. But money cannot be a medium of circulation without being a form of wealth, a contradiction that made monetarism untenable in all its versions—including their versions.

In the case of Marx, however, there is no question of any *logical* contradiction within his monetary theory. His monetary theory is not quite compatible with his theory of value and prices of production in the manner he thought it was. The problem, in other words, is between one part of Marx's theory and another. But the part concerned with monetary theory does not itself have any internal logical problems. Hence, resolving the dilemma faced by Marxist theory is a separate issue altogether that must not detract from the basic correctness of propertyism and its scientific superiority over monetarism.

13

Alternative Interpretations of Keynes

WE SAW EARLIER THAT AGAINST the Walrasian tradition, according to which the value of money, like that of any other commodity, is determined by demand and supply in any period, there is an alternative tradition that holds that the value of money is given from "outside" the realm of demand and supply; I called this the Marx-Keynes tradition. But while Marx saw this "outside" determination in terms of the quantity of labor directly and indirectly embodied in a unit of the money commodity as compared to a unit of the nonmoney commodity (taken as an aggregate), Keynes saw it as an institutionally determined exchange ratio between a unit of money and a unit of labor power (if one may use Marx's term). In other words, the value of money in terms of commodities, according to Keynes, was fixed from outside in any period because the money wage rate was fixed from outside.

This is what ensures that money has a positive, finite, value in terms of commodities in any period. Since the expenditure of labor power is necessary for the production of commodities in general, the value of the latter in terms of the value of labor power, and hence in terms of money, has a lower bound, that is, it can never fall to zero. Likewise, since the relative value of labor power in terms of commodities in general cannot fall to zero if production is to continue (since that would entail zero real/product wages), the money value of commodities cannot become infinitely large. The money value of commodities, in other words, is a positive finite sum by virtue of the fact that the money value of labor power, that is, the money wage rate, is fixed as a positive finite sum in any particular period.

This answer to the question why money has a positive finite value is obviously a sui generis answer, different from the Marxian answer, since it does not postulate that the money value of commodities, and hence by implication the value of money, is given by their respective conditions of production. Indeed, the Keynesian answer presupposes a world of complete fiat or credit money, which the Marxian answer does not: even when the latter was talking about a world with paper money, it usually assumed commodity backing for paper money, which the Keynesian system does not.

Since Marx's monetary theory, for reasons discussed earlier, has remained some-what submerged, it is the Keynesian perception that has been taken generally as providing the opposition to Walrasianism, the debate between the Keynesians and the quantity theorists (who are all, necessarily, theoretically Walrasians) having become the staple of monetary economics for decades. But even this debate has been usually conducted in a highly restricted manner. The question typically asked has been this: Which of the two perceptions, the Keynesian or the Walrasian one, is more *realistic* (not more logically sustainable)? The question is posed this way because Keynesianism has usually been interpreted as postulating a given money wage on grounds of realism, and not logic. The purpose of this chapter is to discuss these alternative interpretations of Keynes and to show how his ideas have been sought to be rendered "harmless" by underplaying his theoretical critique of Walrasianism.

Keynes and Money Wages

The assumption of given money wages in the short period, to which Keynesian analysis is confined, is often taken as an empirical statement about the world, that is, as an alternative "stylization" about the world from the Walrasian one, that is sought to be justified on the grounds of its greater "realism." In other words, a commonly held view is that the Keynesian system questions not the logical basis of the Walrasian system but the "realism" of its assumption of perfectly flexible money wages, and it does so because the real world is characterized by the existence of trade unions that enforce a fixity of money wages.

The implication of this view is not only that the Walrasian system is logically unassailable, and that it therefore represents a perfectly valid stylization of an economy in which all prices are flexible, but also that if trade unions were weakened and money wages made flexible, then the problem of involuntary unemployment would not arise at all. In other words, if it is accepted that in a world of flexible money wages and prices the spontaneous operation of markets eliminates involuntary unemployment, then making the world approximate such flexibility makes very good sense. Involuntary unemployment then becomes a consequence not of the untrammeled functioning of markets but of restrictions upon their functioning.

The conclusion that altering the world into a flexible price one would eliminate involuntary unemployment would follow not only from the views of conventional Walrasians (though a large number of them, especially the monetarists, would not even accept that money wages are in fact inflexible, that the world does not conform to the Walrasian stylization, and that involuntary unemployment at all exists), but also from those of writers such as Malinvaud who talk in terms of a "rationing equilibrium."

There are at least three problems with the theories of rationing equilibrium. First, why and how the fixed prices, which they take as their point of departure, are fixed, is left unexplained by them. In other words, they provide no behavioral basis to their assumption of fixed prices.

Second, what they call "classical" and "Keynesian" unemployment are completely and qualitatively different from what the classical writers or Keynes had actually postulated. For example, "classical unemployment" as expounded by classical writers refers to a situation where the real wage is given. Its downward inflexibility is the cause of unemployment. But the entire output produced at this real wage is exactly what is demanded, that is, there is no rationing of buyers. Likewise, "Keynesian unemployment" according to Keynes refers to a situation where product markets clear but the labor market does not. In rationing-equilibrium theories like Malinvaud's, in contrast, "Keynesian unemployment" entails the rationing of sellers in both the labor and the product markets.

Third, the rationing-equilibrium theories take it for granted that if prices had not been fixed, then a full Walrasian equilibrium would have prevailed with no unemployment of any description.

As a matter of fact, this last proposition was the point of attack by Keynes. Keynes's argument, set out in its complexity in chapter 17 of the *General Theory* was that if the world conformed to the Walrasian stylization where the price of any commodity, including labor power, increased whenever there was excess demand for it and decreased whenever there was excess supply, then there would be no equilibrium in the economy. Not only would there be no Walrasian equilibrium with full employment, but there would be also be simply no state of rest for the economy at all. The fact that the economy does have a state of rest at all is because money wages are given for the period in question. If they were not, then the existence of involuntary unemployment would keep driving the money wage rate and hence the prices down and down, without this fact necessarily resulting in any reduction in involuntary unemployment. It follows that the fixity of money wages is not the cause of involuntary unemployment, that is, is not responsible for the nonestablishment of a Walrasian equilibrium. A Walrasian equilibrium would not be established anyway, not even if money wages were flexible. But if money wages were flexible, then, let alone a Walrasian equilibrium, no equilibrium would be established. The fact that the economy does find for itself a state of rest at all, though not a Walrasian one, is because money wages are given in the period in question.

This can be demonstrated in the context of Keynesian economics in the following manner. Consider a simplistic, rather mechanical model to start with. Let us assume that the minimum ("liquidity trap") rate of interest in the economy is denoted by i', that consumption (in terms of the wage unit) is given by $A + c \cdot Y_w$, where A is a constant, c is the marginal propensity to consume, and Y_w is income in terms of the wage unit. Now, if the elasticity of wage and price expectation is unity, then the position of marginal efficiency of capital schedule becomes completely insensitive to any change in money wages and prices in the economy, so that investment in terms of the wage unit (I_w) becomes a function exclusively of the interest rate, no matter how the wage rate and prices are moving. If in such a world Y^*_w, the full employment income in terms of the wage unit exceeds $[A + I_w(i')] / (1 - c)$, then money wages and prices would keep falling without the economy stabilizing itself at any state of rest. In other words, let alone full employment equilibrium, there would be no equilibrium at which the economy would come to rest.

This, of course, is based on the famous "wage theorem" discussed by Hicks (1974). In any economy where consumption depends exclusively on the level of income and the interest rate is unaffected by any increase in money supply, a reduction in money wages leads to an equiproportionate reduction in prices without any increase in employment, if the elasticity of wage and price expectation is unity. In a world in which, given this nondisappearing unemployment, money wages still keep falling because of it, there clearly would be no state of rest at all.

Now, the first question that can be raised about this concerns the liquidity trap. Surely, the liquidity trap, if it exists, constitutes a rather special case. Are we not making too much out of a special case? Let us therefore first drop the assumption of a liquidity trap. In doing so, however, we become immediately aware of a problem with the Keynesian system.

The liquidity preference schedule showing the amount of money that would be demanded for nontransaction purposes as a function of the rate of interest is supposed to remain unchanged as money wages and prices change. Indeed those who argue about the market spontaneously achieving full employment through money-wage changes (in the absence of a liquidity trap) base their argument precisely on this assumption. A fall in money wages, if accompanied by a *pro tanto* fall in prices, that is, unaccompanied by any rise in employment and output, would reduce the transaction demand for money correspondingly, increasing the amount of money (out of the given money supply) that has to be held in the form of idle balances. With a given liquidity preference schedule, this can happen only through a lowering of the interest rate (again ignoring any "liquidity trap"). Such a lowering of the interest rate in turn is impossible without some effect on investment, employment, and output (we assume away the existence of oligopoly, which would make investment interest-insensitive, in the present context).[1] It follows that any lowering of the money wage rate would stimulate employment, and if the money wage rate is downward-flexible, then a full employment equilibrium would be attained. Underlying this entire argument is the presumption that the liquidity preference schedule itself does not shift when money wages and prices change.

In any economy where there are inherited payments obligations, a reduction in prices, despite being accompanied by a reduction in money wages, increases the real burden of payments obligations and hence increases the chances of bankruptcy among firms. In the money-bonds choice this *must* make bonds less attractive compared to money for any given interest rate, that is, it must shift the liquidity preference schedule outward, no matter what theory we take, whether Tobin (1958), or Keynes (1949), or Kahn (1954), as our explanation for the phenomenon of liquidity preference.

It follows that in a world of inherited payments obligations, we would not have one liquidity preference schedule but a whole family of them, each corresponding to a particular level of the money wage rate. Strictly speaking, the change in the money wage rate rather than the level of it is perhaps an even more potent factor underlying the position of the liquidity preference schedule, but, for the sake of simplicity, let us concentrate on the level only.

A lowering of the money wage rate, then, even as it makes more money available for idle balances, also raises the demand for such balances at any given interest rate. Even if the net effect for a while may be a lowering of the interest rate along with a reduction in the wage rate, eventually the threat of bankruptcy must be strong enough to outweigh any other considerations, so that there would be a floor to the interest rate below which it can not fall, no matter how much money wages are reduced. In other words, exactly the same effect that the liquidity trap is supposed to produce can arise even in the absence of a liquidity trap of the conventional kind, owing to the fact of inherited payments obligations and the consequent threat of bankruptcy in the face of reductions in wages and prices.

The second assumption underlying the wage theorem is unit elasticity of wage and price expectations. While inelastic expectations may mean that money wage reductions have the effect of raising employment (and hence flexible money wages constitute an equilibrating mechanism working toward the attainment of full employment), inelastic expectations presuppose some notion of normal money wages and prices, deviations from which are expected to be self-nullifying. This "normal" must not be confused with the equilibrium level of money wages and prices, since the whole idea is to see if the latter exists at all, and to presume its existence would be illegitimate. The notion of a "normal," therefore, can arise only if there is some independent institutionally given level or range of money wages that the actual figure can transgress only temporarily.

But such an independently given level of money wages violates the assumption of wage flexibility. What is more, even if such an independent money wage rate is assumed to exist, and hence justify, inelastic expectations, so that the actual money wage rate falling below this given rate increases employment, we get from all this a bizarre result, namely that full employment, at which such an economy with wage flexibility would eventually come to rest, would always entail a divergence between the actual and the expected (that is, the independently given fulcrum) money wage rates, in which case this so-called given wage rate loses all meaning. In short, in a world with flexible money wages any assumption of inelastic wage (and price) expectations is illegitimate. (Elastic price expectations, apart also from having little legitimacy, are not even equilibrating anyway.) Without inelastic wage and price expectations, however, there is no reason to believe that money wage reductions, which occur when there is excess supply in the labor market, can at all come to an end.

The third assumption underlying the wage theorem is the postulate that consumption depends on income. With money wages and prices falling, since the real value of cash balances (and of cash denominated assets) increases, does this not have an impact on consumption? There is no reason, however, why we should confine our attention to consumption alone. A wealth effect can be as much on consumption expenditure as on investment expenditure, and just as we have ignored the former until now, we also have ignored the latter. Let us look at the wealth effect on expenditure as a whole, and here the net effect of declining wages and prices is by no means clear-cut.

In an inside-money world, all financial assets, including money, held by economic agents, have as their exact counterpart corresponding liabilities held by other economic agents. The rise in the real value of assets held by some is therefore exactly matched by a rise in the real value of the liabilities held by others, that is, by a corresponding fall in the real value of the latter's net assets. Declining money wages and prices therefore would give rise to larger total expenditure (whether consumption or investment) only if there is an asymmetry of behavior between the losers and the gainers from this price fall, that is, only if the increase in expenditure, if any, by the gainers exceeds the decline in expenditure by the losers.

Besides, even the proposition that the gainers would increase their expenditure is doubtful. Typically such increase, since it is likely to accrue to rentiers, is supposed to take the form of consumption expenditure. But whether declining prices lead to larger consumption expenditure by the gainers via a wealth effect depends on how much wealth they wish to bequeath to the next generation relative to their current wealth. If they wish to bequeath the same amount of wealth to their children as they themselves possess, then there would be no wealth effect on consumption.

On the other hand, the losers from price fall, the firms, are likely to cut back their investment expenditures, a fact not taken into account in the standard Keynesian investment analysis, which sees investment as depending solely on the interest rate and the marginal efficiency of capital. The net effect of declining prices on expenditure decisions via the wealth effect therefore can by no means be taken to be a positive one.

What the foregoing states is that the conclusion arrived at in the simple model of the wage theorem, namely that a reduction in money wages does not eliminate excess supply in the labor market, does not lose its validity when we question its simple assumptions. If this is the case, then unless the economy has some exogenously given state of rest, there would be no state of rest whatsoever. Keynes's belief that the money wage rate is given exogenously provides such a state of rest. It is not that the fact of exogenously given money wages is the cause of unemployment in the economy, but that, given the unemployment that would be there anyway, the economy would not have a state of rest unless the money wage rate was exogenously given.

But why should there be unemployment in the economy at all? Even on this basic question there is much confusion, some of it contributed by Keynes himself.

The Reason for Involuntary Unemployment

It is obvious that involuntary unemployment, as defined by Keynes, arises because at full employment there is an excess supply of producible commodities, and a corresponding excess demand for some nonproducible commodities, which cannot be eliminated through variations in the relative prices between the two. If excess demands and supplies were confined to the circle of producible commodities alone, then we would be facing no more than the familiar problem of the too-many-shirts-too-few-hairpins type, and the question of involuntary unemployment would not arise.[2] But because the excess demand is for a nonproducible commodity and cannot be eliminated through relative price variations, the attainment of full employment becomes impossible.

There are however two alternative possible reasons why relative price variations cannot eliminate this pattern of (negative or positive) excess demand at full employment. One states that there are restrictions on relative price variations, which is why such variations cannot eliminate excess demands. The other states that while there are no such restrictions, the excess demands are insensitive to variations in relative prices.

Corresponding to these two reasons we have two alternative interpretations of Keynes, who of course took money as the nonproducible commodity that experienced excess demand at full employment, corresponding to the excess supply of producible commodities. The first interpretation states that it is the restriction on variations in the relative price between money and commodities, arising from the fixity of money wages, which is responsible for the nondisappearance of excess supply of producible commodities at full employment. But as employment, output and hence income fall below full employment, the excess supply of producible commodities, and hence, by implication, the excess demand for money, begins to disappear until at some equilibrium level of employment it falls to zero.[3]

The second interpretation states that even if there are no restrictions on relative price variations in the form of fixed money wages, the excess supply of producible commodities at full employment would still continue, for reasons we have discussed in the previous section. No amount of relative price variation can eliminate this excess supply, which only a fall in employment to some equilibrium level can. At this equilibrium level of employment the money prices of commodities are given by the exogenously given level of the money wage rate.

The previous section argued the case for the latter view. And there is ample evidence of support for it in chapter 17 of the *General Theory*. In the course of stating it, however, Keynes made certain confusing remarks.

The question Keynes asks in chapter 17, which is as insightful as it is opaque and problematical, is this: What is the special property of money that makes the money rate of interest so significant for the determination of employment? His answer: "The significance of the money rate of interest arises, therefore, out of the combination of the characteristics that, through the working of the liquidity-motive, this rate of interest may be somewhat unresponsive to a change in the proportion which the quantity of money bears to other forms of wealth measured in money, and that money has (or may have) zero (or negligible) elasticities both of production and of substitution" (1949, 234).

The first characteristic mentioned by Keynes, namely the unresponsiveness of the interest rate, together with the fact of the low elasticity of substitution (which makes money a "bottomless sink for purchasing power") ensures that any *ex ante* excess demand for money, corresponding to an *ex ante* excess supply of producible commodities at full employment, cannot be eliminated by variations in money wages and prices. The low elasticity of production implies that money is not itself a producible commodity.

Shortly after saying this, however, Keynes talks of "inelasticity of supply" of money as being the cause of the trouble: "It is interesting to notice that the characteristic which has been traditionally supposed to render gold especially suitable for use as the standard of value, namely, its inelasticity of supply, turns out to be precisely the characteristic which is at the bottom of the trouble" (1949, 236). Keynes is clearly taking inelasticity of supply and inelasticity of production as being synonymous.

The fact that he takes the two to be synonymous is also evident from the following well-known remark: "Unemployment develops ... because people want the moon; men cannot be employed when the object of desire (that is, money) is something which cannot be produced and the demand for which cannot be readily choked off. There is no remedy but to persuade the public that green cheese is practically the same thing and to have a green cheese factory (that is, a central bank) under public control" (1949, 235). After locating the problem in the fact that money cannot be produced, Keynes sees the remedy in having a central bank under public control, which obviously can only supply more money. In other words, supply and production are taken to be identical.

Now, there is a problem in doing so. If money is a produced good, that is, is a product of labor, then an increase in its supply causes ipso facto an increase in employment. On the other hand, if money is not a produced good, then an increase in its supply, through the actions of a central bank under public control does not cause any direct increase in employment. True, it may cause an *indirect* increase in employment, since the typical mode of increasing money supply by banks, through the purchase of securities, entails indirectly an increase in the demand for producible commodities. This is because securities represent claims on capital stock, and by demanding securities, banks raise the prices of existing capital assets relative to the marginal cost of production of new capital goods, thereby increasing the demand for new capital goods. All this however is indirect and hence of limited effectiveness. Banks have certain limits in countering the "bearishness of the public," which Keynes himself underscores through his reference to the "bottomless sink for purchasing power."

Production and supply therefore are not synonymous, since an increase in the supply of a produced good and that of a nonproduced good have very different consequences. Indeed, if the pattern of excess demands at full employment is insensitive to relative price variations, as Keynes himself suggests, then involuntary unemployment would not disappear simply by increasing the supply of (nonproduced) money. For, if it could disappear through an increase in the supply of money, then it could as well disappear through a reduction in money wages and prices, a possibility that Keynes has just denied.[4]

At the risk of repetition, let me restate the argument. Suppose at full employment there is an excess supply of producible nonmoney commodities and a corresponding excess demand for money. Now, if money were a *producible* commodity, then involuntary unemployment would not occur; the economy would be at full employment, though there would be a shift of labor from commodity production to money production. But since money is a nonproducible, that is, nonlabor using, commodity, this cannot happen. On the other hand, reductions in money wages and prices do not induce people to demand more commodities in lieu of money, since the latter, Keynes has argued, is a "bottomless sink of purchasing power." Hence the excess supply of commodities at full employment cannot be eliminated through money wage and price movements and results in an equilibrium with involuntary unemployment. In this case, however, an increase in money supply through an accommodating central bank would scarcely reduce unemployment. Only if the reduction in excess demand for money is brought about in a manner whereby there is a simultaneous reduction in the excess supply of commodities would it help in eliminating involuntary unemployment. Since this cannot happen through labor and other resources being shifted from commodity to money production, the only other possibility for it is if the mode of increasing money supply is simultaneously a mode of increasing commodity demand, for example, if money supply is raised through the process of the government financing commodity purchases by a budgetary deficit covered by bank credit. But Keynes's remark about a "central bank under public control" gives the misleading impression that the fixity of money supply is responsible for unemployment and *any* mode of increasing money supply by banks would automatically reduce involuntary unemployment.

In fact, Keynes's slipping into the fixity-of-money-supply argument as distinct from the inelasticity-of-substitution-of-money-for-other-assets argument as the explanation for involuntary unemployment refurbished the idea that his theory was based on the assumption of wage-rigidity, that it challenged only the assumptions of Walrasianism not its logic.

An Alternative Expression of the Two Interpretations

The matter can be better understood in terms of a distinction that is drawn in Marxist literature between "disproportionality crises" and "overproduction crises" (Sweezy 1946; Kalecki 1971). If the variation in the relative price between two sectors is restricted and the supply of one of the sectors is fixed, then the maximum amount of the other sector's output producible in equilibrium is simply given by the maximum amount of it, which is demanded given the first sector's supply. Suppose, for instance, that the relative price is fixed and at that fixed price the two sector's products are demanded in the ratio of 1:2, then if the first sector (the bottleneck sector) has a maximum supply of 100, the second can supply only 200 in equilibrium. Anything more would create excess supply for its product. The fact that sector 2 would be demand-constrained as a consequence is a reflection of "disproportionality."

Disproportionality has figured prominently in the literature on development, especially development planning. Indeed, a very influential tendency in the macro-economics of developing economies holds that the overall level of employment in the economy, and of course the output and employment in the nonwage goods sector, is determined by the output of the wage goods sector, which, together with the real wage rate, is fixed in the short period (Patnaik 1994).

Disproportionality can also be a cause of involuntary unemployment of the Keynesian kind, that is, where *no* sector with producible output is producing at the maximal level, in the following manner.[5] Suppose at full employment there is an *ex ante* excess supply of the producible commodities owing to an *ex ante* excess demand for some nonproducible commodity, whose supply, together with its exchange ratio with the producible commodities, is fixed. Then, clearly, there would be involuntary unemployment. An increase in the supply of the nonproducible commodity here would increase employment, since *ex hypothesi* it is the fixity of supply of the nonproducible commodity that underlies *ex ante* excess supply of the producible commodities. This case is exactly like the wage goods case in the context of developing economies. Taking money as the nonproducible commodity, this view then explains the existence of involuntary unemployment in terms of the fixity of money supply and of the money wage rate. In other words, the first interpretation of Keynes we mentioned is a disproportionality explanation of involuntary unemployment.

The scope for a disproportionality-based explanation of involuntary unemployment is not confined to a money economy alone, although in a barter economy the nonreproducible commodity, whose fixity of supply acts as the cause of involuntary unemployment, would have to be something other than money. But a barter economy can clearly face involuntary unemployment for *this* reason, that is, because of the fixity of supply of some nonreproducible commodity whose exchange ratio vis-à-vis reproducible commodities is for some reason incapable of sufficient variation (Rakshit 1989).

Disproportionality is indeed the conventional interpretation of Keynes as set out for instance in Hicks's famous IS-LM analysis (1937), which assumes fixity of both money wages and money supply. This assumption of fixed money wages makes his discussion of the classical case highly questionable, since it amounts to studying a flex-wage theory in terms of a fix-wage model; it also makes involuntary unemployment a result apparently of wage-rigidity. Hicks does explore the effects of money wage reductions, but these effects are seen entirely in terms of the position of the LM curve but not of the IS curve. His conclusion about the Keynesian theory being a special theory of something much more general follows entirely from his disproportionality interpretation of Keynes with money wage rigidity at its center.

Overproduction crises, however, are sui generis. They arise because of an insufficient demand for produced commodities that cannot be rectified through price falls of the latter. It is not the rigidity of the latter's price but the inability of price falls to stimulate demand that accounts for overproduction, which of course is an *ex ante* concept that manifests itself in terms of a short-period equilibrium with involuntary unemployment (that is, unemployment despite the workers' willingness to accept a lower real wage).

These two interpretations of Keynes have very simple identification marks: the disproportionality interpretation emphasizes wage rigidity, whereas the overproduction interpretation emphasizes the invariance of the interest rate to changes in money supply in terms of the wage unit.

The fact that Keynes, notwithstanding his confusing references to an inelastic money supply allegedly underlying involuntary unemployment, was actually talking about overproduction rather than disproportionality is clear from his underscoring the insensitivity of the money rate of interest.[6] It is clear above all from his entire discussion of whether land preference in certain societies could hold up investment. No matter whether his discussion on this issue is right or wrong—and we will come to it shortly—there would be no scope for it at all within a disproportionality view. The latter postulates not only fixity of supply of the commodity that is in excess demand at full employment, but also some fixity of its relative price vis-à-vis producible commodities; such a fixity between the price of land and the price of producible goods, however, is inconceivable where wages are not fixed in land units. Hence, on a disproportionality view, no sense can be made of the problem of land preference holding up productive investment.

But the problem makes perfect sense when we see it not in terms of fixity of relative price but in terms of the insensitivity of the excess-demand vector to variations in relative price. And here the matter turns on whether the "own rate of money interest," to use Kaldor's (1964) term, on land declines with a rise in price. While Keynes argued that the "own rate of own interest" on land may be downward-sticky, he did not say anything about its own rate of money interest. Kaldor's argument was that the own rate of money interest would decline with a rise in price owing to expectations of capital loss if the money price of land rises too high.

The point is not whether Keynes was right in his view that land preference could hold up productive investment, or even how a state of rest is arrived at in the market in a situation of unyielding land preference.[7] The point is that his very posing of the problem and his mode of argumentation suggest an overproduction rather than a disproportionality view of involuntary unemployment.

But, if overproduction arises according to Keynes by the fact that money, which is the object of excess demand at full employment, is a nonproducible commodity, then how do we have overproduction in the Marxian system where money *is* a producible commodity employing labor?

Marx and Keynes on Overproduction

Marx saw crises as immanent in the money form. In other words, he did not believe in the possibility of overproduction crises in a barter economy. This is because he distinguished between crises of overproduction and crises of disproportionality, though disproportionality could be the starting point of an overproduction crisis, as Goodwin (1951) was to demonstrate rigorously. Overproduction crises arose because of *ex ante* excess supply of commodities at full capacity production, whose counterpart was an *ex ante* excess demand for money. Crises arose because each exchange was split up into two phases: C-M and M-C, with money inserting itself in the middle. By this reasoning, an *ex ante* excess demand for land or any other nonproducible asset at "full employment" (which, strictly speaking, should read "full capacity use") shows itself as a desire to hold onto more money rather than throwing it into the purchase of producible commodities. It follows that *ex ante* overproduction is synonymous with an *ex ante* excess demand for money at full employment.

This would entail a reduction in commodity prices but if all prices fall pari passu (we are ignoring divergent price movements), then why should there be any output adjustment at all? Moreover if money is a producible good then, given its *ex ante* excess demand, why should it not employ all the labor and resources thrown out of employment from the commodity-producing sectors? The answer to this latter question is that the output of money in the short run is given. It is the answer to the former question that deserves attention.

Marx's answer centers around the fact that inherited payments commitments from the past also enter the picture. If capitalists decide to add to their money holdings, then, while total money holdings would remain the same (since this is nothing else but the total money stock in the economy), what is used for transaction purposes would go down. Now, this could in principle be ensured by an exclusive decline in the money prices of all commodities, with no output effects whatsoever. But with inherited debt commitments, which entail payments commitments, price declines would necessarily mean bankruptcies and hence output and employment declines as well. Of course, Marx did not specify any particular mode of adjustment for such situations; what he would have done, would certainly not have entailed flexible wages being determined by excess demand à la Walras, and need not detain us further. The point is that the fact of money being a producible commodity makes not an iota of difference to the possibility of overproduction crises.

Indeed, in Keynes's entire discussion of the reason for involuntary unemployment, while expectations about the future are given their due role, inherited commitments from the past are not. If they were, then the fundamental Keynesian conclusion about the instability of a system with flexible money wages, being determined though excess demand in the labor market, would have been strengthened and would have been seen as holding under less restrictive conditions than Keynes himself postulated.

Concluding Observations

While the Keynesian explanation for the phenomenon of money having a positive and finite value lies, as we have seen, in the fact that there is one commodity, labor power, whose value in money terms is fixed in any period, Keynes has no explanation of what that value is; nor does he need to, since he is talking about a credit-money world. Thus, while in Marx the value of money in terms of commodities is not just given, but given by the relative quantities of labor embodied in them, Keynesian economics does not go into the question of why money wages may be $5 per day, and not $50, at a particular time.

There are two separate issues here that should be distinguished. The first is the absence of any underlying explanation for the level of the money wage in any period. This is a nonproblem: in a credit-money world there can be no underlying explanation, for such an explanation presupposes considerations foreign to such a world. The second issue is more serious. If the money wage rate, though given in every period (and no matter at what level), showed dramatic fluctuations from one period to the next, the confidence of the wealth holders in the value of money relative to commodities would be undermined, and with it the stability of a system using money. Hence, not only should the value of money in terms of labor power be fixed in any period, but it also must be slowly changing across periods. The important question is: How is this ensured? I will turn to this question later.

14

A Digression on a
Keynesian Dilemma

IN CHAPTER 12 WE EXAMINED a Marxian dilemma, namely that while Marx's theory of money opened up, theoretically, the possibility of generalized overproduction, his theory of *value*, into which his theory of money was integrated, presupposed given production coefficients (thus apparently excluding any effect of demand on output). Marx's resolution of this problem took the form of postulating that the production coefficients, which underlay his theory of value, related to an "average" situation that obtained through fluctuations induced by demand movements, which in turn presupposed that movements in either direction away from the "average" were spontaneously self-correcting. This resolution, however, as I argued in chapter 12, was unconvincing.

In Keynes, who is the other major writer in the propertyist tradition, this problem does not arise, since Keynes does not have a theory of value of the sort that Marx had. He can therefore be consistent in adhering to his theory of money and its logical corollary that "output can settle anywhere" depending on the state of demand.

It would appear then that the Keynesian system is free of the contradiction entailed in assuming the simultaneous existence of idle money balances on the one hand (and hence, by implication, of the possibility of *ex ante* excess supply of all produced commodities) and of some normal capacity output on the other. It is free of this contradiction because it recognizes that output can be *anywhere*, not necessarily at some normal capacity level. But in being free of this particular contradiction, the Keynesian system falls into another one. Or, putting it differently, the fact that Marx assumed the system to be operating on average at some particular normal capacity level had a reason behind it, which was quite distinct from the mere truism that a system of demand-determined output puts a question mark over the labor theory of value. This reason is precisely what is wrong with the Keynesian theory of output determination, which makes output completely open-ended.

The Threshold Level of Output

Let us go back once more to the issue of inherited payments commitments. In any given period firms are obliged to make interest payments on past debt at interest rates that are agreed to in the past and that are, in general, unrelated to the current profit rate. A comparatively lower level of aggregate demand resulting in lower capacity utilization, output, profits, and hence rate of profit therefore increases the possibility, and the incidence, of financial insolvency among firms. And if the level of output falls below a certain threshold, then even simple reproduction of the system is jeopardized.

It may be thought that this is just a transitional problem, that while the lower rate of profit in a recessionary situation does squeeze firms financially on account of the inherited interest payments, the interest rates would be lower on freshly contracted loans. The lowering of the interest rates in response to the lower rates of profit in the recession would not only remove the squeeze on firms after some initial problems, but could also even act as a stabilizing factor that brings the recession to an end. Indeed, Schumpeter's (1952) criticism of Keynes was precisely that the latter did not take into account the possible equilibrating role of interest-rate changes in a recession. Since Schumpeter himself saw interest rate as "a tax on profits," he visualized interest rates declining in response to declines in the profit rate, and possibly to an even greater extent, which therefore conferred on them the role of an equilibrating mechanism.

There are two problems with this argument. The first is that there is a floor to the whole spectrum of interest rates, which is given by the following. The short-term rate has a floor that corresponds to the fact that there is a minimal level of lender's risk. Nobody would part with liquidity unless offered a certain minimal rate of interest that covers this risk. And this minimal rate on the short-term loans then provides a floor to longer term rates, since the latter would entail, in addition, risk-premiums that vary according to the maturity of the loans and are subject to the principle of increasing risk. In short, the entire spectrum of interest rates has a floor and cannot be pushed down arbitrarily. The description of interest as a "tax on profits" may be a qualitatively apt description, but the inference that as a result the interest rates can be pushed down to any level as the profit rate declines is invalid.

Second, as the profit rate declines, since, given the inherited payments obligations, the risk of financial insolvency of firms increases (the question of whether this is a transitional phenomenon is both immaterial and meaningless), the magnitude of lenders' risk increases. The effect of a decline in the rate of profit then is not to make lenders willing to lend at lower rates of interest, but to make them more unwilling to lend even at the prevailing rate of interest, so that even higher interest rates have to be offered to them to make them part with liquidity. The decline in the rate of profit then does not cause an inward shift in the liquidity preference schedule, as Schumpeter and others have argued, but has precisely the opposite effect, namely that it causes an outward shift in it. Movements in the rate of interest, in other words, far from having a stabilizing effect on the system, have a destabilizing effect. As the recession unfolds, instead of the state of credit becoming easier, which could conceivably act as a stimulus for the economy, it becomes more stringent, which has the effect of further aggravating the recession.

While the second of these arguments introduces an element of hysteresis, namely, a reduction in the rate of profit relative to the historically experienced interest rate creates beyond a point serious cumulative instability, or, putting it differently, the system, for its stability, needs to operate at levels of activity which are linked to historically experienced interest rates, the first of these arguments implies that these historically experienced rates themselves must exceed a certain level. The two arguments together imply that the level of activity in any period must not fall below a certain threshold level if the system is to remain viable.

There is, moreover, an asymmetry involved here. While the drying up of credit has an immediate effect on autonomous expenditures and investment, the sheer availability of credit on easier terms because of an improvement in creditors' confidence does not stimulate such expenditures immediately, though it may have a lagged effect. A particular way of visualizing this asymmetry, for example, is this: Suppose investment orders in a particular period bring forth actual investment in the next period, tight credit in the current period owing to lenders' reticence affects not only investment orders but also actual investment of the current period (no matter what the previous period's orders); but easier credit on account of the creditors' greater willingness to lend only increases orders in the current period. The asymmetry, in other words, consists in the fact that orders can be cancelled but cannot be made to fructify immediately.[1]

The implication of this asymmetry is that instability operates only in one direction: below a certain threshold level of activity the economy is unviable, but above the threshold level it can settle down at any particular level of activity. The Keynesian theory of output determination makes sense only above this threshold level of activity. On the other hand, there is nothing in the system to ensure that this threshold level must always be crossed.

Keynesians were wrong in believing that the system could settle down anywhere. Marx had a better intuitive grasp of the capitalist system when he assumed that the system functioned on average at a high enough level of activity: if it did not, then its modus operandi would be seriously undermined and its very viability threatened. But Marx's problem was that he did not advance an adequate theory about *why* the system left to itself would necessarily function at this high enough level of activity. The Keynesians on the other hand while being consistent in maintaining that the system could indeed function anywhere lost sight of the fact that this was not really possible if it were to remain viable. For the viability of the system, the range over which demand-determined equilibrium output can lie must be bounded from below. Marx recognized this but offered no convincing theory about how this was ensured under capitalism. The Keynesians apparently did not cognize this theoretically.

152

The Inflationary Barrier

Just as the viability of the system demands that the level of economic activity must be above a certain threshold, it similarly requires that it should be below a certain level. Paradoxically, it is this latter aspect that has received much attention while the former has been generally ignored. Within the Keynesian tradition, the first person to have discussed this ceiling is Joan Robinson with her concept of the "inflationary barrier": "From the first it was obvious that if we ever reached and maintained a low level of unemployment, with the same institutions of free wage bargaining and the same code of proper behaviour for trade unions that then obtained, the vicious spiral of rising prices, wages, prices would become chronic" (1966, 88).

Keynes, we have seen, answered the question why money had a positive and finite value by suggesting that the price of one commodity ("labor power"), whose use is absolutely essential in any economy, was fixed in terms of it in the short run and was a finite amount in any particular short period. Indeed, the fact that money wages were fixed in any period while real wages could move about depending on the level of aggregate demand was a condition for the stability of the system: "That money wages are more stable than real wages is a condition of the system possessing inherent stability" (1949, 239).

With given money wages, the supply price, and hence the price level, is an increasing function of the level of output, certainly at higher levels of output. This means that the real wages are a declining function of output, at least beyond a certain level of output. This decline in real wages as output increases may cease to be acceptable at a certain point to the workers, who would then press for higher money wages. Any such increase in money wages, if output remains unchanged, must bring about a corresponding increase in the price level, leaving real wages unchanged, which in turn would stimulate further money wage demands, and so on. In other words, implicit in the given money wages postulate is the assumption that the level of activity always lies below a certain limit, which constitutes Joan Robinson's "inflationary barrier."

To be sure, money wage changes take time. We can continue with the assumption that money wages are given in the short run, no matter what happens, and allow for these happenings reflecting themselves only in the next period. In such a case we can tell the preceding story as a dynamic one, which is exactly what the NAIRU theorists attempt to do.

The difference between Joan Robinson's conclusions, arrived at, albeit in a single-period context, and those of the NAIRU theorists however was fundamental. The standard NAIRU story postulates a unique unemployment rate, which alone is supposed to be compatible with a steady rate of inflation, that is, with a state of affairs where the value of money does not zoom up or down. Besides, in several versions of the NAIRU story, including in particular the monetarist version where the NAIRU is taken to be synonymous with the natural rate of unemployment, which is a de facto state of full employment devoid of any excess supply of labor at the going real wage, a stability result is assumed: if the rate of growth of money supply is constant then the economy would automatically tend to settle down at the NAIRU. By contrast, what Joan Robinson was arguing was that as long as the unemployment rate is above a certain level, then for a whole range of such rates there would be no tendency toward any disruption of price stability (the counterpart of such price stability in any dynamic version being steady inflation).

The NAIRU story makes Keynesian demand management in any meaningful sense an impossibility. If there is only one unique rate of unemployment that is compatible with steady inflation, and if the maintenance of any other unemployment rate causes accelerating or decelerating inflation, then it follows that precious little can be done by the government in terms of reducing unemployment. But if the unemployment rate can have a whole range of possible values compatible with steady inflation, subject only to the fact that there is a minimum to it, then the government can intervene through demand management to push it down as close to this minimum as possible.

But then how can one go beyond the NAIRU logic to arrive at a Keynes-Robinson conclusion? The following illustrative model provides an answer.

The workers in any period obtain a certain money wage, deflated by productivity, which we denote by ω. (This deflation by productivity is because we are talking of a sequence of periods; in the single period context, where productivity is given, the variable would simply have been the money wage rate.) ω is determined as follows. The workers always succeed in enforcing an ω that is at least as much as in the previous period; but, where their bargaining strength enables them to obtain a larger amount, they do so. Their bargaining strength is inversely related to the unemployment rate and expresses itself in terms of a certain *ex ante* wage share that they can enforce. It follows then that the ω of any period is the higher of the two: the previous period's ω and the *ex ante* wage share at the expected price determined by their bargaining strength. Denoting by a the *ex ante* wage share that the workers can enforce, and by u the unemployment rate, we can express all this as follows:

$$a = a\,(u) \quad a' < 0 \ldots \tag{i}$$

$$\text{and } \omega = \max\{\, a(u) \cdot p^e; \, \omega_{-1} \,\} \ldots \tag{ii}$$

The actual wage share, or its obverse, the share of profits, on the other hand would depend upon the degree of capacity utilization, since that would determine the identity of the marginal vintage and in general as the margin shifts outward the share of profits would rise. Assuming a positive and unchanging association between the degree of capacity utilization and the rate of employment (Rowthorn 1977), we can then say that the profit share π is given by

$$\pi = \pi\,(u) \quad \pi' < 0 \ldots \tag{iii}$$

The actual wage share or $(1 - \pi)$ is nothing else but the average unit labor cost divided by price, that is, ω / p. We therefore have

$$\omega / p + \pi (u) = 1 \ldots \tag{iv}$$

Finally, as regards the determination of the expected price, we assume a simple adaptive expectation:

$$p^e = p_{-1} \cdot p_{-1} / p_{-2} \ldots \tag{v}$$

From (i) and (iii) there is some $u = u^*$ for which $a(u^*) + \pi (u^*) = 1$. And for all $u < u^*$, the economy would experience accelerating inflation. On the other hand, for all $u > u^*$, we have stable prices, that is, a steady and zero rate of inflation. (All these results presuppose, as in the NAIRU case, that the particular unemployment rate we are talking about is *maintained* through time.)

We can obtain exactly the same result as before from an alternative and more realistic set of assumptions:

$$\omega = a(u) \cdot p^e \ldots \tag{ii'}$$

$$\text{and } p = \max \left[\omega / \{1 - \pi (u)\} ; p_{-1} \right] \ldots \tag{iv'}$$

in lieu of (ii) and (iv) respectively. In the latter case we are simply postulating that the capitalists never let prices decline even when unit labor costs decline, which fits in with the "kinked demand curve" hypothesis (Baran and Sweezy 1966).

The reason for the difference between this formulation and the standard NAIRU formulations is that when the unemployment rate exceeds u^*, the idea that the rate of price increase goes on declining until it reaches negative magnitudes is rejected here. The mechanism of that rejection is either one of the two postulates, namely either that the capitalists never let the price level drop (the "kinked demand curve" hypothesis), or that the workers never let the productivity-deflated money wage rate drop.

The NAIRU theories that attribute stability to NAIRU postulate not only decelerating inflation down to negative levels, but also, in the face of a constant rate of growth of money supply and such decelerating inflation, a progressive recreation of a superabundance of money supply, which has the effect of spontaneously reviving the economy to the unemployment rate u^*. This, however, being exactly analogous to the argument in the single-period case, which held that an increase in money supply in terms of the wage unit can restore full employment, is open to the same objections as we had examined earlier for that case. If there is a floor to the interest rate (apart from the fact that investment may be interest-inelastic), which is perfectly plausible, and if price and wage expectations are not inelastic, which, with adaptive expectations as used in NAIRU theories, they cannot be, then there is no reason why a superabundance of money in terms of the wage unit would automatically stimulate activity. True, if the level of activity is "too high," that is, if $u < u^*$, then accelerating inflation would be difficult to accommodate within a constant rate of growth of money supply, so that some reduction in activity may become inevitable. But even if we accept this proposition and the exogeneity of money supply upon which it is based, this acceptance does not take us beyond Joan Robinson. It does not mean subscribing to monetarism or to the NAIRU theory.

The crucial question, in other words, concerns the other end, that is, whether abundance of money, in conditions of exogeneity of money supply, can stimulate activity. Not only would activity not be stimulated, but the persistence of decelerating inflation down to declining prices in absolute terms would also start reducing activity once the economy has hit the floor nominal rate of interest, since the real rate would then start climbing up (Patnaik 1997). And the position would be even worse if inherited debt obligations are taken into account, since firms would be driven to bankruptcy.

By contrast it is far more plausible to imagine the economy being stuck at any one of a whole range of possible equilibria with involuntary unemployment, each associated with stable prices. These would lie between the lower threshold and the upper ceiling levels of activity that we have been discussing so far. In other words, if the concept of a unique NAIRU itself is unrealistic, that of a NAIRU imbued with the stability property is even more so.

Looking at the matter differently, the concept of a floor to the level of the unemployment rate, below which the system would become unviable appears in Marx as well, but the recognition of this fact did not prevent Marx from recognizing the possibility of overproduction crises. And an overproduction crisis necessarily means a level of equilibrium output where the unemployment rate is higher than the floor level without any self-correcting mechanism. Keynesianism, approaching the question from the other side, that is, from a recognition of overproduction crises to that of a floor level of unemployment, likewise postulates the possibility of multiple equilibria. Far from there being anything naive or illogical about it, as the NAIRU theorists suggest, the charge of unrealism can in fact be leveled against the latter. By the same token, for Marxists to believe that, because there is a floor to unemployment rate, Keynesian demand management is impossible, is to deny the possibility of overproduction crises, which goes against Marx's own argument.

The Range of Possible Equilibria

We saw earlier that there is a threshold level below which output cannot fall in any period (the level itself changing across periods) without damaging the viability of the system. We have just seen that likewise there is a ceiling level above which output cannot rise in any period without damaging the viability of the system. In short, the viability of the system demands that output must lie within this range, which constitutes the range of possible equilibria. The upper limit of this range is given by u^*. The lower threshold is not some unique figure, since it depends inter alia upon the inherited payments obligations. A conceptual characterization of this figure can be given as follows.

Let us continue assuming a monotonic relationship, unchanging across periods, between capacity utilization and the employment rate, that is, $(1 - u) = f(v)$, where v is the degree of capacity utilization, a pure number given by $O / K \cdot \beta$, where β is the technologically given output-capital ratio. If i denotes the average interest rate on the outstanding debt of firms, r the rate of profit, π as before the share of profits (which can also be written as a function $h(v)$ of v) and d the debt-equity ratio, then u^{**} defined as follows would certainly qualify as a threshold.

Since the amount of profits must be sufficient at the very least to cover interest payments on debt,

$$r = \pi \cdot \beta v = h(v) \cdot \beta v = r(v) \text{ must at least equal } i \cdot d / (1 + d).$$

Hence, $u^{**} = 1 - f[r^{-1}\{i \cdot d / (1 + d)\}]$.

At u^{**} the dividend payment is zero. Firms, however, would get into trouble, with share prices tumbling long before a moratorium on dividend payments has been announced. In other words, since equity holders in practice expect a rate of return not too different from r, the actual threshold level of activity would be even higher than suggested by u^{**}, which therefore has no more than an illustrative role.

But no matter how exactly this threshold is defined, it exists, and so does the range within which possible equilibria must lie. There is nothing in the system, however, to ensure that the actual equilibrium would in fact lie within this range. In other words, while for the viability of the system it is essential that the equilibrium level of output must lie within a certain range, there is no inherent tendency in the system to ensure that it actually does so.

There is more to it than that. The notion of a ceiling on activities that spontaneously comes into operation is not necessarily a far-fetched one. We have seen that there may be some basis for the belief that if the unemployment rate falls below u^* then the accelerating inflation that would occur would force a reduction in the level of activity back to u^* if the rate of growth of money supply can somehow be pegged at a constant exogenous magnitude. Even if one does not believe in money supply being exogenous, and even if one does not believe in the spontaneous effect of accelerating inflation, via discouraging investment decisions, in reducing the level of activity down to u^* once it has exceeded that benchmark,[2] one can still accept the fact that the economy cannot sustain itself at or below the unemployment rate u^*. The reason is what business cycle theorists have been talking about for years. The self-propelling tendency of investment via the multiplier-accelerator mechanism which carries the economy to u^* or even lower rates of unemployment, would mean, once labor shortages appear (if for no other reason), that there would be a downturn as well, which would carry the economy downward beyond u^*. (Of course, if perchance there is no such self-reversing mechanism during the boom, and the economy is doomed to experience high rates of growth together with accelerating inflation, then the argument that follows is further strengthened; postulating a self-reversing mechanism is not a necessary part of my argument).

However, when the economy moves *down*, the self-propelling tendency of investment, acting in a downward direction, may carry it *below* a level of activity corresponding to unemployment rate u^{**}, in which case it would keep going down without any self-reversal mechanism coming into operation. Of course the economy's downslide may get arrested before it reaches the lower threshold u^{**} (or some other), owing to the operation of strong exogenous stimuli on investment capable of counteracting the endogenously propelled downslide, but there is no particular reason to expect that this would happen. What is more, if the economy does go below the lower threshold, even exogenous stimuli would cease to be of any consequence, since their capacity to call forth investment would be severely jeopardized if firms were threatened with bankruptcy.[3]

It follows that not only is there a range such that if the equilibrium output does not lie within it the system becomes unviable, but there are also tendencies working in the direction of pushing the system out of this range. These tendencies, to recapitulate, arise from two factors: first, the basic asymmetry inherent in the fact that the self-reversing mechanism that operates during upswings does not do so during downturns; and second, exogenous stimuli that could counteract the operation of self-propelling downward movements of the economy themselves cease to operate when the downturn carries it below some threshold activity level. As a result, even if equilibrium output may lie within the viability range for some single period or even for a succession of such periods, there is a tendency to take it out of this range.[4]

A brief discussion of the dynamics of the system in a situation where the exogenous stimuli do not operate will clarify the point. Let us consider the following simple system:

$$n_{t+1} = n_t + b \cdot (v_t - v_0)\, n_t \ldots \tag{i}$$

where n refers to the net investment per unit of capital stock in the period denoted by the subscript, v, as before, to the level of capacity utilization, and v_0 to the desired level of capacity utilization.

$$v_t = O_t / K_t \cdot \beta \ldots \tag{ii}$$

where O refers to *gross* output, β to the technological output-capital ratio, and K_t to the capital stock at the beginning of the period t. Assuming that all wages and a proportion

c of gross profits are consumed, that the share of gross profits in gross output is a constant μ (we are ignoring "ratchet effects" for the moment), and that I denotes gross investment, we have

$$O_t = I_t / \mu(1 - c) \ldots \tag{iii}$$

Finally, we assume "radioactive decay" of capital stock at the rate δ, so that

$$K_{t+1} - K_t = I_t - \delta \cdot K_t \tag{iv}$$

and $n_t = I_t / K_t - \delta \ldots$ $\tag{v}$

This system admits two steady state solutions: $I / K = \delta$; and $I / K = \beta.\mu \cdot v_0 \cdot (1 - c)$, corresponding to which the growth rates are 0, and $\beta\mu \cdot v_0 (1 - c) - \delta$. The latter corresponds to Harrod's warranted rate and is an unstable solution; the former is a stable solution and represents simple reproduction. The behavior of the system conforms to Kalecki's (1962) proposition that in the absence of exogenous stimuli the system will settle down to simple reproduction. The net rate of profit in this state is given by $\delta c / (1 - c)$.[5] If this rate is below the minimum rate of profit associated with the threshold unemployment rate u^{**}, that is, $\beta \cdot \mu \cdot f^{-1}(1 - u^{**})$, which is perfectly plausible, then a weakening of exogenous stimuli as the system goes below u^{**}, makes its viability problematical (see the next section).

Some may object at this point that we have not taken into consideration the autonomous components of demand. Since these, such as the autonomous consumption of the capitalists (or their hangers on) or the autonomous expenditure of the state, are unaffected by the level of current output, they ipso facto provide a floor to the level of activity in any period (Hicks 1950; Kalecki 1954). But while the fact of autonomous expenditures providing a floor to the level of activity is undeniable, its significance for our present argument is limited. Two points in particular should be borne in mind in this context. First, we are concerned with spontaneous self-correcting mechanisms that keep the level of activity in an economy within a specified range. Autonomous demand components may keep the economy within this range, but they would not necessarily do so. Their keeping the economy within this range, in other words, would be a coincidence, not a necessary phenomenon, unless we believe that they are used deliberately as countercyclical discretionary measures, which they are not under "classical" capitalism. Second, what appear autonomous are themselves usually based on the belief that the downturn in the economy is only a transitional phenomenon. An understanding of the basis of this belief therefore has to be located outside the sphere of autonomous expenditures themselves, and the Keynesian problem lies in the fact that it provides no theoretical basis for such a belief within the model of a capitalist economy.[6]

Kalecki on the Trend

What has just been said is in contrast to Kalecki's discussion of the trend. Kalecki's model differs in its details from what has been assumed here, but it is not these differences but the contrast in basic perception that accounts for the different results.

Kalecki came to two conclusions: first, in the absence of specific exogenous stimuli, a capitalist economy would settle down at a state of simple reproduction; and second, exogenous stimuli, such as innovations, introduce a positive trend into the system. The basic difference between Kalecki's analysis and what has been discussed here lies in the fact that Kalecki implicitly assumes that a capitalist economy is viable at any rate of profit, while we have been arguing that there is a minimum to the rate of profit and hence to the level of activity, slipping below which would make the system unviable.

Consider the state of simple reproduction. The gross rate of profit in simple reproduction is $\delta / (1 - c)$ and the net rate is $\delta c / (1 - c)$. We mentioned earlier that there is a floor to the short as well as the long-term rates of interest. We can visualize the former as the minimum compensation for parting with liquidity and the latter as this minimum plus the minimum risk premium charged on a long as compared to a short-term loan. If the spectrum of actual rates is less than these, then the economy would be characterized by absolute liquidity preference (this argument is different from what was mentioned above in the context of the determination of u^{**} where we considered firms with a specific history and specific debt obligations). Now, if the *net* rate of profit $\delta c / (1 - c)$ is less than the minimum long rate *plus* the minimum risk premium that a capital asset as compared to a long-term loan must cover, then nobody would hold the capital asset; every capitalist would try to convert it into money, for which there would be an absolute preference, by letting gross investment fall below δ. In other words, simple reproduction itself would become impossible.

Underlying Kalecki's proposition about simple reproduction being an equilibrium position, therefore, is an implicit assumption, namely that $\delta c / (1 - c) > r_{min}$. Since there is no reason why this condition should necessarily be satisfied, the economy may not be capable of settling down even at simple reproduction; the system, in other words, may be unviable.

Now, even if there are exogenous stimuli giving rise to a positive as opposed to a zero trend, exactly the same kind of condition must be satisfied for it to be an equilibrium, namely the net rate of profit must exceed r_{min}. The validity of both Kaleckian propositions therefore becomes doubtful once we introduce the possibility of absolute liquidity preference.

But even if the positive trend caused by exogenous stimuli is a viable one in the sense of the net rate of profit on it exceeding r_{min}, there now emerges the additional problem of access to it. And here we go back to historical time. Firms with concrete histories, with particular debt obligations, may find that the historical interest rate at which they had borrowed is so much in excess of the equilibrium rate of profit (that is, the rate of profit along a trend sustained by exogenous stimuli) that they cannot stay at the equilibrium but move further down. Once they do so, however, the risks associated with capital assets increase, so that it is no longer a question of the equilibrium rate of profit covering the *minimum* risk premium. On the contrary, the risk premium demanded when the economy is in the throes of a depression may be so high that the equilibrium rate of profit cannot cover it; the economy in such a case does not recover, does not get back toward equilibrium and becomes unviable.

The interest rate, or more generally the state of credit, does not play any prominent part in Kalecki's analysis. Consequently, he does not consider a number of problems such as the possibility of absolute liquidity preference, which makes the so-called equilibria untenable, or the inaccessibility of equilibria even if they are tenable in the narrow sense. Once we reckon with them, then the issue of output determination acquires far greater complexity than even Kaleckian-Keynesian analysis, which has grappled with it to greater purpose than other strands of economic theory, has hitherto invested it with. Putting it bluntly, all strands of economic theory, including even the Kaleckian-Keynesian strand, have seriously flawed theories of output determination.

Concluding Observations

If the "Marxian dilemma" discussed in chapter 12 refers to the inadequacy of the theoretical attempt to explain both the possibility of generalized overproduction and the operation of the system, on average, at some "normal capacity" level, the "Keynesian dilemma" refers to the inadequacy of the theory to explain why a system subject to generalized overproduction should still experience a level of activity that falls within a particular range beyond which the system becomes unviable. Discussing these dilemmas, however, points only to the incompleteness of propertyism, an issue taken up in the last part of this book; it does not negate the superiority of propertyism over monetarism or Walrasianism in general. Propertyism, in short, represented a huge step of scientific advance over monetarism and demand-supply theories generally (though the two traditions developed not one after the other but in a parallel fashion, a fact overlooked in the usual classical-Jevonian dichotomy), but this scientific endeavor has to be carried forward to overcome its incompleteness. This requires a change in our perception of capitalism itself as a unit of analysis.

15

Marx, Keynes, and Propertyism

IN THE REALM OF ECONOMIC THEORY, narrowly defined, Karl Marx made two revolutionary advances: one relates to his theory of surplus value, and the other to his theory of money. The fact that surplus value is appropriated even when there is equivalent exchange among "free" agents entering into a voluntary contract, the fact that it arises in the sphere of production and is only realized in the sphere of circulation, the fact that it arises because labor power becomes a commodity, and the fact that its arising in the sphere of production implies that the Darwinian struggle for survival among capitalists results in a continuous tendency to revolutionize methods of production, were all momentous results derived from the first of his theoretical discoveries. Even though these discoveries went far beyond Ricardo, Marx's starting point in this particular theoretical quest was Ricardo. Or, putting it differently, what he said was an enormous advance over what Ricardo had said, what he said sorted out and clarified some of the ambiguities that Ricardo's theory had contained (such as Ricardo's telescoping of the spheres of production and circulation), but what he said did not directly contradict what Ricardo had said.

His other advance was no less pathbreaking, and it was largely in opposition to Ricardo. The fact that money is not merely a medium of circulation but constitutes a form of holding wealth, the fact that this shows itself in the existence of some wealth all the time in the form of money (the perpetual existence of a hoard), the fact that this presupposes that the value of money is determined from outside the realm of demand and supply (and hence constitutes a negation of the quantity theory), and the fact that this necessarily gives rise, contrary to what J. B. Say had argued, to the possibility of generalized overproduction, a phenomenon Ricardo had denied while adhering to Say's law, were also equally momentous discoveries. Here, Marx's starting point arguably was James Steuart, but certainly not Ricardo, whose views in these respects he continuously attacked. And his successor was Keynes, though the latter and his followers would repudiate this claim, as would Marxists in general. Of course, the worldviews of Marx and Keynes were vastly different, but we are talking here only of economic theory narrowly defined, and, as Joan Robinson once said, among different political-ideological positions there may very easily be a common core that is scientific (1960). The fact that a Marxist writer, Michael Kalecki, who was an engineer by training and whose introduction to economics was by way of Marx's *Capital*, arrived at the so-called Keynesian revolution independently, does support the view that there is a commonality of perception between Marx's views in this sphere and the Keynesian position.

Marx, as argued in chapter 12, sought to reconcile his two momentous discoveries through an ingenious conceptual innovation, the "average state," but this is not a very convincing resolution of the problem, so that there still remains a tension at the heart of his analysis. But this issue, which I discuss in the next part of the book, is not germane to the present discussion. The fact that Marx has been bracketed only with Ricardo, whether with approval (e.g., Dobb's [1973] reference to a Ricardo-Marx tradition) or disparagingly (e.g., Samuelson's [1957] reference to Marx as a "minor post-Ricardian"), only underscores the total neglect that the second of his momentous theoretical advances has suffered. Indeed, so overwhelming has been the attention focused on his first theoretical advance and its affinity with Ricardo, that it has been implicitly assumed, notwithstanding Marx's copious, explicit, and emphatic discussions on the subject, that his theory of money, too, is no different from Ricardo's. Not only is this view erroneous, but it has also obscured Marx's theoretical achievement, distorted his theoretical system, and delayed the theoretical recognition of the problem of effective demand by almost three-quarters of a century until Keynes came on the scene. To be sure, it can be legitimately argued that the Great Depression had to occur before the problem of effective demand could be taken seriously, but we are not talking here of the broad acceptability of the relevance of a problem. A whole theoretical discourse remained closed because the nonmonetarist (propertyist) theory of money and the associated theory of effective demand, which had already figured extensively in Marx's work, remained neglected.

Marx and Keynes

To be sure, a lacuna remained in Marx's second theoretical advance, namely, that while he saw clearly the possibility of the emergence of generalized overproduction, owing to people's desire to hold a larger amount of money (or, in Keynesian language, owing to an increase in liquidity preference), he did not analyze how the economy would actually behave in such a situation. In other words if there is an *ex ante* excess supply of commodities and an *ex ante* excess demand for money when the economy functions at, say, full capacity utilization, then how would output and employment actually behave?[1] Where would the economy come to rest in such a situation? Or if we use "equilibrium" to refer to this state of rest, then what would be the equilibrium position of the economy when it cannot be at full capacity owing to an *ex ante* excess supply of commodities at full capacity (or "full employment" in Keynesian language, which does not incidentally refer merely to a particular state of the labor market). Keynes answered this question through his theory of the "multiplier," and Kalecki through his postulate that only as much surplus value would be produced as can be realized. But Marx gave no such rule, and indeed he did not analyze the off-full-capacity behavior of the economy at all. He recognized only the possibility of the economy slipping below this level of activity without examining where it would come to rest in any single period when it does slip below this level.

But if Marx's system had the lacuna that it did not examine single-period output determination, it also had an advantage over the Keynesian system in specifying quite unambiguously the need for outside determination of the value of money. His great merit lay in recognizing that the principle governing the determination of the equilibrium-exchange ratio among commodities was fundamentally different from the principle governing the exchange ratio between money on the one side and the world of commodities on the other. This is where he differed fundamentally from Ricardo, and this proposition was completely foreign to the Walrasian system. It was inadequately recognized within the Keynesian system itself, even though it underlies that system. Indeed, if Keynesianism had clearly asserted from the beginning that the rules governing exchange ratios within commodities had to be different from the rules governing the exchange ratio between commodities and money, that any system (such as the Walrasian one) that postulated that these two sets of ratios were determined by the same rules necessarily had to be logically flawed, then much confusion could have been avoided. The entire interpretation of Keynesian theory as being based on a fixed money wage rate whose validity for theory lay allegedly in its empirical pertinence could have been skipped. The fixity of money wages would have been seen as an assumption introduced not for its empirical pertinence but for its theoretical necessity, without which the exchange ratio between money and commodities remained indeterminate.

The proposition that the fixity of money wages in Keynes is what determines the value of money relative to the world of commodities also points to a deeper conclusion. It is customary to distinguish between "commodity money" and "fiat" or "credit" money," the former consisting of precious metals, or paper money backed by precious metals, and the latter consisting of pieces of paper with little intrinsic value and no commodity backing whatsoever. But labor power *is* a commodity under capitalism, so that the fixity of the money wage rate is tantamount to the fixity of the value of money relative to one commodity, labor power. The fiat money world, in short, is no different from a commodity money world: instead of a unit of money being exchangeable for a given quantum of gold, we have, in a fiat money world, a unit of money being freely exchangeable against a given quantum of another commodity, namely labor power. A monetary world necessarily requires, according to the propertyist view, the fixity of the value of what is used as money vis-à-vis *some* commodity, be it gold or silver or labor power. In either case we have, as it were, a commodity backing for money; so, to call only one of these a "commodity money" world is arbitrary. Fiat money is as much commodity money as money fixed against gold; it is just that the commodities in the two cases are different. The world has never succeeded in getting out of commodity money.

Nicholas Kaldor (1964) once argued that the acceptability of fiat money arose from the backing of the state for it, the fact that taxes and other payments to the state could be made in it. There is however a difference between juridical acceptability and economic acceptability. State backing can at best confer upon fiat money juridical acceptability, but for it to actually function in the economy in a meaningful manner something more is needed and this something is the fact that it has commodity backing, of the commodity labor power, through the fixity of the money wage rate in any single period.

Wage Share and the Value of Money

While the Marxian and the Keynesian perceptions converge on the need for some commodity backing for money, there is a very important difference between them. Keynes took the money wage rate as fixed in any period and the money price level of commodities as varying according to the state of aggregate demand. Marx, on the other hand, took (in the "average state" that was his conceptual time-period of analysis) the money price level as fixed (by the conditions of production), and the money wage rate as varying according to the state of aggregate demand (which determined the ratio of the reserve army of labor to the active army). A rise in aggregate demand relative to full employment output lowers the share of wages in the former case and raises it in the latter.

This difference arose from the difference in perception between the two approaches on which particular commodity (commodities) provided the backing for money. If the commodity was labor power, as in Keynes, then the level of aggregate demand could affect only the prices of nonlabor commodities; on the other hand if the commodity backing for money came from the nonlabor commodities, then the level of aggregate demand could affect only the price of labor power, that is, the money wage.

This had an obvious implication for the theory of distribution: that strand of the theory of distribution which took off from Keynes saw the share of wages as *declining* as the level of aggregate demand increased relative to full employment output, while the Marxian tradition saw the share of wages *increasing* as the level of demand increased relative to full employment output. Solow and Stiglitz (1968), though concerned not with the Marxian perception but with the neoclassical one, which comes to a similar conclusion about real wages rising at full employment as aggregate demand, and hence by implication the demand for labor, increases, argue that the difference between this conclusion and the opposite one arrived in the neo-Keynesian tradition by Kaldor (that real wages fall in the stated situation), has to do with which market, the product or the labor market, responds faster to an increase in demand. What they fail to see is that this entire issue, of what happens to the share of wages when aggregate demand increases, is intimately linked to the theory of money. And that precisely because it is linked to the issue of the value of money, one can say with certainty that the very presumption of full employment under capitalism is wrong, that full employment defined as a state of affairs where there is an absence of an excess supply of labor at the going real wage[2] can never be attained under capitalism,[3] a point that constitutes a criticism of Kaldor as well, who also assumes full employment.

If the commodity backing for money is seen to be given by the commodity labor power, through the fixity of money wages, then clearly, as Joan Robinson's concept of the "inflationary barrier" expressed it, a reduction in unemployment below a certain threshold would destabilize the wage unit and hence negate the possibility of money having a positive value. The economy can therefore never reach full employment, since full employment, as defined here, is incompatible with money having a positive value. On the other hand, if the commodity backing for money is given by gold, which has a fixed exchange ratio with the nonlabor commodities taken as a whole, then the reduction in unemployment below a threshold, by *increasing* the money wage (and hence the real wage), would lower the rate of profit below what capitalists consider an acceptable level. This would put a stop to the accumulation of capital in the form of productive assets and hence create a surge in the reserve army of labor.[4] Thus, no matter whether we accept the Marxian or the Keynesian perception of the commodity backing for money, stability in the value of money is incompatible with a state of affairs where there is an absence of excess supply of labor at the going real wage rate. "Full employment" in this sense, let alone being either the actual state of affairs or the centre of gravity toward which the actual state of affairs tends, cannot even occur at the peak of the boom. It is incompatible with capitalism (except under special circumstances such as fascism, when the workers are kept under the extreme regimentation provided by terror).[5] The propertyist position, in contrast to monetarism, not only postulates the possibility of generalized over production, not only sees capitalism as a demand-constrained system, not only sees unutilized capacity and unemployment as the average state of affairs under capitalism but also rules out any clearing of the labor market at any time, even at the peak of the boom.

Part 3

The Incompleteness of Propertyism

16

The Incompleteness of Propertyism

WHAT DETERMINES THE VALUE OF MONEY relative to the world of nonmoney commodities in any period? And why does money have a positive and finite value? Economists have answered these related questions in two distinct ways. The monetarists provide one answer that, in its modern version, has its roots in the Walrasian system; it states that the value of money, like that of any other commodity, depends upon its demand and supply. There is of course a basic difference between money and any other commodity. This consists in the fact that for any other commodity (other than free goods) there is a positive excess demand at zero price, which is why it has a positive equilibrium price. Money has the peculiarity that at zero price it has zero demand and hence negative excess demand. But as long as this is only a matter of discontinuity of the excess demand function, which has this peculiar property of having a negative value only at zero price, but, a positive value at all positive prices close to zero, and the usual downward sloping shape for all nonzero prices, then its price can be determined like that of any other commodity.

The excess demand function for money would have this usual shape for all positive prices of itself if its demand depends on the money value of commodities. The old Cambridge assumption of a constant k linking the demand for money to the level of money income ensured this. But why there should be such a constant k is inexplicable. If "real balances" are taken as a commodity like any other for which there is demand because they yield "utility" to the holder, then this demand has to be determined through an optimization exercise which, there is no reason to believe, would yield a constant k. What is more, insofar as other forms of holding wealth can also yield some of the benefits yielded by real balances, the amount of such balances held for any given level of real income cannot also be independent of the rate of return on these other forms of wealth. And finally, even when such balances are held, in an "inside" money world where money is issued against private debt, a change in the value of money would not necessarily have any impact on the demand for commodities in the aggregate.

The alternative approach is to link the demand for money to the money value of commodities by bringing in the transaction motive. But why there should at all be any transaction demand for money within a Walrasian system is not clear, since all transactions are supposed to occur only at equilibrium prices and the availability or otherwise of money simply does not enter the picture. Some authors, such as Clower (1967), have sought to modify the Walrasian system to allow for the existence of a transactions demand for money, by introducing a temporal separation between sale and purchase. In such a case a constant k can at least be visualized.

But this route entails assuming only a medium of circulation role for money. The moment we recognize that money is also a form of holding wealth, the assumption of a constant k becomes logically unsustainable. And money must be a form of holding wealth in a money-using economy. Indeed, even its medium of circulation role logically entails that it is a vehicle for carrying wealth. Hence, a strict Chinese Wall between the medium of circulation and the form of wealth roles of money cannot be built. If money acts as the one, then it must ipso facto act as the other. In such a case, since there are also other forms of holding wealth, the ratio between the demand for money and the level of income cannot be independent of the rates of return earned on these other forms. In other words, k cannot but be a function of the rate of return on competing wealth forms. Or, looking at it differently, the demand for money must depend upon a comparison at the margin between the rate of return earned on competing assets with the implicit rate of return on money.

Now, suppose we start from an equilibrium and there is a chance increase in the value of money, that is, a chance fall in the money prices of commodities. Monetarism would say that this would give rise to an increase in the demand for commodities. But this cannot happen through the so-called real-balance effect, since this effect, whose magnitude and direction are uncertain, ceases to operate altogether if money is of the inside variety. The only way that this chance fall in the money prices of commodities would stimulate larger demand for them in an inside-money world is by changing the rate of return comparison at the margin between different wealth forms. Only if the relative rates of return move in the correct direction can we get back to the original equilibrium. The chief instrument through which this can happen is the variation of the current prices of commodities relative to their expected prices. If when the current price falls, the expected price remains unchanged, or falls less, then holding commodities becomes more attractive, since they promise larger capital gains. In short, inelastic price expectations are the main route through which a deviation in money prices of commodities from their original equilibrium levels can be self-correcting. In an inside-money world, inelastic price expectations are what the Walrasians in general, and the monetarists in particular, would have to bank upon.

But in a Walrasian universe there is no reason for price expectations to be inelastic. Inelastic price expectations presuppose some restriction on the range of expected price movements, and this is possible only if some price that is consequential for other prices is somehow tethered, which violates the assumption of perfect price flexibility. If no price is sticky and all prices are flexible, then there is no reason for inelastic price expectations, in which case in a world with money (of the inside variety at least) and with price flexibility, any chance deviation from equilibrium will not be self-correcting. The Walrasian equilibrium in such a case ceases to be a meaningful concept; hence a demand-supply explanation of the value of money ceases to be valid.

The second answer to the question of why money has a value, and a positive and finite one at that, invokes not demand and supply but the fixing of this value from outside. This is the strand we have called propertyism. In Marx, the value of money in any period, defined not as a stretch of arbitrarily chosen historical time with certain conceptual properties but as a conceptual entity corresponding to the average state of affairs within a complete cycle, is determined by the relative quantities of direct and indirect labor embodied in a unit of money compared to a unit of the basket of non-money commodities. In Keynes, the value of money in any period, defined in the first sense, is given by the fact that the money wage rate per unit of labor is fixed. The superiority of propertyism consists in its cognition that the value of money relative to the world of commodities cannot be determined by demand and supply. This cognition constitutes a tremendous theoretical insight, and Marx can rightly be given the credit for this scientific discovery.

This insight in the case of Marx was particularly remarkable since he was not talking about an inside-money world, in the context of which the real-balance effect ceases to hold and the demand-supply explanation becomes palpably inadequate. He was talking about a commodity-money world, and yet he made this discovery; he could do so because he saw money as "money-capital," that is, as property, which can be held, up to any amount, and whose desired depletion is determined by independent decisions on productive investment rather than any utility maximization.

When wealth can be held in the form of money, Say's law does not hold, and the possibility of generalized overproduction of all produced commodities arises. And the fact that the value of money in any period is given from outside entails that changes in demand in the period under consideration (given the respective definitions of the term by Marx and Keynes) do not affect the value of money relative to the "benchmark" commodity (in terms of which the value of money is given from outside). This can happen only if the system is a demand-constrained one. The role of money as a wealth form, the determination of the value of money from outside, the possibility of generalized overproduction, the normality of the system being demand-constrained, and hence the normality of an element of unemployment over and above the unemployment that would exist anyway (at full capacity output) even if Say's law habitually held: all these features are logically interconnected. Propertyism highlights these interconnections and makes room for them within its theoretical corpus. No matter, what limitations it may have as a general tendency or in its particular incarnations, its scientific superiority over other tendencies, including Ricardo's eclectic monetarism and the latter-day Walrasian monetarism, is indubitable.

The Incompleteness of Propertyist Theory

Notwithstanding its scientific superiority, propertyist theory, too, remains incomplete. We have seen this in the case of both Marx and Keynes, but incompleteness is not just a feature of the analytical structures erected by these two authors; it afflicts all of propertyism since, as we will see, its roots lie deeper, in the very concept of an equilibrium within the universe of a closed capitalist economy, which propertyism has not gone beyond.

The incompleteness of the Marxian system, it may be recalled, arose from the fact that while the theory of value, and hence the theory of money based upon it, assumes certain given conditions of production independent of demand, the fact of money being a form of wealth holding entails that the economy be demand-constrained; if an economy is demand-constrained, then its output changes with demand, in which case the production coefficients cannot be taken to be independent of demand. Marx's solution to this conundrum was ingenious: he defined the production coefficients as referring to an average state of the economy subject to cyclical movements. But, for this to be meaningful, departures in either direction from this average state of affairs must be intrinsically self-correcting. Marx did not demonstrate this.

Kalecki had a theory of price that avoided this particular problem. Like Keynes, he took the level of money wages as given in any period, and like Marx, he took the level of money prices, which were a mark-up over unit prime costs, as also given independent of demand. But the reason that demand does not affect prices is because the unit prime cost is assumed to be constant. While demand would certainly affect average fixed cost and hence overall average cost, it would not affect the unit prime cost in oligopolistic conditions. Kalecki assumed such a market situation and therefore got, for any period, a value of money independent of demand.

But in the Kaleckian system, like in the Keynesian system, with its focus on a single period, if output can really settle anywhere, then the viability of the system is not guaranteed. What ensures that a demand-constrained system continues to remain viable period after period is a question that is not answered.

The problem more generally can be stated as follows. Since the propertyist tradition sees the economy as demand-constrained, if the level of demand, dependent essentially upon the level of investment, can take any value, the economy can settle anywhere; in such a case the viability of the system is not assured. On the other hand, if demand is taken as fluctuating within a certain range, so that the economy does not settle anywhere but remains confined to this range, then some theory of self-correction of departures from some average level is needed to explain why demand remains confined to this range. No such theory exists.

This is not just a case of insufficient theorizing, of a mere theoretical gap that happens to exist which can be filled in time. No such theory exists because no such theory can exist. Since a reduction in demand feeds on itself, causing over time lower levels of investment and hence still lower levels of demand, it is a characteristic of demand-constrained systems that movements in downward or upward directions tend to be cumulative. Harrod (1939) who had introduced the idea of a "warranted rate of growth," that is, a rate of growth that, if realized, persists, had talked of the "knife-edge" property of this growth path: if an economy falls off it, then it keeps moving away from it. He had believed that this knife-edge property only gave rise to cyclical fluctuations around the warranted rate, but this belief was wrong. With such knife-edge property, not only would the generation of cycles need exogenously given "ceilings" and "floors," but the trend around which such cycles would be generated would be the zero trend rather than the warranted growth path (Kalecki 1962). Of course, the existence of exogenous investment stimuli, of which innovations are usually considered the classic example, would impart a positive trend to the economy. But there are two problems with such a picture of capitalist dynamics.

First, the pace at which innovations are introduced into the production process is not independent of the state of demand in the economy, so that innovations are not truly exogenous. The reason is the following. When the level of demand is relatively higher, producers would also perceive it to be more responsive to a lowering of price, since the fear of retaliation by rivals would be less; hence they would be more willing to build up additional productive capacity embodying new processes or turning out new products (Patnaik 1972). For any given stream of new processes and products becoming available, the stimulus to investment therefore would be greater at higher levels of demand than at lower levels. This has two implications: one, when the economy is in a downturn, the stimulus provided by innovations is unlikely to pull it up before much damage is done, a view amply supported by the experience of the Great Depression (Lewis 1978); and two, innovations can not be considered a particularly strong bulwark against the zero-trend syndrome. If the trend imparted by innovations to a capitalist economy is itself insubstantial and if significant downward movement of a cyclical type is superimposed upon it, then it follows that there is no effective barrier against the system becoming unviable.

One can of course argue that self-limiting cycles, or, what comes to the same thing, self-correcting departures in either direction from central position, *can* characterize a demand-constrained system, since there are bound to be lagged effects on the functioning of the system. Writers from Kalecki to Samuelson have invoked such lagged effects to explain the phenomenon of self-limiting cycles. But even if such cycles are self-limiting, the explanation of a positive trend continues to be problematical, once we cast doubts on the exogeneity of the innovation stimulus. Cycles, superimposed on a zero or low trend, would not prevent the system from becoming unviable. We would still be left with no explanation for the viability of the system.

Three other exogenous stimuli have been discussed in the literature, apart from innovations. One is the existence of autonomous consumption and investment. Here however we must draw a distinction. Autonomous expenditure that is of relevance to the present argument must be distinguished from expenditure that is insensitive to short-term fluctuations. The latter may appear large in any period, but to infer from it that autonomous expenditure is large would be erroneous. The following example focusing only on autonomous consumption would clarify the point.

If the consumption in any period is given by

$$C_t = a + b \cdot Y_{t-1} + c \cdot Y_t,$$

and investment (we ignore depreciation) is given by

$$I_t = d \cdot (Y_t - Y_{t-1})$$

which is a simple accelerator, then, assuming that $(1 - c)$ exceeds both b and d, the system would settle down at a stationary state where the level of income is given by $a / (1 - c - b)$. The actual autonomous consumption that determines the level of floor activity is a, but the consumption that would appear autonomous *in* any period, that is, that is undertaken even if the level of income in that particular period is zero is $(a + b \cdot Y_{t-1})$. In other words, different elements of consumption respond to income changes with lags of different lengths. If we take the floor level of activity corresponding to the level of expenditure, which is truly autonomous (in the preceding example, a), then this level may well be below the threshold level mentioned in chapter 14 and hence incapable of ensuring and explaining the viability of the system.

The second exogenous stimulus is incursion into precapitalist markets. We will discuss this in the next chapter; we keep it out of the picture here since we are focusing on a capitalist economy in isolation, which has provided the core universe of analysis in all strands of economic theory. The third is the state, which, even though it belongs outside the economic base, is nonetheless an integral part of a closed capitalist economy. And state expenditure can indeed be a major source of stimulus behind a positive trend under capitalism. Goodwin (1991) sees state intervention as the main instrument limiting the progressive departure of a capitalist economy in either direction from a central position. But while the state can play such a role and has done so in recent years, it has not traditionally played such a role. True, state demand has always been an important component of aggregate demand, but deliberate and systematic intervention by the state in a countercyclical fashion to keep the economy from moving away from a central position has never been the norm.

Indeed, even during the Great Depression there were several plans, such as the Kindersley, Francqui, Keynes, and ILO ones, that proposed a simultaneous deficit-financed expansion of government expenditures in the major capitalist countries, supported by a jointly contributed fund to help countries tide over payments problems, as a way out of the crisis. But these plans were shot down, since no one was willing to countenance budget deficits. State nonintervention in stimulating activity in short was de rigueur. In Britain even earlier, in 1929, Lloyd George had proposed a borrowing-financed public works program to overcome unemployment, which then stood at 10 percent (it was to reach 20 percent later), but this was shot down in a white paper of the British Treasury, which argued that public works so financed would crowd out private investment (or capital exports): the new employment created through public works therefore would be accompanied by loss of employment elsewhere, resulting in no net addition to total employment. The fallacy of the treasury view was obvious, and it was exposed by Richard Kahn in his celebrated article in 1931 on the "multiplier": since savings depended on income, to assume a fixed pool of savings, as the treasury view did, was to assume in effect that employment and income could not be augmented, that is, that the economy was at full employment (Kahn 1931).[1] The treasury view was arguing against a plan for reducing unemployment by assuming that unemployment did not exist at all! Underlying this opposition however was the belief in the doctrine of "sound finance," and hence of state nonintervention in matters relating to the level of activity.

The instances we have just cited may be attributed of course to the hegemony of financial interests whose opposition to state activism in matters relating to the level of activity is well known (Kalecki 1971). But it is not as if before the era of finance capital, state intervention in demand management was commonly accepted and the emergence of finance capital brought about a change in this regard. Capitalist economies, even though nourished by state intervention in crucial ways, have not seen state intervention in demand management until the post–Second World War period.

State intervention in this regard moreover is not just empirically untrue; it is theoretically inadequate as well. In chapter 14 we saw that there were two thresholds to the level of activity. There was a lower threshold such that if the level of activity went below it, the system became unviable owing to too little realized surplus value. And there was an upper threshold such that if the level of activity reached it, then the system became unviable owing to an inflationary spiral (an undermining of what Keynes called the "wage-unit"). Now, the viability of capitalism requires not just that the system be kept within these two bounds, but, even more fundamentally, that the interval between these two limits be a nonempty set. There should in short be a range of activities within which the economy can move.

This is not an innocuous requirement. Shortage of inputs, of material means of production, especially those whose output, for natural reasons, takes considerable time for augmentation, may well mean that the inflationary barrier in an isolated capitalist economy is reached at a level of activity that is too low in terms of the surplus value that is realized. In any such case, state intervention can do precious little within the normal rules of the game with regard to the functioning of capitalism (that is, without recourse to explicit coercion on labor and union-bashing, characteristic of fascism) to ensure the viability of the system.

Notwithstanding all these possible hurdles to its viability, capitalism has functioned reasonably smoothly for a long time. Marx's postulate that departures of the level of activity in the system from a central position in either direction are self-correcting may not have been theoretically established, but it has been a fact of life. The incompleteness of propertyism consists in the fact that it has no explanation for the apparently regular functioning of the system.

Concluding Observations

The set of interrelated propositions that we have called propertyism, namely that the value of money relative to nonmoney commodities is given from outside the realm of demand and supply, that this is the basis for money being a form of wealth, that this opens up the possibility of generalized overproduction in violation of Say's law, and that this underlies the fact of capitalism being a demand-constrained system, together constitute a tremendous insight into nature of the capitalist system. At the same time, however, the system also shows remarkable regularity in its functioning. The limitation of propertyism consists in the fact that it cannot explain the coherence of the system. This limitation, we will see in the next chapter, arises because it analyzes the system in isolation, as a closed, isolated phenomenon. Propertyism, in short, still has not broken sufficiently with the so-called mainstream theory with which it shares this perspective on capitalism, seen theoretically as a closed, isolated system. Overcoming the limitations of propertyism requires breaking out of this perspective.

17

A Solution to the Incompleteness

CHAPTER 16 ARGUES THAT while the propertyist tradition was superior to the Walrasian-monetarist one, both by virtue of its avoiding the logical flaws of the latter and in terms of its ability to cognize and explain certain observed facts about capitalism, such as generalized overproduction, which the latter was theoretically incapable of perceiving, it nonetheless was theoretically incomplete. To explain this incompleteness we defined two thresholds, a lower and an upper threshold, to the level of activity in the economy. If the economy falls below the lower threshold, then the magnitude of realized profits (and hence ipso facto the rate of profit) becomes too low to maintain the viability of the system; on the other hand, when it reaches the upper threshold, which constitutes the "inflationary barrier," the wage unit ceases to be stable and thereby undermines the viability of the system in a different way.

Now, the incompleteness of propertyism manifests itself in at least three ways. First, it does not adduce any mechanism within the system that would ensure its remaining within the range of activity levels defined by these two thresholds. On the contrary, since it perceives capitalism as a demand-constrained system (a fact that constitutes its theoretical strength), and since demand-constrained systems, if anything, have a self-propelling tendency to move further and further away from a central position (a tendency highlighted by the multiplier-accelerator models), it should perceive the system as prone to becoming unviable. Not only has it not done so, but it has not even adduced any reasons to explain why the system has actually functioned reasonably smoothly over long stretches of time.

Second, it does not adduce any internal mechanism that would even ensure that the two thresholds are separated at all by a range of viable levels of activity, that they do not overlap, or that the rate of profit, even when the economy is at the "inflationary barrier" level of activity, is not already below what is necessary for the viability of the system.

Third, the longer-term tendency in capitalism is for the upper threshold to come down. The emergence of oligopolistic collusion among capitalists and the growth of trade unions among workers imply that the inflationary barrier appears at a lower level of activity than earlier (Galbraith 1968). The lower threshold u^{**}, too, is likely to come down for a different reason: since shareholders in practice are not substantially different from creditors and basically expect a rate of return not too different from the interest rate, the interest rate may be taken as the lower threshold rate of profit. The rate of profit being the product of the profit margin and the output-capital ratio, the increase in profit margin entailed in the rise of monopolies and oligopolies would mean, for any given level of the interest rate,[1] a reduction in the output-capital ratio at the lower threshold, which means a reduction in the degree of capacity use or level of activity. The lowering of both thresholds with the emergence of monopoly capitalism implies that even when the economy is within the viable range, the level of unutilized capacity is in general larger.

Together with this lowering of both threshold levels of activity (or degree of capacity use) however, something else happens. We saw in chapter 14 that if there were some exogenous stimuli internal to the capitalist sector, then it would not settle down at simple reproduction but would have a positive trend with a positive rate of profit. Now, any rise in the degree of monopoly will increase the profit margin, and lower the stable positive trend.[2] Correspondingly, it would lower the rate of profit associated with this stable positive trend. Thus while the lower threshold rate of profit does not change (it approximates the minimum interest rate as just mentioned), the rate of profit associated with the stable positive trend gets reduced, so that the viability problem discussed earlier gets accentuated with the longer term tendencies of capitalism. Propertyism does not explain how, in the context of this perennial tendency of the system to sink into unviability, it continues to remain viable.

Propertyism does not explain these phenomena because it cannot. And it cannot do so, not because of any specific failing on its part, but because, like other theoretical traditions in economics, it too looks at capitalism as a self-contained and isolated system. We saw in chapter 16 that none of the usually mentioned stimuli, which operate from within the capitalist system, can explain why the system continues to remain viable despite being demand-constrained. The theoretical impasse therefore consists in this: in a closed capitalist system the viability of the system cannot be explained by propertyism; on the other hand, abandoning propertyism amounts to theoretical retrogression.

The obvious way out of the impasse is not to abandon propertyism but to abandon the closed-economy model, a solution that is also empirically defensible. Capitalism, even though it has been theorized from the very beginning as a self-contained and closed system, has always been a system integrally linked to its surrounding precapitalist formations. It has never been a closed system, and yet its description in all theoretical models attempting to explain its modus operandi, has been that of a closed system. Once we abandon this theoretical position, each of the three objections to the propertyist argument, as it stands, would disappear.

Precapitalist Markets

The first problem, namely, restricting and reversing the self-propelling character of movements of the economy from a central position, so that the economy operates within the two thresholds and remains viable at all times, is obviously resolved by recourse to precapitalist markets. There is, however, a misunderstanding here that needs to be removed.

Rosa Luxemburg who was among the first to theorize about the need for precapitalist markets for the realization and capitalization of surplus value produced within the capitalist sector, argued as if the entire surplus value had to be sold within the precapitalist sector, which provided in return the material elements of constant and variable capital, apart from labor power itself. Her argument was that the market for the preexisting levels of constant and variable capital, which got used in production during the period in question and needed replacement, and for that element of surplus value that consisted of capitalists' consumption, could be provided within the capitalist sector itself. But for the unconsumed element of surplus value, which, under the simplifying assumption of negligible capitalists' consumption (since consumption is not the capitalists' goal anyway), would approximate the total surplus value, no preexisting market existed within capitalism and hence a market had to be found outside, in the precapitalist sector. Capital accumulation, therefore, was based on exchange not so much between the two great departments of production within the capitalist sector as Marx had visualized in his famous reproduction schemes, but between the capitalist and the precapitalist sectors.

This particular argument of Luxemburg presupposes that there is no preexisting desire for investment within the capitalist sector. If capitalists had this desire to start with, then the unconsumed part of the surplus value could get realized within this sector itself. Bukharin made this point forcefully but drew an erroneous conclusion from it. His witticism against Luxemburg's argument, "If one excludes expanded reproduction at the beginning of a logical proof, it is naturally easy to make it disappear at the end; it is simply a question of the simple reproduction of a simple logical error," even though not an inappropriate riposte to her claim that *no* part of the unconsumed surplus value could be realized within the capitalist sector, missed her basic position that *sustained* investment was inexplicable in a closed capitalist economy, a position elaborated by Kalecki (1962) and discussed in earlier chapters (see Patnaik 1997 for a detailed account). The point is that while incursions into the precapitalist markets were necessary to keep investment in the capitalist sector going, these incursions were in the nature of a *stimulus*. Incursions into precapitalist markets provided the condition for investment within the capitalist sector, and hence for the realization and capitalization of surplus value within this sector. But the entire (unconsumed) surplus value did not have to be realized outside of it. Or putting it differently, the qualitative importance of precapitalist markets was crucial, even when their quantitative significance was limited.

Indeed, one can visualize the following logical possibility (just as one can visualize the Luxemburg case of all unconsumed surplus value being realized abroad as a logical possibility but not a logical necessity). The very existence of precapitalist markets where the capitalist sector can sell (apparently) any amount at the going price would provide the capitalists with an inducement to invest that would be so strong that *no actual* sales in the precapitalist market are undertaken: the internal demand within the capitalist sector fueled by this confidence in the absence of any market constraint is enough to remove the need for any outside sales. The existence of precapitalist markets here is essential even though the actual recourse to such markets is negligible. To be sure, this would not happen in reality, but if the capitalist sector makes inroads into precapitalist markets whenever there is a downward movement in the level of activity, which in turn keeps this movement in check, then this fact would explain how the system remains within the range of viable levels of activity and why departures from a central position remain restricted and get reversed.

It is not even necessary that such incursions should take the form of export surpluses as several authors, such as Bukharin (1972), Kalecki (1971), Dobb (1972), and Sweezy (1946), have argued. These authors saw precapitalist markets not as a stimulus but as a location for surplus realization. Once we see its role as a stimulus, then it follows that even if exports are matched by equivalent imports, it can still provide the basis for maintaining the level of activity in the capitalist sector. (The historical discussion of how incursions into precapitalist markets sustained capitalist development at the core is taken up in chapter 19.)

By the same token, even when imports equal exports within the precapitalist sector, there can be unemployment and deindustrialization contrary to what many authors believe. The reason for this differs however from the reason for which balanced trade increases the level of activity in the capitalist segment. In the latter case the reason is the stimulus provided to investment (or capitalists' consumption) by the sheer availability of the precapitalist market even when trade is balanced (Patnaik 1972). In the case of the precapitalist segment, however, since investment is insubstantial (otherwise the segment would not be precapitalist), the mechanism for deindustrialization with balanced trade works differently. To see this, let us assume that there are 100 peasants each producing 0.8 units of corn and 0.2 units of raw materials (corn and raw material are of equal value and this value equals 1), and consuming 0.5 units of corn; the remainder, amounting to 30 units of corn and 20 units of raw material, goes as rent to landlords who in turn employ 60 artisans, at the wage rate of 0.5 units of corn, to produce, together with the 20 units of raw material, luxury goods for them. Now suppose the landlords exchange 25 of their rent income (consisting in physical form of 15 units of corn and 10 units of raw materials) for imports of luxury goods, which they prefer to the domestically produced luxury goods and which they consume. Then, even though trade is balanced, 30 artisans (exactly half of the original number) would become unemployed and the value of domestic luxury goods output would fall by half to 25. Thus deindustrialization and unemployment arises even with balanced trade.[3]

The standard textbook presentation on the benefits of trade assume full employment before and after trade and preclude unemployment-creating deindustrialization. But, as the example shows, this is fallacious: if the 30 workers thrown out of employment cannot access land (which either is in short supply or whose harnessing for production may itself require investment that is beyond them), they would linger on as a pauperized mass. Trade in this case would have improved the "welfare" of the landlords but contributed to an accentuation of mass poverty, which is what happened in history with colonial trade (Bagchi 1982).

Labor Reserves in Precapitalist Surroundings

Encroachments into precapitalist markets thus have the effect of creating a pauperized mass in those societies. This constitutes for capitalism a distant labor reserve. Traditionally, the reserve army of labor has been identified with what exists in the proximity of the active army, that is, with the labor reserves located in the midst of the capitalist sector proper. But once we recognize the necessity for the interaction between the capitalist and precapitalist sectors for the viability of the former, then it follows that, in addition to the reserve army located in the midst of capitalism, there is also a distant reserve army located within the precapitalist sector, which does not retain its pristine nature but gets transformed through interactions with capitalism.

This distant reserve army plays a crucial role under capitalism, a role that is as yet insufficiently recognized. This role consists in the following: first, like any reserve army it constitutes a pool of available labor from which the capitalist sector can draw at will when the need arises. Drawing on this pool takes the form not just of the use of immigrant labor (which was a pronounced phenomenon during the postwar boom), but also of the establishment by metropolitan capital of production units in the distant regions (which has been a less pronounced phenomenon under capitalism, except in specific areas like mines, plantations, and manufacturing for the local market).

Second, the labor reserves created within the precapitalist sector are a key element in ensuring the stability of the value of money. We discussed earlier the concept of the "inflationary barrier" introduced by Joan Robinson. More recent literature has talked of a nonaccelerating inflation rate of unemployment (NAIRU). It has been argued, typically, that if the rate of unemployment falls below the NAIRU, then the economy experiences accelerating inflation, while if the rate of unemployment exceeds NAIRU, it witnesses decelerating inflation turning eventually into accelerating deflation. Even if this latter proposition is ignored, which would happen for instance if sellers agree to avoid price cuts even when unit prime costs fall, the idea that a reduction in unemployment below a certain level causes accelerating inflation is reminiscent of Joan

Robinson's inflationary barrier. Now, all such conclusions are based on the presumption that below the NAIRU, workers, if they anticipate inflation correctly, cannot be made to accept the "leavings of profits," that is, the remainder of output after the capitalists have taken the minimum profit-share acceptable to them at that level of aggregate demand. This undermines the stability of the wage-unit, and hence of the value of money, below NAIRU.

The matter can be expressed quite simply through the following model (Patnaik 1997), though the conclusions are not specific to the model. This model has already been given in chapter 14 and is further elaborated here to explicate the role of the precapitalist sector. Suppose the workers succeed in obtaining a money wage rate, which, at the expected price, gives them a wage share whose relative size varies inversely with the unemployment rate. If labor is the only current input and the price level is a markup over the unit prime cost, then we have

$$p(t) = p^e(t) \cdot \omega(u)(1 + m) \ldots \omega' < 0 \tag{i}$$

where p is the price, p^e the expected price; ω the wage share, which is a function of unemployment rate u; and m the markup.

If we take simple adaptive expectations, whereby the expected inflation of the current period is the same as the actual inflation of the previous period:

$$p^e(t) = p\,(t-1) \cdot p(t-1) \,/\, p\,(t-2) \ldots \tag{ii}$$

then it follows that there is a unique rate of unemployment u^* at which there can be steady inflation. At $u < u^*$ there will be accelerating inflation and at $u > u^*$ there will be decelerating inflation. This u^* is given by

$$u^* = \omega^{-1}(1 \,/\, (1 + m))$$

The idea of decelerating inflation leading to accelerating deflation seems far-fetched. If we modify (i), quite realistically, to

$$p(t) = \max\,[p(t-1); p^e(t) \cdot \omega(u)(1 + m)] \ldots \omega' < 0 \ldots \tag{i'}$$

to express the fact that collusive behavior would eliminate actual price falls, then we can have a whole range of NAIRUs, namely all $u \geq u^*$, of which u^* is the smallest. Any lowering of the unemployment rate below u^* generates accelerating inflation.

But the capitalist sector also imports primary commodities from the precapitalist sector against which it has to offer its own products. There are therefore three claimants upon its products: the capitalists, the workers they directly employ, and the precapitalist producers who indirectly service their needs. If the terms of trade can be turned against these precapitalist producers, then the NAIRU can be correspondingly reduced, or, putting it differently, for any given level of the terms of trade between the capitalist and the precapitalist sectors, there is a corresponding NAIRU. Now, turning the terms of trade against the precapitalist producers is synonymous with lowering the real wages of the workers in the precapitalist sector (or the real incomes of pre-capitalist petty producers), who are engaged in producing the primary commodities. If they can be made to accept the "leavings" of both the profits and the wages in the capitalist sector, that is, if their share can be lowered sufficiently, even when inflation is correctly anticipated, to accommodate the claims of the workers and the capitalists in the capitalist sector, then the NAIRU can be lowered arbitrarily without undermining the wage-unit in the latter sector and hence the value of money. And if those produc-ers are located in the midst of a vast pauperized mass, which we have called the distant labor reserve or the distant reserve army of labor, then they would be in no position to enforce any minimum *ex ante* real wage claims at the anticipated rate of inflation. They constitute, in other words, the "shock absorbers" of the system. Their share in the out-put of the capitalist sector is compressible without engendering accelerating inflation. And this contributes to stability in the value of money.

In terms of this model, this can be expressed as follows.

$$p(t) = [p^e(t) \cdot \omega(u) + a \cdot \pi(t)](1 + m) \ldots \omega' < 0 \ldots \tag{i''}$$

where a is the physical amount of primary product, produced in the precapitalist sector, used per unit of the product of the capitalist sector and π the price per unit of it in terms of the capitalist sector's money. The primary commodity price in turn can be visualized as a markup (say by oligopolist traders) over the unit wage cost, the markup factor being $(1 + h)$. The workers in this sector are unorganized and weak, because of being located within a vast pauperized mass. They succeed, let us assume, only in obtaining the same share in the capitalist sector's commodity as they did in the previous period at the current period's expected price of that commodity. And let us assume the same expectation formation function for them as for the capitalist sector's workers. Since the previous period's share for them, which is the residue after all other claimants have taken their shares, is $[1 / (1 + m) - \omega(t - 1)] / (1 + h)$, we have

$$a \cdot \pi(t) = [p^e(t) \cdot \{1 / (1 + m) - \omega(t - 1)\} / (1 + h)](1 + h) \ldots \tag{iii}$$

From (i''), (ii) and (iii), it follows that

$$p(t) / p^e(t) = 1 + (1 + m) [\omega(u) - \omega(t - 1)\} \ldots \tag{iv}$$

Now, $p(t) / p^e(t)$ is the same as $\omega(u) / \omega(t)$, so that (iv) can also be expressed as

$$\omega(u) - \omega(t) = \omega(t)(1 + m)[\omega(u) - \omega(t - 1)] \ldots \tag{v}$$

Obviously, $\omega(u) > \omega(t)$ for all t, for otherwise there would be no tendency for accelerating inflation to start with. Since it is also the case that $\omega(t)(1 + m) < 1$ for all t, as long as there is a positive price for the primary commodity, it follows from (v) that for any u maintained over time, the share of the workers in the capitalist sector would converge to $\omega(u)$. Hence, the capitalist sector, if it is surrounded by a precapitalist sector saddled with a vast pauperized mass, created through interactions with itself, can have steady inflation and maintain any level of activity over time. There is no inflationary-barrier level or minimum NAIRU level of activity.

Let us now come back to the second problem of incompleteness of propertyism that we noted before. There was, we had seen, nothing in the system, conceived as a closed isolated system, to ensure that the minimum level of activity needed for viability was below the inflationary-barrier level of activity (or the minimum level of the NAIRU). But once we see the capitalist economy as surrounded by and interacting with the precapitalist sector, where large labor reserves get built up through this interaction, the very notion of an inflationary barrier level of activity, or of some minimum NAIRU level of activity, becomes irrelevant, since the unemployment rate can be pushed as low as possible without undermining the wage-unit in the capitalist sector. This can be effected by turning the terms of trade against the primary producers, who are price takers and whose real incomes are always compressible to the required extent. The second instance of incompleteness of the propertyist argument therefore is resolved, like the first, when we see the capitalist sector as existing not in isolation but necessarily in interaction with its precapitalist environment.

The Absorption of Parametric Changes

If there are parametric changes, such as for instance an increase in the degree of monopoly, on account of greater collusion among capitalists, whose numbers shrink through the process of centralization of capital highlighted by Marx (a process that does not stop even when precapitalist markets are available), or an increase in the bargaining strength of the workers employed in the capitalist sector (resulting in a rise in the $\omega(u)$ function), these changes get absorbed at the expense of the precapitalist producers without causing any threats to the stability of the system. We had discussed earlier that the upper threshold level of activity has a tendency to move down for reasons such as the rise in the degree of monopoly, and that this would accentuate the problem of unviability. But the upper threshold level of activity itself does not exist if the capitalist sector is ensconced within a precapitalist setting. And there is no question of its coming down since the parametric changes introduced by the emergence of monopolies and oligopolies get absorbed at the expense of the precapitalist producers without causing any threats to the stability of the system.

Equation (v), it should be remembered, holds no matter what the degree of monopoly m happens to be and what the function $\omega(u)$ happens to be. Hence a rise in m or in $\omega(u)$ does not negate the conclusion drawn earlier that the capitalist sector can stabilize itself at any level of activity without causing accelerating inflation. The existence of a pauperized mass in the precapitalist surroundings of the capitalist sector implies that the terms of trade can be turned against the primary producers located within those surroundings, with impunity. Of course, this "turning" the terms of trade is not a deliberate or planned act. Capitalism is not a planned system. But it is the outcome of an objective process that no one deliberately sets up.

All the instances of incompleteness of propertyism therefore disappear the moment we see capitalism as a system ensconced within a precapitalist milieu. Nonetheless two caveats are in order here. First, from the proposition that a higher wage share of the workers in the capitalist sector can be accommodated, without causing accelerating inflation, through a squeeze on the wage share of the workers in the precapitalist sector, it should not be concluded that the workers in the capitalist sector "exploit" those in the precapitalist sector. The outcome of an objective process over which the workers have no control whatsoever (and even the capitalists do not) should not be confused with a direct social relationship. (This issue is discussed again in the next chapter.) Second, while having a vast pauperized mass located in a distant outlying region is a necessary condition for the stability of the value of money, and hence of the system, it tends to lose its effectiveness over time. This is because parametric increases in the degree of monopoly, or in the product wage in the capitalist sector relative to productivity, progressively reduce the share of the claims of precapitalist primary producers over the output of the capitalist sector. With the decline in this share, the ability of the system to resolve its problems at the expense of the precapitalist producers becomes increasingly blunted. This problem becomes particularly serious in view of the fact that there are commodities like oil whose price has little to do with the cost of production. A rise in this price, brought about independently, may destabilize the wage-unit in the capitalist sector, since it becomes increasingly difficult, for the reason just mentioned, to stifle the inflationary consequences of such an increase in oil price, by pushing the burden on to the shoulders of the precapitalist commodity producers. We return to this issue in later chapters.

Concluding Observations

Rosa Luxemburg had seen the encroachment of the capitalist sector upon the precapitalist sector as a means of resolving the problem of realization and capitalization of the unconsumed portion of the surplus value produced within the former. She had seen this encroachment as taking the form of an assimilation of the precapitalist sector within the capitalist one, leading eventually to a complete disappearance of the former, a limit point where, even as Marx's reproduction schemes come into their own, accumulation ironically becomes impossible, resulting in a collapse of the system. Even though her insight into capitalism's need for encroaching upon the precapitalist surroundings remains unparalleled for its prescience, the details of her argument are unsustainable on at least two counts. First, as already discussed, the entire unconsumed surplus value does not need to be realized and capitalized through sales to the precapitalist markets. The role of the latter is of a stimulus for accumulation, not of a receptacle for unconsumed surplus value. Second, she sees the precapitalist sector not as lingering on as a ravaged entity containing a vast pauperized mass of displaced producers, but as an entity that disappears over time. The latter scenario is neither the experience of history nor a necessary corollary of theory.

On the contrary, while the need for the stimulus provided by precapitalist markets for the process of capital accumulation cannot be overstated, the encroachment engendered by this need, precisely because it takes the form of a vast lingering mass of pauperized precapitalist producers existing within a ravaged precapitalist sector, fulfills another fundamental role. It ensures the stability of the wage-unit within capitalism, keeps the inflationary barrier at bay, and hence stabilizes the value of money. Luxemburg's insight was precious, but the links between the capitalist and precapitalist sectors are far more fundamental, far more integral, to the functioning of the capitalist sector than even she recognized.

Notwithstanding the formal sophistication of the Walrasian-monetarist theory, the alternative propertyist tradition marked a tremendous advance in our understanding of the nature of capitalism. Its break from the mainstream theory, however, remained incomplete precisely because it adopted as its theoretical paradigm the same one which the Walrasian-monetarist tradition had adopted, namely a closed capitalist economy spontaneously achieving a state of equilibrium both in the single period and over a sequence of periods. This position was not logically tenable, and its adoption circumscribed the revolutionary theoretical potential of propertyism. When we break out of this assumed universe and see capitalism as necessarily ensconced within a precapitalist sector, in constant interaction with it but not assimilating it, we not only overcome the logical problems associated with propertyism as it stands but also come closer to an understanding of what happened in history.

18

Capitalism as a Mode of Production

THE RESOLUTION OF THE DILEMMA that lies at the center of propertyism, in both its Marxist and Keynesian versions, consists in visualizing capitalism not as a closed self-contained system but as one ensconced within a precapitalist setting. The recognition of this as a fact of outstanding importance characterizes Marxist theory. But this fact is not given any space within the theoretical system. Indeed, there is a paradox at the center of Marxist theory. Nobody wrote as perceptively on the working of colonialism as Karl Marx did, not just on its overall historical implications, but also on the mechanics of its economic functioning: many have even noted a remarkable resemblance between Marx's writings on the economics of colonialism in India and those of Dadabhai Naoroji, the "grand old man" of Indian nationalism, who provided the basic theoretical foundation for India's anticolonial struggle through his celebrated "drain theory" on the appropriation of surplus from India by Britain.[1] And yet in the entire corpus of Marx's theoretical writings on the "law of motion of modern society" there is no role for colonialism.

This is not just an omission that can be explained in terms of the usual "had-Marx-lived-he-would-have-taken-care-of-it" kind of argument; its roots lie deeper. Indeed, it is instructive that in the entire Marxist tradition, with the notable exception of the Luxemburgist stream, there is no theory of colonialism, or more generally, theory of imperialism that actually locates the phenomenon of imperialism (in the inclusive sense of covering both the quintessentially colonial and the subsequent periods) in the law of motion of the capitalist mode of production. In Marx's own theoretical writings, colonialism figures only in the discussion of the "primitive accumulation of capital," but once capitalism has gone beyond this stage, colonialism is assigned no further role.[2] The classic writings of Lenin and Bukharin, even though they keep imperialism as their central focus, are concerned solely with the monopoly phase of capitalism and hence make no attempt to provide a theory of imperialism in the inclusive sense just referred to.

The reason for this omission lies in a conceptual conundrum: if capitalism exploits its domestic workers to extract a surplus value and also needs a precapitalist appendage for ensuring its realization and capitalization, an appendage where producers are dispossessed in the process, then there are two different types of exploitation occurring simultaneously. The theoretical relationship between these two different types of exploitation is not clear, and their simultaneous occurrence goes against the basic Marxist proposition that capitalism is fundamentally a system of exploitation of workers in the sphere of production.[3] In other words, one cannot retain every other aspect of the classical Marxist analysis of capitalism, and simply "add on" a proposition about capitalization of surplus value requiring exchange with the precapitalist sector; the acceptance of this proposition must necessarily be accompanied, for logical consistency, with a reconstruction of the overall perception and analysis of capitalism as a mode of production.

The Usual Perception of a Mode of Production

As was mentioned earlier, at the beginning of the *Communist Manifesto* we come across a set of binary opposites: "freeman and slave, patrician and plebeian, lord and serf, guildmaster and journeyman, in a word, oppressor and oppressed." The *Manifesto*, as is well known, belongs to a phase of Marx's work when several of his key theoretical concepts had not yet been developed; nevertheless the concept of a mode of production characterized by the antagonism between the producers on one hand and the appropriators of surplus on the other is a continuation of this perception of a binary opposition. A mode of production is an integrated complex of social relations of production corresponding to a certain level of development of the social productive forces. The key to these relations of production lies in property relations, which in turn can be understood by looking at the mechanism of appropriation of surplus from the direct producers: "property relations" refers juridically to the pattern of claims on social product, their essence being the claim on surplus.

Embedded in this entire set of well-known arguments emphasizing the primacy of the sphere of production, however, is an implicit perception of a "closed system," a system "ideally" seen as an isolated, self-contained entity, within which the drama of class struggle is played out in accordance with its inner law of motion based on its own specific contradictions. The interaction of this essentially self-contained entity with the "outside" world can act at best as a catalyst, *through* its effect eventually on the basic contradiction and the central class struggle between the class of direct producers and the class of appropriators of surplus; but it is not per se essential for understanding the inner law of motion of the mode of production. The concept of the mode of production, because it focuses on production and gives primacy to the sphere of production, is necessarily associated with the analytical exploration of a self-contained entity.

This, of course, is the strength of Marxism, its point of departure that makes it so powerful a tool of analysis. A theory that would attempt to look at everything at the same time in the name of comprehensiveness would end up being a mere description and no theory. A theory that would start at some other end, for example, from the sphere of exchange, would have at best a set of disjointed insights but would miss the historical process. A theory to be meaningful at all must have structured determinations; for it to have insights into the historical process these structured determinations must give primacy to the sphere of production, which is what Marxism does. The problem, however, is that, when it comes to capitalism, this perception precludes any analytical role for imperialism. Marx's theoretical treatment of capitalism as a self-contained entity, which has been often attributed to his Ricardian lineage is thus embedded in something deeper, namely, the traditional concept of the mode of production.

A consequence of this "closed system" analysis, other than the theoretical damage done to the cause of the oppressed in the colonial countries, is the unwarranted hostility toward Keynesianism among Marxist economists. The reference here is neither to the social philosophy and political outlook of Keynes, which Marxists would naturally reject, nor to the precise conceptual building blocks of Keynesian economics, such as "propensity to consume," which are methodologically unacceptable to Marxian economics, but to the Keynesian conclusion about the role of effective demand. Given Marx's trenchant critique of Say's law, the Keynesian emphasis on effective demand should have been easily acceptable to the Marxian tradition, but it was not. The Keynesian revolution, despite the fact that one of its coauthors was a Marxist economist, Michael Kalecki, an engineer by training whose introduction to economics was via Marx's *Capital*, was for a long time rejected (or at best considered inconsequential) because of its focus on the "sphere of circulation." Much of Marxian economics operated as if Say's law held, despite Marx's demolition of it.

This was hardly surprising: by arguing the possibility of generalized overproduction, and yet locating it within a context of self-regulating cyclical fluctuations, Marx had effectively downgraded this possibility. Marx had demolished Say's law, but Say's law crept into his own analysis through the back door, by the resolution he provided to the dilemma of reconciling within the conceptual universe of a closed capitalist system the observed fact of its being reasonably stable with his own theoretical demonstration of the intrinsic possibility of its instability. He could have overcome this dilemma by jettisoning the conceptual universe of a closed capitalist system, as Rosa Luxemburg did.[4] That, however, would have gone against his concept of a mode of production where the focus was on the relationship between classes, especially the two binary opposites, that is anchored in the production process, which is specific and *internal* to the system.

This concept itself is valuable and must be retained, but in the context of capitalism at any rate the perception of the system as a whole cannot be coterminous with this basic concept alone. The capitalist system is much more than the capitalist mode of production analyzed by Marx.

Marx's Own Departures from the Usual Concept

This suggestion is not as outlandish as may appear at first sight. Indeed within Marx's *analysis* itself (and not just in the factual clothing of the analysis), there is the glimpse of a conceptual universe of the capitalist mode being ensconced within a precapitalist setting. This appears when he is discussing the concept of the reserve army of labor. The capitalists exploit the workers in the process of production. By definition, the unemployed, belonging to the reserve army of labor, are not exploited (which prompted Joan Robinson's remark that for a worker the one thing worse than being exploited by capital was not being exploited by it). But while the reserve army is not exploited in the same manner as the active army, it is exploited by the system nonetheless in a different way. What is more, the reserve army does not consist simply of the openly unemployed. It consists of different elements, some of which are even employed but outside the system.[5] Even Marx in other words, while analyzing the closed capitalist system, recognizes, not just descriptively but also analytically, the existence of a universe outside the system but obviously linked to it, in the sense that the workers employed outside constitute a reserve army that can always be drawn into the active army inside.

This point acquires greater weight when we recognize that Marx's notion of the reserve army, as it stands, is somewhat restricted in scope. Capitalism actually requires a far larger reserve army for its functioning than even Marx recognized, for a reason we have discussed earlier. Let us recapitulate this reason.

Marx's analysis of money refers to a commodity-money world where money is a produced commodity like any other, and its value relative to the world of commodities is determined by their respective conditions of production. (This, as we saw, is different from Ricardo's theory of commodity money, where the relative exchange ratio between money and the world of commodities changes with the change in the wage rate as well.) For any given conditions of production, a rise in money wages, it follows, results ipso facto in a rise in real wages (a conclusion common between Ricardo and Marx, notwithstanding their other differences). We can therefore use the terms *money* and *real wages* almost interchangeably.

The role of the reserve army in the Marxist theoretical tradition is, among other things, to keep down the rate of growth of the wage rate relative to productivity, so that (1) the rate of profit is always positive and (2) any tendency for the rate of profit to decline in the accumulation process is spontaneously arrested through an appropriate expansion in the reserve army caused by a decline in the pace of accumulation as a result of the decline in the rate of profit (Goodwin 1967). In short, the role of the reserve army is to keep down wages relative to productivity, not necessarily to ensure that the level of wages does not increase, but rather to ensure that the share of wages does not. (Many writers postulate the wage share as being a monotonic function of the ratio of the reserve to the active army, but the precise nature of this relationship is not germane to the current discussion.)

In a world where money is not a produced commodity, the value of money relative to commodities is determined by the fact that the value of one commodity, labor power, in terms of money is fixed in the short run and changes slowly in the long run (which was Keynes's argument). And since the expenditure of labor power is essential for the production of every commodity, this ipso facto fixes the relative value of money with respect to all commodities.[6] In other words, the level of money wage rate determines the value of money relative to commodities; the stickiness of the money wage rate prevents any violent fluctuations in this relative value.

This stickiness presupposes that a significant section of workers acts as a price taker. For workers to act as price takers, it must be the case that they are not organized. Keynes, who correctly postulated the stickiness of money wages as a condition for the stability of the capitalist system (1949, 239), attributed this stickiness not to the fact that workers, or a substantial section among them, are unorganized, but to the existence of "money illusion" among organized workers, that is, among the trade unions themselves, who supposedly do not notice a decline in real wages since their attention is focused exclusively on the money wages. But this was a weak and patently untenable argument, and monetarism was quick to seize upon it for staging a successful revival from the position to which it had been reduced as a consequence of the Keynesian onslaught: it introduced the concept of a natural rate of unemployment, which denied any scope for successful state intervention in demand management of the sort that Keynesianism had argued for. The rigidity of money wages, at least of a certain section of workers (which is quite enough for the stability of the system) arises because they are unorganized. Workers act as price takers because they are unorganized. And they remain unorganized because they live amidst a reserve army of labor.

The notion of a reserve army that restrains the bargaining strength of trade unions and ensures that the share of wages does not increase and the notion of a reserve army that ensures that a substantial section of workers remains unorganized are two very different entities. Workers remain unorganized only when they constitute part of a vast pauperized mass, in whose context it is not even clear that the term *reserve army of labor*, which suggests at least periodic or potential active duty, is at all applicable. If we do use the term, then we must recognize that keeping workers unorganized, and hence trapped as price takers, requires a much larger reserve army of labor than what would be necessary merely for ensuring that real wages do not rise faster than labor productivity secularly. Since Marx, who first proposed the notion of the reserve army of labor, confined himself only to its latter role, and not its role in stabilizing the "wage unit," his concept is somewhat restricted.

Capitalism requires that even if there are autonomous reasons for a fall in real wages, resulting in a fall in wage share, even then the stickiness of money wages is not disrupted. The reserve army, therefore, must be large enough to ensure that a significant section of the workers cannot enforce any particular *ex ante* wage share.[7] They should not be able to defend some particular level of real wages relative to productivity by jacking up money wages whenever there is a fall below that level (so that hyperinflation is prevented). They must be part of a vast pauperized mass.

The very vastness of this mass strengthens Marx's insight about the outside location of the reserve army. The enormous amount of reserve army required for this denouement (of keeping the wage unit steady), cannot be geographically located within the metropolitan capitalist economies without giving rise to major social upheavals; it has to be located geographically outside. What is more, it must also be located sociologically outside the capitalist system, within modes of production other than the capitalist one, strictly defined, but which are linked to the capitalist mode of production (just as Marx had visualized in the case of his concept of the reserve army). It follows, on the basis of this argument, that the simultaneous existence of other modes of production surrounding it is a condition for the existence of the capitalist mode of production itself.

Of course, this simultaneous existence is necessary not for this or that particular reason. Its necessity arises not merely for the sake of finding an external market to stimulate accumulation; nor does it arise merely for the sake of stabilizing the system by preventing accelerating inflation when the system does experience a high enough level of activity. (Such accelerating inflation would occur if *all* workers whose products were used by capitalism could enforce *ex ante* wage shares.) It is not one reason alone but a whole range of reasons. And for this whole range of reasons the overall functioning of capitalism requires that it be linked to other modes of production; it thrives by sponging on them, by making them subservient to its own will.

The Specificity of the Capitalist Mode

Thus the concept of a mode of production, defined in terms of its internal appropriation mechanisms, and hence as an epistemologically self-contained entity, which may be relevant for earlier modes of production, is not relevant for capitalism, since it tends to detract from its linkages with other modes of production with which it must simultaneously coexist. This is not to critique the concept of the mode of production or to belittle Marx's gigantic labors in unraveling the law of motion of capitalism, starting from an analysis of the origin of surplus value within it, but merely to underscore the insufficiency of even that Herculean effort.

This is necessary for one very important reason. Marx and Engels had written in the *Manifesto*: "The bourgeoisie, by the rapid improvement of all instruments of production, by the immensely facilitated means of communication, draws all, even the most barbarian, nations into civilization. The cheap prices of its commodities are the heavy artillery with which it batters down all Chinese walls, with which it forces the barbarians' intensely obstinate hatred of foreigners to capitulate. It compels all nations, on pain of extinction, to adopt the bourgeois mode of production; it compels them to introduce what it calls civilization into their midst, i.e. to become bourgeois themselves. In one word, it creates a world after its own image" (Karat 1999, 93). The clear suggestion here is that the revolutionary nature of the bourgeois mode of production necessarily results in its universal diffusion, a suggestion that reappears in Rosa Luxemburg as well, who developed a whole theory of the breakdown of capitalism on the argument that when capitalism had become the universally prevalent mode of production, expanded reproduction would become an impossibility. Even though the Sixth Congress of the Communist International had rejected this suggestion and recognized the fact that in third-world countries integration into the orbit of world capitalism did not lead to a replication internally of the capitalist mode of production (it had adopted the thesis that "pauperization of the peasantry" in the third world did not lead to its "proletarianization"), this "diffusionism" has been a persistently recurring theme within the Marxist tradition. Our argument not only rejects diffusionism but also amounts to saying that the capitalist mode, contrary to common belief, can exist *only* within an environment of precapitalism, which does not remain in its pristine form of course, but is molded, shaped, and dominated by capitalism and made to cater to its needs.

The capitalist mode, it follows, is both revolutionary and yet not quite revolutionary enough. It does break down the insulation of existing precapitalist societies; it does ruthlessly draw them into the vortex of its own accumulation process, but not necessarily by creating within them, in a dominant form, the structures of the bourgeois mode of production itself. They are transformed and hegemonized by metropolitan capitalism, but they themselves are never transformed into predominantly bourgeois societies. They may replicate within them the dichotomy characterizing the system as a whole, by having an enclave of capitalism, but this is very different from their transformation into bourgeois societies.

While this fact may be accepted by many, the question may be asked: Why should we not be content with encapsulating it within some other concept, for instance, "the capitalist world system"? Why should we insist on retaining the concept of the mode of production at all? The answer to this question is as follows: concepts, and the theories using them, are of value essentially as aids to praxis. The preference for one concept over another must ultimately be determined by the degree to which it aids praxis, more specifically the degree to which it helps in carrying forward the struggle for emancipation of the people by making possible the concrete analysis of the concrete conditions. Nothing that has been said earlier questions the validity of Marx's basic insights into the dynamics of the capitalist mode of production; it merely wishes to locate that dynamics within a larger totality. To understand that dynamics, to identify the plethora of classes located within this larger totality, and to see the changes in the interrelationship between these classes, the concept of the mode of production is absolutely necessary. Without it, one would be in the realm of mere description, albeit "rich description," but not in the realm of analysis.

While retaining the concept of the mode of production, however, we must recognize that the capitalist mode of production is always located within a cluster, surrounded by precapitalist modes of production that are hegemonized but are nonetheless very clearly extant and by no means obliterated. The tendencies immanent to capitalism, unraveled by Marx, operate surely, but in a manner refracted by its interactions with this surrounding universe. Exploitation within this totality is of diverse forms: there is above all the exploitation of workers directly employed by capital through the appropriation of surplus value; there is the exploitation of the metropolitan reserve army, which is kept in depressed living conditions and has the role of keeping down the bargaining strength of the trade unions in the metropolis; then there are the unorganized workers in the periphery, who are exploited through unequal exchange and made to act as price takers so as to sustain the stability of the value of money; finally, there is the vast pauperized mass amidst whom these unorganized workers are placed which is also exploited, through even more depressed living conditions than the metropolitan reserve army, and upon whom the system rests ultimately for its stability. In addition to these, there are of course the different forms of exploitation by the precapitalist hegemonic classes.

Recognizing this complex totality seems to be a much better way of proceeding than treating capitalism as a self-contained mode of production like the earlier ones, and hence missing out on the phenomenon of imperialism (in the inclusive sense). We should therefore not change in any basic sense the concept of the mode of production; we have to remove from it the connotation of a self-contained entity by recognizing that the capitalist mode, unlike the previous ones, exists necessarily by hegemonizing but not eliminating these previous ones. No mode of production that is so dependent on the world market, that comes into existence by constituting a world trading system, could be meaningfully cognized as a self-contained entity.

Concluding Observations

Let us now pull together the different strands of the argument of this chapter. The basic concept of Marxist analysis is the mode of production. Since it takes as its point of departure the production process in any society and the manner of extraction of surplus from those engaged in direct production, the mode of production is seen essentially as a self-contained entity, and the law of motion governing it is worked out within this perspective. This procedure, applied universally by Marxist analysts across all modes, is particularly evident in the analysis of capitalism, which has been seen as a mode of production epistemologically on a par with any other, and one on which Marxist analysis has been particularly focused. The result of this has been that imperialism, not just in Lenin's sense but also in the more inclusive sense that incorporates the colonial phase as well, which has been a constant feature of capitalism, has not figured centrally in the Marxist analysis of it: (leaving aside the monopoly phase) it figures only in discussions of primitive accumulation, and in concrete analyses of capitalism, but not in its law of motion, in the basic theory of its functioning.

There are, however, overwhelming reasons to believe that it must figure there, that capitalism cannot be analyzed as a self-contained system on a par with earlier modes. Once we recognize, as Marx did, the possibility of a demand constraint leading to generalized overproduction, then, as Rosa Luxemburg had pointed out, we have to look for exogenous stimuli to explain accumulation as a sustained process; and the main exogenous stimulus is export to precapitalist markets (even when trade is balanced with these markets). The fact that capitalism has performed on average with a reasonable degree of stability should not be taken as proof of its inherent stability; the fact that capitalist economies have generally succeeded in keeping overproduction crises in check does not constitute proof of their *ex ante* impossibility. In other words, the fact that in a situation where capitalism has actually been ensconced within a precapitalist setting it has performed reasonably cannot be used to deny the necessity of such a precapitalist setting. Its necessity for the dynamics of capitalism consists in the fact that it must provide exogenous stimuli for sustained accumulation and for playing the role of a shock absorber. Pointing out the weakness of *narodnik*-style arguments about the impossibility of capitalism in a particular country, arguments that constitute distorted (because they are epistemologically erroneous) conclusions from this proposition about exogenous stimuli, cannot be used to deny the validity of this proposition.

In addition, there is this fact. Already in Marx, the concept of the reserve army, as it appears, points implicitly to the existence of other modes of production alongside and dominated by capitalism. The scope of this concept as it appears in Marx is itself somewhat restricted. Its role there is confined to one of keeping down the bargaining strength of workers, so that the rise in real wages relative to productivity is kept in check. In a fiat money world, however, the stability of the system requires that the money wages of at least a substantial section of workers should be sticky in the short run and change slowly over time, which would happen if these workers act essentially as price takers. When workers act as price takers, they themselves are usually underemployed, that is, can be said to belong to some sort of a semireserve army; what is more, they do so only when they are surrounded by vast unutilized labor reserves, which is usually the case in third-world economies from whom capitalism draws much of its raw materials and primary commodities. The reserve army that capitalism typically operates with, therefore, is much larger than what Marx had visualized, and typically this reserve army is split into two parts, a smaller one that exists in the metropolis, and a much larger one that exists in the periphery ensconced within modes of production that are different from capitalism but are nonetheless subjugated by it, and hence different too from their own pristine forms.

Capitalism therefore necessarily exists within a complex environment, within a cluster of precapitalist forms. While many recognize this fact, the theoretical devices they advance for cognizing it, such as "the capitalist world system," tend to do away with the Marxist concept of the mode of production. Such doing away is unwise, since it amounts to throwing the baby out with the bathwater. A much better way out of this theoretical problem is to retain the concept of the mode of production, to retain and build on all the insights that Marx derived from this concept, but to recognize that capitalism, contrary to the ruthlessly single-minded revolutionary nature usually attributed to it, functions throughout its life within an environment constituted by a cluster of precapitalist modes of production, which it alters, transforms, dominates, and exploits. The notion of exploitation, it follows, must also be broadened to take account of the different types of exploitation prevalent under capitalism, apart from the basic extraction of surplus value. The solution to the apparent contradiction between the concept of the mode of production and the theory of imperialism is not to abandon the centrality of either but to recognize theoretically a phenomenon that has been on view for long, namely that the capitalist mode has some very specific characteristics attached to it, one of which is the fact that it never exists in isolation.

19

Money in the World Economy

I HAVE SO FAR CONFINED this discussion to a universe of one single unified capitalist economy. In such an economy, I argued, the value of money had to be given from outside the realm of demand and supply. Such outside determination of the value of money not only undermined Say's law and opened up the possibility of generalized *ex ante* overproduction, but it also entailed that the system was basically a demand-constrained one. I then argued that for such a system to be viable, in the sense of remaining within a range of activity levels where it earned the "minimum rate of profit" necessary for its survival without engendering accelerating inflation, it needed to be surrounded by a precapitalist sector. Such a precapitalist sector, constituting its environment, could alone provide the stimulus for investment needed to keep the system above the minimum rate of profit by being available for deindustrialization; it could also, because of the pauperized mass of displaced small producers created through such deindustrialization, act as a shock absorber for any inflationary pressures arising within the capitalist sector, and thus prevent any possibility of accelerating inflation, no matter what the activity level might be.

This entire discussion, however, presumed a single unified capitalist core, ensconced within a precapitalist sector, but itself constituting a single entity. But the moment a multiplicity of countries constituting the capitalist core is introduced, this model does not suffice. Let us examine this.

Commodity Money and the International Economy

The fixing from outside of the value of money takes the form, in Marx's work, of the money prices of commodities as a whole being fixed; and this is supposed to be in accordance with the relative quantities of labor directly and indirectly embodied in a unit of money compared to a unit of the aggregate commodity. In Keynes it takes the form of the money wage rate being fixed. These two perceptions correspond respectively to the labor-embodied and the labor-commanded measures of the value of money. They are adequate when we are talking of a single economy or one integrated capitalist economy where—leaving aside skill differentials, which are separately handled and pose no special problem in the present context—the term *labor* has a clear meaning. But when we are talking about several national economies across which there is no mobility of labor, we are talking not about one labor but several different national labors. Even if the money wage rate is fixed in each of these economies in terms of its own currency, the relation between these different currencies remains indeterminate, so that we still do not have a notion of money in the world economy. Putting it differently, to have a notion of money in the world economy, as distinct from a mere ensemble of currencies, the fact of money wages being fixed in each economy is not enough. What is logically needed in addition is either an independent basis for the determination of the relative valuation of the different national labors, or an independent fixation of the relative prices of the various national currencies. (These two, to be sure, are not necessarily delinked from one another, that is, if the currency prices are fixed independently, then the wage rate in each country in terms of its own currency may be such as to ensure a certain relative valuation of its labor compared to others.) Once the relative prices among the ensemble of currencies are fixed, they can of course be expressed in terms of any one of them. But this is a purely formal point. The basic issue is that the considerations hitherto emphasized in our discussion of the value of money are no longer sufficient when we talk about a capitalist world economy.

For instance, among the many currencies in the capitalist world economy, there is usually one that acts as the principal unit of account, as the principal medium of circulation and as the principal form of wealth holding, thus fulfilling the role of world money. The substantive questions that arise are: Which particular currency plays this role? What enables it to play this role? How is the value of "world money" with respect to the world of commodities determined? How are the relative prices between the different currencies determined? How are these relative prices between the different currencies preserved? Why does one particular currency playing this role yield its place to another? What are the contradictions arising out of this peculiar nature of "world money" where it is both money of the world as well as the currency of a particular nation? And so on. We will not be able to answer all these questions, and we must confine ourselves instead primarily to developing an approach to the study of world money.

A capitalist economy, we saw, needs to hold its wealth, to a greater or lesser extent, in the form of money. Indeed, there would not even be any transaction demand for money, unless money was also a form of holding wealth. This is because any separation of purchase and sale, which the transaction demand for money presupposes, implies that there is a certain transitional period when wealth is held in the form of money, a fact underscored by Marx's concept of "money capital" into which "commodity capital" is transformed, and which in turn is transformed to "commodity capital."

In a world in which there are no currencies at all but only commodities, one commodity from among them would have to be set aside to serve the role of a wealth-holding medium; and typically it would be that commodity whose expected rate of change of relative price, less the relative carrying cost, is the highest. Putting it differently, if all commodity prices are expected to move more or less in tandem, then that commodity would be chosen as the money commodity that has the lowest carrying cost. Gold typically has been the money commodity, since it has a very low carrying cost. And because of this very fact, namely the low carrying cost, which has made it a favorite form of wealth holding, its price is generally expected not to fall relative to the world of commodities, thus reinforcing its position as the money commodity.

In a world of currencies, that particular currency would be chosen as money that is "as good as gold" in the minds of wealth holders. Throughout history, until very recently, this "as good as gold" status has been enjoyed by particular currencies by virtue of their being statutorily enshrined as being freely convertible to gold. Under the gold standard, the pound sterling, which was the leading currency of the time, had a fixed price vis-à-vis gold at which it was freely convertible; and so, in principle, were the other currencies, which had fixed exchange rates vis-à-vis the pound sterling. Under the Bretton Woods system, the U.S. dollar was freely convertible into gold; other currencies were not directly convertible into gold and were not necessarily freely convertible into the U.S. dollar, but nonetheless had fixed exchange rates relative to the U.S. dollar. In short, in the past the world economy has always been on a commodity-money system, apart from brief interregnums like the period between the collapse of the gold standard and the establishment of the Bretton Woods system.

I mentioned earlier that within a single capitalist economy, even when we do not apparently have commodity money, since the value of the fiat money vis-à-vis commodities is fixed through the fixing of the money wage rate, that is, of the exchange ratio between money on the one hand and the commodity labor power on the other, we still remain trapped within a de facto commodity-money system. In other words, even when there is no de jure commodity money, there still is de facto commodity money. But the moment we think of the capitalist world economy, we have always had until very recently (on which more later) both de jure and de facto commodity money. There are two separate fixings here: the value of the leading currency (the one that is "as good as gold") is fixed relative to gold; and the value of this currency (and hence of gold) is fixed relative to the world of commodities. (In addition, of course, the value of the other currencies is fixed in terms of the leading currency, but that is a separate issue that I will discuss later.)

The basic criterion for a currency to be considered "as good as gold," and hence to be a medium of wealth holding, is that its price must not be expected to fall too much (at a rate offsetting its relative carrying cost advantage) in terms of commodities, of which gold is a representative. This requires in turn that the money wage rate (relative to productivity) in that economy should be relatively sticky, that the degree of monopoly in that economy should be slowly changing, and that the prices of primary commodities imported into that economy should not experience any sudden or sharp increase. At the same time, that economy must have a level of activity that ensures its viability in terms of its earning a certain minimum rate of profit. In short, what I said earlier about the capitalist sector as a whole, namely that it must have a level of activity that ensures its viability without engendering accelerating inflation must hold in particular for the leading capitalist economy; and the role the precapitalist environment was supposed to play in achieving the stability of capitalism in this sense must be played by it specifically relative to the leading capitalist economy. Putting it differently, the imperialist relationship of the capitalist sector to the precapitalist sector must be mediated in particular through the leading currency country. The picture of interaction between the capitalist and precapitalist sectors drawn earlier does not necessarily, in a world with several capitalist countries, translate into a multiplicity of similar relationships between each core country and its own precapitalist hinterland; rather, it entails that the capitalist countries, many of which have no colonies or precapitalist adjuncts, relate to the precapitalist sector of the world and enjoy the benefits (for them) of such interaction, through their relations with the leading capitalist country, which does necessarily have this precapitalist adjunct.

It follows that the leading capitalist country must be the strongest imperialist power of the time. Indeed, it is this latter characteristic that makes its currency the leading currency. Wealth holders would have the maximum confidence in that country's currency, which is so backed up by a precapitalist hinterland that its level of activity remains reasonably high without there being any fears of accelerating inflation on the horizon. And the most powerful imperialist country of the time fulfils these requirements the best. Not surprisingly, its currency acquires the status of the leading currency.

To say that the leading currency constitutes the stable medium for holding wealth without which a capitalist world economy cannot function is not to say that it plays this role exclusively. It is never the case that this currency (and assets denominated in terms of it) alone constitute a wealth-holding medium. Other currencies (and assets denominated in terms of them) constitute forms in which wealth is held. But they do so only insofar as their relative value in terms of the leading currency is not expected to change secularly (notwithstanding short-term fluctuations). Of course, this need not be the case if wealth holders face restrictions in shifting from one currency to another, but if such restrictions do not exist or can be surreptitiously violated, then several different currencies can coexist in which wealth can be held, provided that their relative values, barring temporary fluctuations, are expected on the whole to remain unchanged.

Marx observes, "All historical experience ... shows that, where two commodities function as legally valid measures of value, it is always one of them only which actually maintains this position" (1971, 76). Of course, if the relative values of the two are fixed, then they are in effect transformed into only one commodity. Exactly the same holds in the world economy. When more than one currency functions as a form of wealth holding, this can only happen if their relative values are more or less fixed. This was the case under the gold standard and, barring exceptional situations where currencies were allowed to depreciate, under the Bretton Woods system as well (even though there were restrictions on capital flows). The normal state of affairs in the capitalist world, in other words, has always been an approximate fixity of the relative prices of the different leading currencies.[1]

In such a situation, how has the balance of payments equilibrium been established in individual capitalist economies? This problem, of reaching balance of payments equilibria in a regime of more or less fixed exchange rates, has not, however, been as serious as one might imagine for one very important reason, namely, that the leading currency country typically runs a current account deficit against the other capitalist countries, at least after a certain stage in its leadership career. In the beginning the leading country has a technological edge over the others. It not only outcompetes the others but also uses this fact to export capital to the others, thus giving rise to a process of diffusion of industrial capitalism. But after a certain stage, as its rivals come up, its current account surplus with them is transformed into a current account deficit.

The fact of the leading capitalist country running a current account deficit has been explained in a variety of ways. It is argued, for instance, that this is one way of meeting the demand, including for transaction purposes, for money as represented by the leading currency. Likewise, its running a current account deficit has been seen as a way of enabling its rivals to pay back the loans they had incurred earlier. But while such implications of the leading country's running a current account deficit are indisputable, they do not necessarily constitute the *reason* for running such a deficit. For instance, the money demand of the rest of the capitalist world could be met entirely through capital account transactions, without necessarily involving a current account deficit. Likewise, loan repayments to the leading country by those countries that had borrowed earlier can also take the form, from the leading country's point of view, of purely capital account transactions; they need not entail a current account deficit by the leading country. The causes for that deficit have to be located elsewhere.

For any given level of real aggregate demand in the capitalist world, there would be an amount of equivalent output (if we assume for simplicity that trade between the capitalist and precapitalist sectors is balanced). But the distribution of this demand across the different countries would be different from the distribution of output, which after all is the cause for current account deficits and surpluses across these countries. The distribution of output and hence the pattern of current deficits would depend, among other things, upon the relative money wage (say in terms of the leading currency) per efficiency unit of labor in the different capitalist countries.

Three things, in short, affect the pattern of current deficits: exchange rates (which are fixed), the vector of money wages (in local currency), and the vector of labor productivities. Now, newly industrializing economies, precisely because they do not have a large stock of inherited old equipment, possess on average a more up-to-date equipment stock compared to earlier industrialized economies. (This has been referred to as the "penalty of the early start" argument.) But the money wage differences between the two (at the prevailing exchange rates) are not usually all that pronounced. Hence the unit labor costs (expressed in the leading currency) are typically lower in the newly industrializing economies than in the earlier industrialized ones. This accounts for the current account deficit of the leading country. And since this difference has a material impact only after a certain amount of time has elapsed, this current account deficit comes into being only at a certain stage of the leading country's leadership career.

Since it is the leading country that typically runs a current account deficit, the fact of fixed exchange rates scarcely poses any serious problem as far as balance of payments adjustments are concerned: indeed the very need for such adjustments scarcely arises. The leading country which runs the deficit need not make any adjustments: its currency, being " as good as gold," will simply be held as an asset by the creditor economies (which at the most may wish to hold some currency-denominated assets rather than currency itself), unless its deficit becomes so large that it creates demand-pull inflationary pressures in the capitalist world economy (as happened during the Vietnam War; see Kaldor 1976). But as long as the system remains demand-constrained, sustaining the deficit poses no problem to the leading economy. As far as the rival capitalist economies are concerned, since, as a group, they run a surplus, there is no need for them to make any exchange rate adjustments. Particular countries among them may have current account deficits requiring some exchange rate adjustments, but this does not constitute a problem for the system as a whole.

The problem, as far as the entire monetary arrangement that characterizes the capitalist world economy is concerned, arises from an altogether different source. But before discussing that, let me clarify a point.

The Diffusion of Capitalist Development

We have so far considered the question of the sustainability of current account imbalances in a fixed-exchange-rate regime, such as is necessary if wealth is to be held in several currencies (or currency-denominated assets). We now turn to the role of such imbalances. By running a current account deficit, the leading country provides a market to the newly developing ones, which are emerging as its rivals. Its current account deficit, therefore, is a mechanism for the diffusion of capitalism from the leading country to a host of others. The leading country runs this deficit and thereby facilitates such diffusion, not out of any altruism, but because, by accommodating the ambitions of the newly industrializing countries, it stabilizes the capitalist world economic order under its own leadership. The fact that the deficit arises at all has to do with considerations relating to wages and productivity, mentioned earlier; but the fact that the leading country tolerates this deficit and allows it to persist has to do with its desire not to destabilize the system of which it is the leading economy.

Even Keynes missed this point. Discussing the peace-promoting potential of state intervention in demand management, he says (1949, 381–382), "War has several causes. Dictators and others such, to whom war offers, in expectation at least, a pleasurable excitement, find it easy to work on the natural bellicosity of their peoples. But, over and above this, facilitating their task of fanning the popular flame, are the economic causes of war, namely, the pressure of population and the competitive struggle for markets. It is the second factor, which probably played a predominant part in the nineteenth century, and might again, that is germane to this discussion ... under the system of domestic *laissez-faire* and an international gold standard such as was orthodox in the latter half of the nineteenth century, there was no means open to a government to mitigate economic distress at home except through the competitive struggle for markets."

Remarkably, however, it is precisely in the latter half of the nineteenth century that wars arising out of the competitive struggle for markets were conspicuous by their absence. The Crimean War and its sequel, the wars of German and Italian unification, can scarcely be attributed to the competitive struggle for markets. On the other hand, where competitive struggles for markets (or raw materials) were involved, the division was accomplished peacefully, such as the partition of Africa or of China. (The subjugation of the Philippines, though brutal, does not also fit into Keynes's pattern.) The point is that Pax Britannica was established when Britain already had an empire, and it was sustained because Britain kept its own markets open for other capitalist countries, while encroaching on the markets of its colonies.

The problem with the leading country running a persistent current account deficit vis-à-vis its rivals is not that it cannot finance it; we have just seen that it can. The problem is that ceteris paribus it progressively reduces the leading economy into a debtor economy, which eventually becomes too high a price to pay for its leadership. But this problem is overcome through imperialism. The leading economy which typically is the most powerful imperialist economy ensures that corresponding to its current account deficit against its rival capitalist economies, it manages to show an equal or even larger current account surplus with its colonies, whose current surplus to its rivals in turn, built up from primary commodity exports, is used to offset its own deficit. Thus the leading economy does not get into a debtor status because of its control over colonial markets and sources of revenue.

Let us consider an example. If the rival R has a current surplus of 100 with the leading economy L, and if the colony of the leading economy C has a current surplus of 100 with R, then all that L has to do is to arrange a current surplus of 100 with C. In this case, L would have kept its market open for R, thereby accommodating R's ambition and stabilizing the system under its own leadership, without getting into any debtor status.

Three points have to be borne in mind in this context. In the example, we have not incorporated any capital exports. If C has a current account surplus of 200 with R and if L manages to have a current account surplus of 200 with C, then L would actually be making capital exports worth 100 vis-à-vis R. Historically capital exports from the leading economy, Britain, to the tropical colonies was of a very limited magnitude, confined only to some investment in plantations, mining, and the like. Much of the capital exports went first to continental Europe, and later to the temperate regions of white settlement, in other words, to the group we have designated as R. And it follows that as long as the leading country can arrange to have an appropriate amount of current surplus vis-à-vis the colonies, it can not only balance its current account but also even make capital exports to the same group of countries with which it has a current account deficit.

Second, the phrase "arranging a current account surplus vis-à-vis the colonies," which I have repeatedly used, is an apt one. For the leading metropolitan economy, the colonial market is a wide open one where any amount of sales can be undertaken at the expense of the local precapitalist producers (causing deindustrialization). It is, in the words of British economic historian S. B. Saul (1970), "a market on tap."

But that is by no means all. We have so far been talking about sales being undertaken by the leading economy in the colonies. Suppose no sales are undertaken whatsoever but an amount of surplus value worth 200 is simply appropriated without any quid pro quo from the colonies. Formally, of course, it would appear as payments being made for the provision of administration by the leading country (though no one ever asked it to do so) or as gifts from C to L. Now, in this case again, capital exports worth 100 would have been made by L to R even though L has a current account deficit vis-à-vis R. True, in this case L would have had no means of offsetting the contractionary effects of its current deficit against R, but nothing prevents L from using its colonial market, which is on tap to sell 100 of its products in addition to the appropriation of 200 of surplus value. In this case, if C's current surplus with R increases by this 100, capital exports worth 200 would have been made by L to R, even while providing markets to R, sustaining the economic order, maintaining its own domestic aggregate demand, and avoiding debtor status. (True, surplus appropriation hurts the market, but if the colonial domain is large enough, both can be accomplished in desired magnitudes.)

Third, this kind of indirect balancing of accounts, at the expense of the third world, essentially tropical, colonies (as distinct from the temperate regions of white settlement, which may have been juridically classified as colonies), is precisely what is meant when referring to the "mediated" relation between the metropolis and the colonies. It is not the case that every metropolitan country has a direct relationship with some colonial possession of its own. Rather, the colonial relationship for most of them, including of those who have colonial possessions of their own, is largely mediated through the leading country. They become indirect beneficiaries of the colonial relationship of the leading country. If the leading country accesses markets in colonies while its own market is open to its rivals, if the leading country balances its accounts by making the colonies produce essential raw materials and sell these to its rivals, then these rivals also gain from the leading country's colonialism.

Colonialism, therefore, has complex ramifications. This is true even as regards its role. We had seen in chapter 17 that precapitalist markets, located essentially in the colonies, provided a stimulus for investment even when actual trade with this sector was balanced, a fact ignored by the critics of Luxemburg. But as the preceding discussion shows, quite apart from providing this stimulus, quite apart from preventing downturns from gathering momentum, and quite apart from housing labor reserves that effectively prevent accelerating inflation no matter what the level of activity, the precapitalist sector plays at least two additional roles: first, it yields surplus value to the capitalist sector, not just through such well-known processes as "unequal exchange" but also through the latter's exercise of direct administrative control. And second, trade with the precapitalist sector in colonial conditions makes possible the management of current balances within the metropolis. In the preceding example, where R does not want L's goods but does want C's goods, their current balances can still be settled by L selling to C and C selling to R. So, colonial trade makes it possible to change appropriately the form of goods: one set of metropolitan goods is transformed into another that is demanded within the metropolis itself.

This is why the state within the capitalist sector, even when it takes upon itself the role of demand management (as it did in the post–Second World War years) cannot be a substitute for the precapitalist sector. Contrary to what several authors like John Strachey (1959) had argued, namely that state intervention eliminated the need for imperialism, the complex ramifications of the relationship between the metropolis and the colonies, or between the capitalist and precapitalist sectors, cannot be replicated in the relationship between the capitalist sector and the state (which, as we will see, has been a major problem facing postwar capitalism).

What this means is important: Since the acceptance by the leading country of a current deficit against newly industrializing countries is predicated "normally" upon the leading country entering the "wide open markets" of its colonies and unleashing "deindustrialization" there, the diffusion of development toward some countries is associated with the retrogression of others. Under capitalism in other words the process of spread of "development" from its original core to some other countries is accompanied by "deindustrialization" and retrogression of still others. Diffusion cannot be a process that would gradually encompass all countries, since the condition for its encompassing some is that others retrogress.

Crises in the World Monetary System

It is only when the leading country is unable to sustain its current account deficits, and consequently the leading currency can no longer retain its position in the eyes of the wealth holders of being "as good as gold," that the international monetary system gets into crises. Under the gold standard, as we have seen, the role of Britain's colonial possessions, notable among them India, was crucial. They provided markets on tap for British goods such as textiles, which were not demanded in the advanced country markets; and surplus value was extracted from them through the use of the administrative apparatus (a process referred to in Indian nationalist writings as the "drain of wealth"), for capital exports to the temperate regions of white settlement such as the United States, Canada, Australia, New Zealand, and South Africa, which were the sites for diffusion of capitalist development (Bagchi 1972). It follows that the demand stimulus for the old capitalist core came, during the late nineteenth and early twentieth centuries, not so much from the tropical colonies as from the "expanding frontiers" of capitalism, as Keynes (1919) and Hansen (1938, 1941) have argued. These expanding frontiers, too, meant encroachments on the precapitalist setting, but of a different kind from those made on the tropical colonies. The role of the tropical colonies was to provide the wherewithal for capital exports (through the "drain") and to provide the commodity form in which such exports could be made. If this change of commodity form had not been possible, then not only would Britain not have been able to undertake the capital exports, but she would have also found it difficult to sustain her current account deficit vis-à-vis her rival capitalist countries, in which case the gold standard would have become unsustainable. The sustainability of the gold standard therefore owed much to the availability of Britain's colonial empire.

By the same token, in the post–First World War period, when there was massive Japanese encroachment upon Britain's colonial markets in Asia and Britain was forced to seek an alliance with the local colonial bourgeoisie by making some room for them through tariff protection, to ward off this Japanese challenge, these colonies could no longer play the same role as before (Patnaik 1997, 2006). The fact that the "return to gold" at par in 1925 could not be sustained was because of Britain's loss of control over Asian markets in the interim: the pound sterling appeared overvalued because the old mechanism for sustaining it in the face of current account deficits against her rivals could no longer work. Domestic wage deflation to shore up the pound sterling led to the general strike in 1926. Finally, the gold standard had to be abandoned in 1931.

The collapse of the Bretton Woods system likewise was linked to the unsustainability of the U.S. current account deficits. The United States did not have the advantage that Britain had, namely having an extensive colonial empire. But the United States had long run a trade surplus, which in the postwar period was accompanied by a current account deficit mainly because of her large expenditure on overseas military bases. But since the dollar under this system was statutorily "as good as gold" ($35 per ounce of gold), and since the U.S. military expenditure was seen as protecting the capitalist world as a whole against the threat of Communism, other countries were more or less obliged to hold on to the dollars pouring out of the United States. But its current account deficit widened during the Vietnam War, which not only enlarged the inflow of dollars into the rest of the world, which the latter had to hold, but also created excess demand pressures that made the holding of such dollars relatively unattractive at the same time. The U.S. current deficit could no longer be sustained, and the Bretton Woods system collapsed. The fact that President de Gaulle of France took the lead in refusing to hold dollars has misled many into attributing the collapse to his intransigence. The real underlying problem was the unsustainable U.S. current account deficit.

The Oil-Dollar Standard

It may appear at first sight that the capitalist world economy in the post–Bretton Woods era has at long last done away with commodity money, and with fixed exchange rates. Appearances, however, are deceptive. It is no doubt true that no currency in the present system is linked to gold. But there *is* a leading currency, the U.S. dollar, which in the minds of wealth holders all over the capitalist world still constitutes a stable medium for holding wealth. Indeed, the system simply cannot function without such a medium in whose stability there is pervasive confidence. This was amply demonstrated during the crisis years of the Bretton Woods system (marked by Nixon's delinking the dollar from gold), when there was a rush to commodities resulting in an explosion in their prices. The fact that the dollar still constitutes the leading currency presupposes that there is confidence in the stability of its value relative to commodities. In the present context, when international mobility of finance has undermined Keynesian demand management, and hence the levels of unemployment are in general higher than before (and the strength of trade unions much lower than before), the possibility of a threat to the value of the dollar through an autonomous increase in the dollar price of labor power in the leading country is remote.

As regards the primary commodities, again in the period since the mid-1970s, marked by the absence of demand management, and by expenditure deflation by states in conformity with the predilections of globalized finance capital, nonoil commodity prices have on average, through fluctuations, fallen in absolute terms in many instances, and certainly with respect to any index of manufacturing price. The prospects of an increase in these prices to an extent that threatens the position of the dollar as the wealth-holding medium appear remote. Besides, the weight of these commodities in the gross value of output in the advanced capitalist world is so small (through the systematic manipulation of the terms of trade against them over the years), that the cost-push effects of such commodity prices are also negligible.

That leaves oil, a primary commodity of critical importance both for production and for consumption in the metropolitan capitalist economies, and one whose price is fixed by a powerful cartel. The threat to the position of the dollar, or indeed to that of any leading currency in today's world, arises from the possibility of an increase in oil prices. It may be thought that if oil prices increased in terms of all major currencies, then there should be no specific threat to the dollar: true, wealth holders may wish to move from currencies and currency-denominated assets to oil, but since they cannot possibly gain access to oil in requisite quantities as a wealth-holding medium, no threat arises to the dollar as such. This view, however, is erroneous. The point is not whether wealth holders gain access to oil in requisite quantities; the point is what their effort to move into oil does to oil prices and hence to the entire price system in the capitalist world, and what this in turn implies for the role of money as a wealth-holding medium. There can be little doubt that the instability generated by a possible move from dollars to oil will be vastly destabilizing for the capitalist world as a whole.

There is an argument that states that it is not the price of oil that is crucial, but whether the oil producers hold their wealth in dollars or not. It is certainly true that if ceteris paribus oil producers move out of dollars to some other currency, then the position of the dollar will be jeopardized. It is also true that if with a rise in the price of oil the oil producers who are beneficiaries of such an increase decide to hold their wealth in the form of dollars, then this fact will help in restraining any possible destabilizing effect of the oil price rise on the role of the dollar. But *how* the oil producers hold their wealth is an additional factor over and above *what* happens to oil prices. The importance of the former does not negate that of the latter.

It follows that the post–Bretton Woods system is a dollar standard whose viability is based on the stability of the price of oil in terms of dollar. Stability of course does not necessarily mean absolute stability. A rise in the price of oil that does not have a significant or persistent effect on the domestic inflation rate in the leading country and leaves inflationary expectations unchanged is unlikely to undermine confidence in the dollar, but this will be the case only if the price rise is supposed to be either temporary or once-for-all, not if it is persistent. It follows that the present currency arrangement hinges crucially on the stability of the price of the dollar in terms of oil, in the sense at least of the absence of persistent declines in it, which is why it can be called the oil-dollar standard. No matter what the de jure situation, the world has not moved away from commodity money.

Likewise, insofar as the dollar is not the exclusive medium for wealth holding and wealth is also held in other currencies, it must be the case that, notwithstanding short-term fluctuations, the general expectation must be that these currencies will not depreciate against the dollar over a certain time horizon. The dollar, too, must not be expected to depreciate against these currencies over this horizon, for, if it did, it would not be the leading currency. In short, notwithstanding short-term fluctuations in currency values, the medium- to long-term expectation must be that the relative exchange rates between currencies that continue to provide the medium for wealth holding would remain more or less unchanged. That is, even though the capitalist world is on a regime of floating exchange rates, the expectation among wealth holders must be no different from what would be the case if it was on a fixed-exchange-rate regime.

To generate such expectations the nonleading countries must be pursuing deliberate policies to boost "investor confidence" in their currencies, such as expenditure deflation by the government and relatively more attractive interest rates. The leading currency in short is ipso facto worthy for wealth holding; the nonleading currencies, in which much wealth is nonetheless held, have to be made worthy through specific finance-friendly policies. This distinction between the leading and nonleading currencies is clear from a comparison of the dollar with the euro. The euro is a rival of the dollar and appears strong, sometimes even stronger than the dollar, and it certainly constitutes a medium of wealth holding. But to keep the euro that way, the European countries have to curtail fiscal deficits while the United States runs huge deficits, and they have to put up with much higher levels of unemployment than does the United States. While they may enjoy a current account surplus vis-à-vis the United States, they still do not feel emboldened to pursue expansionary fiscal policies to bring down their high unemployment rates.

There are some currencies, especially third-world currencies, in whose case no amount of finance-friendly policies would induce wealth holders to consider them as worthy instruments of wealth holding. This very gloomy expectation about their future value becomes self-fulfilling. Since they are not considered worthy, the tendency, again over a period of time, is for wealth to move out of such currencies. This tends to depreciate the currencies and hence strengthen further the gloomy expectations about their future value. Such economies should have capital controls and not allow free inflow and outflow of finance (Patnaik 2002). If they do allow such free flows, then the secular tendency is for their currency values to depreciate faster against the leading currency than what would be warranted by the differential inflation rates between the countries in question and the United States.

We can therefore think of a hierarchy of currencies in the world economy. At the top is the leading currency, the dollar. Below it there are a host of currencies that also constitute wealth-holding instruments, but in their case, unlike in the case of the leading currency, keeping them "worthy" requires an effort, in the form of contractionary policies for the economy. Finally, there are the third-world currencies that are doomed to secular real depreciation, and from whose economies wealth is bound to drift away; their only hope lies in imposing capital controls.[2]

One implication of the secular real depreciation of these currencies is that the commodities they produce witness a secular decline in their terms of trade, for reasons having nothing to do with the real economy but arising solely from the behavior of finance capital.

Concluding Observations

The current international monetary system, notwithstanding its apparent novelty compared to what has prevailed in the past, shares de facto the same general features as the earlier systems. We have examined it until now, however, as a coherent entity, and hence as a frozen entity. But is this entity losing its coherence? The recent decline in the value of the dollar, both in relation to oil and to other currencies, notably the euro, gives the impression that the oil-dollar standard is on its way out. Paradoxically, this decline of the oil-dollar standard has come in the wake of efforts that were meant to achieve the exact opposite, namely a strengthening of it by capturing the oil reserves of Iraq for the leading capitalist power; but the Iraq invasion did not turn out as planned. Even so, the United States remains the most powerful capitalist economy in the world, and the hegemonic capitalist power in terms of military might. A displacement of the dollar from its dominant role in the international monetary system is by no means imminent. Moreover, the United States itself may not be averse to a decline in the value of the dollar relative to other currencies to improve its competitiveness, followed by a new period of stability and dollar hegemony. Hence, while a question mark does remain over the immediate future of the oil-dollar standard, it is premature to write obituaries to it. But the real issue relates to something else, not the immediate prospects of the oil-dollar standard, but the political consequences of the attempt on the part of the United States to defend it.

20

Capitalism and Imperialism

OUR INQUIRY INTO THE VALUE of money has brought us a long way. A recapitulation of some of the important signposts along this journey may be useful here. The standard explanation of the value of money, which has a long lineage going back at least to David Hume but in its modern form is rooted in the concept of a Walrasian equilibrium, is in terms of demand and supply. This "monetarist" explanation states that the excess demand for money is a function, representable by a downward-sloping curve, of the value of money relative to the world of nonmoney commodities; the equilibrium value of money is where its excess demand is zero. This explanation, however, is logically flawed: since money is a form in which wealth is held, the demand for it must depend upon expectations about the future, and the stability of any equilibrium based on demand and supply requires inelastic price expectations; but price expectations can be inelastic only if some prices are sticky, which violates Walrasian premises.

The alternative explanation of the value of money, which we have called propertyist, starts from sticky prices and is logically superior: it sees the value of money as being given from outside the realm of demand and supply. In Marx it is given by the relative quantities of labor directly and indirectly embodied in a unit of money and a basket of nonmoney commodities; in Keynes it is given by the fixity of the money wage rate in any period. Such outside determination of the value of money necessarily entails the possibility of *ex ante* generalized overproduction (or "involuntary unemployment," in Keynesian language); more generally, it entails that the system is demand-constrained.

Notwithstanding its profound insights, propertyism does not go far enough. While it recognizes capitalism as a demand-constrained system, its conceptual universe is confined to a self-contained capitalist system. Now, if a system is demand-constrained and self-contained at the same time, it would not be viable. Propertyism as it stands cannot explain the viability of the capitalist system, the fact that it functions, apparently quite coherently, for long stretches of time at its metropolitan core. The system needs a minimum rate of profit for its viability, and hence a minimum level of activity. If the actual activity level falls below this, then it ceases to be viable; on the other hand, if the level of activity crosses a threshold, then it is afflicted by accelerating inflation and a collapse of the value of money. There is absolutely no reason why a spontaneous, self-contained, demand-constrained system should stay within these limits, which is why the propertyist position as of now is incomplete.

It can be completed only if we see capitalism as ensconced within a precapitalist setting, whose production and trade pattern it bends to suit its own requirements, from which it derives the stimulus for investment, and whose conversion into a repository of substantial labor reserves (created through the deindustrialization it unleashes there) prevents any accelerating inflation in the capitalist sector, no matter what the level of activity. It follows that interaction with the precapitalist sector is what keeps the capitalist sector viable, always experiencing a level of activity that ensures the minimum rate of profit without engendering accelerating inflation. The propertyist theoretical structure becomes complete once we introduce into it at a conceptual level the phenomenon that has been an actual part of history, namely the capitalist sector's existence within, encroachments upon, and interactions with, the precapitalist sector. And this phenomenon has been associated with imperialism. Lenin reserved the term *imperialism* to refer to the monopoly phase of capitalism, but we use it in a more inclusive sense to refer to the whole ensemble of relationships, within capitalist countries and with countries located in the precapitalist sector, that has always been associated with capitalism, and of which the relationships in the monopoly phase are one particular manifestation. Capitalism can never exist without imperialism in this inclusive sense. It is quintessentially a mode of production that is not self-contained. This does not nullify Marx's analysis about capitalism as a mode of production; it only suggests that the validity of that analysis arises inter alia from the fact that capitalism exists within a precapitalist setting.

A Comparison with Rosa Luxemburg's Theory of Imperialism

Rosa Luxemburg was certainly the first author to have argued that continuous encroachment on the precapitalist sector was *essential* for the dynamics of capitalism. Even though Marx wrote more than almost anyone else located in the metropolis on the exploitation of the colonies under capitalism, this sensitivity did not get reflected in the core of his theoretical analysis, which took a self-contained capitalist economy, consisting only of capitalists and workers, and divisible only into departments of production, as its point of departure (Patnaik 2006).

Indeed, one can go further. To date, Rosa Luxemburg is perhaps the only author of note to have argued the theoretical necessity of the precapitalist sector for capitalist dynamics. A large number of Marxist and third-world nationalist writers have under-scored the historical fact of colonial exploitation. Many, including early undercon-sumptionists like Fritz Sternberg, have argued the contingent necessity of colonial markets (though this is not true of later underconsumptionists such as Baran and Sweezy), but this "contingent necessity" must be distinguished from theoretical necessity: the latter suggests that the isolated capitalist system is incomplete per se, that colonial markets, and imperialism in general, are necessary not as an antidote to a tendency toward underconsumption but for the very operation of the law of motion of capitalism. Exactly the same can be said for the other strand of argument about the necessity of imperialism, namely the one that sees it as an antidote to a falling ten-dency of the rate of profit. Leaving aside the issue of whether such a tendency actually exists or not (see Patnaik 1997 on this), this argument, too, proposes the "contingent necessity" of imperialism, that imperialism is a possible antidote (one among many) to some tendency of capitalism. Rosa Luxemburg, by contrast, talked of the theo-retical impossibility of capitalism existing in isolation. This book follows Luxemburg in arguing the same basic case.

It is particularly necessary therefore that the difference between the present argu-ment and that of Luxemburg should be clarified. Let us begin by recapitulating the basic problems with her argument. There are three such problems: first, she consid-ers it essential that the entire unconsumed surplus value of the capitalist sector must be realized through sales to the precapitalist sector and converted into material ele-ments of additional constant and variable capital obtained from this latter sector. This is unnecessary. If the precapitalist sector is to provide the stimulus for investment, then it is not necessary that the whole of the material elements of investment should be procured from there. Indeed it can provide this stimulus simply by being available, by being "on tap," even when no sales actually occur in this sector (though occasion-ally when the system experiences a downturn the "market on tap" may be used for stimulating a new boom). And if the precapitalist sector is used for changing the mate-rial form of commodities in order to remove mismatches between what is demanded and what is supplied in the capitalist sector, then there is no reason why the amount sold to the precapitalist sector should equal the unconsumed surplus value; it could be more or less. Thus whichever way we look at the matter, her proposition of the entire unconsumed surplus value being realized through sales to the precapitalist sector makes little sense.

The second problem with her argument arises from her view that the capitalist sector's encroachment on the precapitalist sector takes the form of an assimilation of the latter. The fact that this encroachment may take the form of leaving behind a vast pauperized mass of precapitalist producers, continuing to linger on in a subjugated precapitalist sector, though fleetingly acknowledged by her, is not her central vision. This, however, is what happened in history. It was reflected, as is well known, in the thesis of the Sixth Congress of the Comintern that in the third world there was pau-perization of the peasantry, but not proletarianization.

The third problem is her theory of collapse. If encroachment by the capitalist sector takes the form of assimilation, so that the precapitalist sector gradually ceases to exist, then a time would inevitably come when the world would be a single self-contained capitalist economy exactly the way Marx had visualized in his analysis. And since encroachment on the precapitalist sector is essential for capitalist dynamics, there can be no such dynamics when there is no more precapitalist sector. The system would collapse, even though Luxemburg was quick to add that long before this limit point was reached, it would have been overthrown.

While there were important political reasons for her advancing a theory of collapse, having to do with the inner-party struggle within the German Social Democratic Party between the "revolutionary" and the "revisionist" wings, it is methodologically unacceptable. It invokes a mechanical notion of inevitability that is foreign to a scientific inquiry. Lenin (1975) had expressed himself against any such mechanical notion of inevitability: "There is no such thing as an absolutely impossible situation for capitalism." Much the same idea was expressed by Althusser (2003) when he said, "Socialism is necessary but not inevitable." A theory of collapse, like a machine grinding to a halt, constitutes an inapt analogy for a mode of production.

But there is an internal unity in Luxemburg's vision of capitalist dynamics, of which a collapse constitutes the logical denouement. It is not enough to believe in the other parts of Luxemburg's theory but to reject the notion of a collapse. One has to replace the totality of her theory by an alternative totality, even while appreciating her prescience in recognizing the centrality of interactions with the precapitalist sector for capitalist dynamics. The argument of this book, while generally following the direction charted by Luxemburg, differs from her on all the three critical issues, namely, the role, the implications, and the denouement of the interactions with the precapitalist sector.

Historically, a very important contribution of the colonies to the rise of capitalism was the drain of surplus from them to the metropolis, which Marx himself had recognized and written about. But we will deliberately abstract from this, since our concern is with the theoretical essentiality of the precapitalist sector. This essentiality arises because the precapitalist sector provides a reserve market for capitalism and the reserve army of labor that underlies the stability in the value of money. The existence of this reserve market provides the stimulus for investment; it also makes possible the requisite change in the material form of commodities that is necessary for avoiding demand-supply mismatches within capitalism and hence for keeping the boom going. Market signals are not enough to avoid such mismatches, as the Walrasians believe, since many of these commodities are simply not producible within the capitalist core.

Likewise, the precapitalist-sector reserve army plays a very different sui generis role that the internal reserve army within the capitalist sector cannot. If the prospect of nonaccelerating inflation is to be kept at bay without restricting the level of activity, then it must be that a group of producers or workers should exist who act as price takers (Patnaik 1997). This presupposes a hiatus within the workers serving the needs of capitalism. If one group is to act as price taker while another does not, then labor mobility must be restricted across the two groups. And this is ensured if one group is located within the precapitalist sector, thus being geographically and sociologically distant from the other. It follows then that corresponding to the two groups of workers there must be two distinct reserve armies, one located internally and the other located within the precapitalist sector forcing that sector to act as a shock-absorber for the capitalist system.

The implications of such interaction too are different from what Luxemburg had suggested. Since the existence of such a reserve army, which makes the workers of this sector act as price takers, willing to accept the "leavings" of the capitalist sector in lieu of what they provide to that sector, is essential for the survival of capitalism, the question of the precapitalist sector progressively disappearing through assimilation into the capitalist sector simply does not arise. Indeed, such assimilation would negate the very usefulness of the precapitalist sector. Hence the interaction is such as to ensure the persistence of a degraded precapitalist sector with a vast pauperized mass located within it, of which an active part produces raw materials or low-value-added activities for the capitalist sector. The implications of the interaction are not in the direction of making the world fully capitalist; rather they serve to reproduce the dichotomy between the capitalist sector and the degraded precapitalist sector (different from its pristine form).

On the question of denouement, it is clear that there is no question of a "collapse" of the system because of the disappearance of the precapitalist sector. But there is a sense in which the precapitalist sector ceases to play its role effectively over time. This is not because it is assimilated but precisely because it is degraded as it lingers on. There are at least three ways in which the capitalist system, propped up with the support of the surrounding precapitalist sector, finds these props inadequate as time passes. These three ways, in fact, constitute the three problems faced by capitalism today.

The Stimulus of Precapitalist Markets

Precapitalist markets, even when their quantitative significance from the point of view of the capitalist sector is limited over any period of time, provide nonetheless a stimulus for investment because they constitute reserve markets. Even if capitalists are not directly conscious of these reserve markets, their availability truncates downturns and revives the economy much sooner than would have been the case otherwise; and this very fact keeps up the tempo of investment. But to play this role effectively, the precapitalist markets must have a certain minimum size relative to the capitalist sector; and the very history of encroachment upon such markets and the degradation inflicted on those economies erode the size and significance of precapitalist markets.

Their capacity to provide any stimulus for investment within capitalism therefore dwindles over time

This in itself should not matter much, since, in the postwar years at any rate, state intervention in demand management emerged as a significant phenomenon in capitalist countries; and with such management the need for any external stimulus disappears. True, state intervention for stimulating demand is not as advantageous for capitalism as precapitalist markets. Since the latter simultaneously releases inputs used up earlier in precapitalist production, it is doubly advantageous for capitalism. But leaving this aspect out, purely from the point of view demand stimulation, state intervention would do as well. John Strachey's position that with the advent of state intervention capitalism's need for an empire had become obsolete should scarcely come as a surprise.

But the postwar years of state intervention were only a passing phase for capitalism. Such intervention became possible only under the twin pressure of the socialist threat and domestic working class resistance to any return to the old ways (which had witnessed the Great Depression) in the aftermath of the war. As the immediacy of these threats receded, as inflation began to reemerge on the scene as a sequel to prolonged near-full employment, and as a new kind of finance capital, which was international in nature, emerged as a major feature of capitalism, especially with the removal of restrictions on cross-border financial flows that had characterized the Bretton Woods system, capitalist states started withdrawing from the ambitious project of demand management. Finance capital is always hostile to state activism in matters of employment and level of activity; indeed, it is hostile to any state activism except in defense of its own interests. And when finance is "globalized," while the state is a nation-state, this hostility acquires a spontaneous effectiveness. Finance capital, including what originates in the country in question, simply leaves the country if its caprices are not respected. And the effectiveness of this opposition undermined Keynesian demand management, except in one country, the United States.

Precisely because the U.S. dollar is the leading currency, considered by wealth holders all over the capitalist world to be "as good as gold," the need for the United States to bow to the caprices of finance capital does not arise. In the event of its not doing so, there is nowhere that the wealth holders can shift their wealth to, since no other currency enjoys the same status. Even if some wealth holders do shift their wealth, they would not be followed by others, so that the question of the dollar sliding because of state intervention in demand does not arise. This is why the United States alone of all the capitalist states can afford to run a large fiscal deficit as it has been doing of late, while all others have even found it prudent to tie their own hands by having statutory ceilings on the ratio of fiscal deficit to GDP. So, while state intervention in demand management is generally in retreat, the United States can afford to be an exception to this rule. But the United States is also a nation-state. It cannot become a surrogate global state and pursue demand management for world capitalism as a whole. It follows then that taking the world capitalist economy as a whole, the days of Keynesian demand management to achieve near-full employment are over.

Since no more "open frontiers" exist to which migration can occur from the capitalist core, since the significance of precapitalist markets has dwindled owing to the continuous degradation of this sector, and since state intervention, except by the United States over a limited domain, is undermined because of the ascendancy of international finance capital, capitalism in the contemporary epoch exhibits a general tendency toward a slowdown. The stimuli that existed in an earlier period are no longer available to it.

The Problem of Current Balances

Imperialism's opening up of the precapitalist markets of the colonies served not only as a stimulus for investment in the capitalist sector; even more important, it resolved the problem of current balances. This problem has received little theoretical attention till date, since the focus has always been on the problems of investment stimulus, of underconsumption and of disproportionality (where there is a mismatch between the pattern of supply coming from the two great departments and the pattern of demand). Indeed the disproportionality problem is often seen as the central theme of Rosa Luxemburg's theory (though, in our view, while all three themes—disproportionality, underconsumption, and investment stimulus—figure in her work, centrality must be accorded to the problem of investment stimulus). The current balance problem, as already discussed, arises from the fact that the leading country has to run a persistent current deficit vis-à-vis its rivals from a certain point in its leadership career to preserve the international arrangement of which it is the leader; but if it is progressively indebted in the process, then its leadership position is threatened. The solution to this problem is found through colonial markets.

During the late nineteenth and early twentieth centuries, Britain, the leading capitalist country of the time, which presided over the gold standard, ran a persistent current account deficit against its rivals of the time (taken together), but "engineered" for itself a current account surplus with the colonies, and used the current account surplus which the colonies had in turn with its rivals, not only to settle its deficit but to make substantial capital exports. India, as already mentioned, played a key role in this, and Britain's current account surplus vis-à-vis India was "engineered" not only through the exports to its "wide open" market of British goods not wanted in the metropolitan countries, but also through the politically imposed "drain" of Indian surplus to Britain.

I mentioned earlier that the investment stimulus provided by the precapitalist market was superior, for capitalism, to that provided by the capitalist state, since it released inputs at the same time. There is a second reason for this superiority arising from this problem of current balances. In the face of a current account deficit, the level of activity in the leading country can be maintained through an appropriate fiscal deficit, but this still does not negate its growing net indebtedness. This growing net indebtedness can be offset only through a current surplus by the leading country with some third country, which *ex hypothesi* can only be the precapitalist sector. Putting it differently, this current balance-offsetting role of the precapitalist market is perhaps even more crucial than its investment-stimulating role, since in the latter role there are alternatives to the precapitalist sector but not in the former.

But as the size of the precapitalist sector vis-à-vis the capitalist sector declines, and with it the potential significance of this sector in playing either of these roles, then, even if the capitalist state can provide the necessary investment stimulus, the current balance problem remains unresolved.

This is precisely what we find today. The United States as the leading capitalist country has a current account deficit with respect to rival capitalist countries and the newly industrializing countries (taken together). As far as the potentially contractionary effect of the current deficit on its domestic level of activity is concerned, this can be taken care of, and has been, through an appropriate fiscal deficit, which, the United States, as the leading capitalist country with a currency "as good as gold," can afford to run. But this still does not prevent its growing net indebtedness. Such indebtedness not only poses a threat to the dollar, but is also not to its liking as a *nation*, since its creditors may at some point insist on converting their financial claims into other forms of assets, such as land or real capital, causing a "denationalization" of its real assets.

At the same time there are very few policy options before the United States for eliminating this deficit. Protectionism on its part would dismantle the international trade arrangement over which it presides. A permanent depreciation of the dollar, achievable only through common agreement among the major capitalist countries, would entail significant capital losses for wealth holders everywhere and undermine future confidence in the dollar as a form of wealth holding (though the United States, as mentioned earlier, may not be averse to it as a measure of last resort). Expansion of rival economies, since the chief means of achieving it would be through an enlarged fiscal deficit, would face opposition from international finance capital. Global Keynesian solutions, which entail that rival capitalist countries, instead of running a current account surplus with the United States, do so with the poor economies of the third world and finance it through grants, require a degree of "altruism" that is absent under capitalism. As a result, the United States is currently engaged in pressurizing, not its major capitalist rivals, but the newly industrializing countries of Asia, to appreciate their currencies. This is a typical "beggar-my-neighbor" policy that would thwart whatever diffusion of industrial activities is occurring from the capitalist core to the newly industrializing countries of the third world.

In a sense, this is an attempt to recreate what had come to pass under the old colonialism, namely alleviating the current balance problem of the leading capitalist country through creating unemployment in economies amenable to control and manipulation. But there are two obvious problems with this strategy. First, in the absence of direct colonial rule, such control and manipulation are not easy to effect. Second, even if this part of the U.S. current deficit is eliminated, the deficit vis-à-vis its rival capitalist powers would still remain with all the potentially adverse consequences mentioned above (unless the appreciation of Asian currencies is so high as to cause a large U.S. current surplus with them, which is impossible without direct colonization). Thus the absence of colonial markets "on tap," both because direct colonization in today's world is no longer tenable, and because the precapitalist sector is already so degraded that its market can scarcely play any significant role in this sense (no matter how attractive these small markets may be per se), entails a serious problem for capitalism.

The Sustenance of the Oil-Dollar Standard

I argued in chapter 19 that the post–Bretton Woods system can be characterized as an oil-dollar standard, and that contrary to common belief the world capitalist economy had not moved away from commodity money. The viability of the dollar as the leading currency arises not so much from its use in international transactions (including oil transactions), or even from the fact that oil producers hold their wealth largely in dollars or dollar-denominated assets (though this fact does help in sustaining the dollar); it arises above all from the expectation that the price of oil in terms of dollars is unlikely to undergo any major secular change. And this expectation in turn is based on the belief that, as the most powerful capitalist power with a global reach, the United States would not allow a secular increase in the dollar price of oil. Of course, even if oil prices increased but the prices of other primary commodities could be pushed down appropriately to counterbalance the effect of this, then the importance of oil per se would be greatly diminished, but the significance of the other primary commodities in the value of goods produced (or consumed) in the advanced capitalist world is already so low (thanks to the long history of adverse terms of trade for these commodities) that any inflationary pressures arising from increased oil prices pose a threat to world money that cannot be offset by reductions in other primary commodity prices. This is why oil is so important.

Controlling the dollar price of oil is easily accomplished if the United States controls the bulk of the world's oil reserves. It is immanent in the oil-dollar standard that it should attempt to do so, through diplomatic manipulations if possible, but force if necessary. The fact that at this moment there is an enormous effort on the part of the capitalist world, especially the United States, to control the world's oil reserves, can scarcely be doubted. Indeed much of contemporary world affairs, including the war in Iraq, can be explained in terms of this quest for oil, and its substitute, natural gas. Much has been written on the thesis that the primary motive for the war in Iraq is the desire to control the enormous oil reserves of Iraq, and it need not be repeated here. The point of departure of the present work is to argue that this desire for control is not just because oil is a commodity of outstanding importance in the lives of the people in the advanced countries; it is also closely linked to the monetary stability of the capitalist world.

But this quest for control is fraught with contradictions whose roots again lie in the fact that the world has gone beyond the days of colonial rule. The case of Iraq illustrates this. The occupation of Iraq was prompted largely by the desire to control its enormous oil reserves, which would have permitted the United States to keep oil prices in check and removed all doubts about the stability of the dollar, which has been under some cloud owing to the massive U.S. current account deficits. But the very resistance encountered in Iraq has been responsible inter alia for a stiff rise in the price of oil, which, even though it may not threaten the dollar immediately (since it is expected not to persist), does pose a serious potential threat. And if the United States, in order to shore up the fortunes of the dollar, invades oil-rich Iran, it is likely to find that this decision, too, would backfire. In short, the leading capitalist country appears to be getting caught in a peculiar dialectic: every effort on its part to remove threats from the dollar potentially worsens the situation for it and gives rise to further efforts to ensure its stability with similar damaging consequences. The basic reason for this lies in the fact that U.S. efforts to acquire colonial-style control over oil-rich economies face stiff resistance in a world that no longer resembles the pre–First World War universe, and where third-world nationalism, having achieved political decolonization, is not going to succumb so easily to a recolonization drive. All this poses a serious threat to the sustenance of the oil-dollar standard.

The Assault on Petty Production

The encroachment by capitalism upon the precapitalist sector constitutes an assault on petty production. The deindustrialization and unemployment that the penetration of capitalist products into the precapitalist market engenders; the "drain" of surplus from the precapitalist sector, financed by taxation of the peasantry under a regime of political control; the imposition of a pattern of division of labor where the precapitalist sector is made to produce primary commodities whose terms of trade have a secular tendency to decline; these are all mechanisms for degrading the position of petty producers. But this process is carried several steps forward in the era of late capitalism. One obvious element here is the exhaustion of available land. As "open frontiers" become closed, expropriation of settled peasants becomes the chief mechanism for obtaining land for various uses under capitalism, including for setting up large luxury estates for the financial class that Hobson and Lenin had talked about. Such expropriation no doubt characterizes the entire history of capitalism: the so-called open frontier, after all, meant the expropriation of American Indian tribes. But in the earlier period when the density of population on land was relatively lower, the magnitude of displacement was correspondingly smaller compared to what occurs in late capitalism.

The second complementary mechanism is through a carrying forward of the terms of trade decline for primary producers. Abstracting from cyclical fluctuations, there

can be three possible reasons for a decline in the terms of trade for primary producers. The first is when for any given level of (average) activity maintained over time in
the capitalist sector, there is a rise, as far as this sector's products are concerned, in the
magnitude of markup, or in indirect taxation by the state, or in wage claims relative to
labor productivity. The second is associated with a change in the average level of activity in the capitalist sector itself. And the third is when there is a secular depreciation
of the real exchange rate of the primary producing countries caused independently by
capital account transactions, notably a secular transfer of wealth out of the backward
economy in a situation where financial liberalization has made such transfers possible.
These cases are examined through a model of price formation in the appendix to this
chapter. The interesting proposition that emerges from that discussion is that if we
start from a state where a certain level of activity with a steady rate of inflation associated with it has got established, then a change in activity level in either direction
worsens the terms of trade for primary producers.

We saw earlier that the rise to prominence of international finance capital has
resulted inter alia in a slowing down of the growth rate of the capitalist world and in
a lower average level of activity. This has been associated with a rise in the share of
surplus in output, together with a reduction in the share of wages and a worsening of
the terms of trade for primary producers. Indeed the decline in the terms of trade is a
result of the lower level of activity consequent upon the pursuit of state expenditure
deflation in order to cater to the caprices of globalized finance. While the advanced
capitalist countries have protected their own minuscule remaining peasantry through
massive subsidies, the peasantry in the periphery has suffered enormously, an indi-
cation of which is the suicide of thousands of peasants in India. In short, the period
of late capitalism, associated with the rise to dominance of globalized finance, has
dealt crushing blows to the peasants and petty producers in general and in the process
undermined its own social stability.

Concluding Observations

While Rosa Luxemburg might not have been correct in predicting a collapse of capitalism, she was again remarkably prescient in her surmise that the continued degradation of the precapitalist reserves upon which capitalism subsists would engulf capitalism in intensifying problems. Its attempts to overcome these through coercion
would bring forth increasing resistance, which the assault on petty production would
further add to. But unless the different strands of this resistance are combined and
channeled toward transcending capitalism and building a humane society, it may take
all kinds of destructive forms, such as terrorism, religious fundamentalism, and reactionary utopianism. Such a humane society would necessarily be a socialist society, but
one where, unlike in the case of the socialism that appeared in the first round on the
world stage, the people would not be depoliticized under a dictatorship of the party,

but would take charge of their own destiny within a democracy, that is very different from bourgeois democracy, where they enjoy the maximum freedom of direct intervention. The praxis for building such a society is not a matter of choice; it is a matter of necessity. Resistance to capitalist aggrandizement is bound to occur and is occurring anyway. The point is what form it takes: the fruitless, unproductive, paralyzing form of religious fundamentalism and terrorism that promises permanent pain, or the productive form of bringing mankind together in a new and humane order. The more clearly and quickly we see that the real choice is confined to these two options, that lingering capitalism increasingly submerges mankind only in brutality and unfreedom, the more we can abbreviate the period of painful and fruitless terrorism. Not long ago there was talk of capitalism being the "end of history." If this was so, then the history with which it ends is a negation of humanity. Humankind's quest for freedom would surely put an end to such reactionary daydreaming just as surely as it transcends the reactionary resistance to it.

Appendix: Factors Underlying Secular Movements in the Terms of Trade

The purpose of this appendix is to show how the three factors mentioned in the text as affecting secular changes in the terms of trade might operate. Let v denote the level of capacity utilization in the capitalist sector, an index of the magnitude of aggregate demand relative to full capacity output. The price in the manufacturing sector is determined as follows:

$$p(t) = \text{Max}\left[p(t-1) \cdot (1 + m\,(t-1)); \{a \cdot w'\,(v(t)) \cdot p(t-1) + w''(v(t)) \cdot 1 \cdot p(t-1)\,(1 + m(t-1))\}(1 + \pi\,(v(t)))\right] \ldots \qquad \text{(i)}$$

This can be interpreted as follows. The price of the capitalist sector's product in the current period is the higher of the two magnitudes: one, the previous period's price projected into the current period at the rate of inflation experienced from time zero until the previous period, which is $m(t-1))$; two, the markup over current unit prime cost by a factor π, which itself is an increasing function of v. The unit prime cost in turn consists of two elements: one is the unit labor cost, which is a product of the labor coefficient l, and the money wage rate, which is given by multiplying the real wage claim of the workers, w'' (an increasing function of v), with the expected price, which is a projection into the current period of the previous period's price at the inflation rate experienced from time zero until the previous period, that is, $m(t-1)$. The other element of unit prime cost is the imported raw material cost, which is arrived at by multiplying a, the physical amount of raw materials per unit output, w', the per capita real income claim (which is an increasing function of v) of raw material producers on the capitalist sector's product, and $p(t-1)$. There is no expected inflation term in the raw-material producers' claim, since their weak bargaining strength prevents this. (This is a way of incorporating the "price taker" assumption).

The story can be told as follows. In any period, pricing is based on a markup principle for high levels of capacity utilization. But at lower levels of capacity utilization, the markup principle is replaced by a ratchet effect on price (more precisely, a ratchet effect on the rate of inflation). When the markup principle holds, (i) can be expressed as

$$r(t) = [\{a \cdot w'(v) + l \cdot w''(v)\}(1 + \pi(v)) - 1] + l \cdot w''(v) \cdot m(t-1)$$
$$\cdot (1 + \pi(v)) \ldots \tag{ii}$$

which, for given v, makes the current rate of inflation, $r(t)$, a linear function of the rate of inflation from time zero until the previous period, $m(t-1)$. Obviously this latter rate would continue into the current period if $r(t) = m(t-1)$.

For every level of v there is a different linear function, since both the intercept and the slope are functions of v. The intercept is positive when the *ex ante* claims of the three claimants on the capitalist sector's output, namely the workers, the capitalists, and the raw-material producers, add up to more than one. If they add up to one, then the intercept is zero, and if they add up to less than unity, then the intercept is negative. The slope of the function $l \cdot w''(v)(1 + \pi(v))$ is likely to be less than one, since it is the sum of the *ex ante* claims of only a subset of the claimants: it represents only the claim of the workers and only a part of the claim of the capitalists. With a positive intercept, the linear function must intersect the 45-degree line from the origin. And the point of intersection gives the rate of steady inflation for any given v. As v rises, the rate of steady inflation increases.

Effect of Changes in v on the Terms of Trade

The price dynamics of the system are shown in figure 20.1 and can be stated as follows. Suppose we start from some historically given rate of inflation. If at the prevailing v the steady rate of inflation is higher, then the rate of inflation will increase to arrive at this steady rate. Likewise, if we start from some steady rate corresponding to a given v, and there is a sudden increase in v, then the rate of inflation will increase. During any period of increase in the rate of inflation, the terms of trade move against the raw-material producers. Hence, if v increases and this brings about an increase in the rate of inflation, then the terms of trade would deteriorate for the raw-material producers during the entire period when inflation is increasing. They settle down at a lower level when the inflation rate stabilizes at a higher level. On the other hand, if v increases but there is no increase in the rate of inflation, since the steady rate is less than the historical rate, then there would be an improvement in the terms of trade of primary producers.

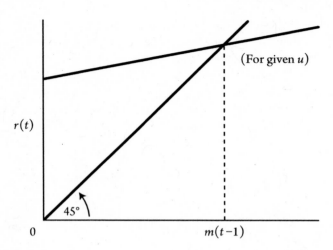

Figure 20.1

Likewise, a reduction in v improves the terms of trade of primary producers if it is associated with a lowering of the inflation rate, but it lowers the terms of trade if the rate of inflation remains unchanged.

To sum up, whether a change in v improves or worsens the terms of trade depends upon its effect upon the rate of inflation. An increase in v improves the terms of trade if the rate of inflation remains unchanged, but worsens it if the rate of inflation increases; a reduction in v lowers the terms of trade if the rate of inflation remains unchanged but improves it if the rate of inflation decreases.

Effect of Changes in Parameters

Now suppose at any given v, there is an increase in $\pi(v)$ and in $w''(v)$. (The possibility of $w'(v)$ rising is remote since the primary producers are price takers). Then the intercept and the slope of the linear function (ii) increases, and hence so does the steady rate of inflation at that v. If this means an increase in the rate of inflation, since the new steady rate now exceeds the original inflation rate, the terms of trade would move against the primary producers; the process would go on until the economy settles at the new steady rate when the terms of trade would stabilize at a lower level. On the other hand, if any change in parameters leaves the inflation rate unchanged, since both the old and the new steady rates are lower than the original rate of inflation, then there would be no change in the terms of trade. Again, the criterion is whether the inflation rate increases or not.

In principle, we can talk of a reduction in $\pi(v)$ and $w''(v)$. The former is extremely rare, associated perhaps with antitrust drives, which have been few and far between.

The latter associated with the weakening of trade unions is more common. The effects of such changes can be easily seen from the model.

Effect of Changes in Exchange Rate

The exchange rate has so far not figured in our price-formation discussion. This is because we have assumed for simplicity that primary producers directly demand a certain part of the capitalist sector's output. In fact, their perception of their real income is in terms of their own product, and this is translated into a certain claim upon the capitalist sector's product. The exchange rate enters into this translation; a depreciation of the exchange rate is analogous to a reduction in $w'(v)$. Alternatively, we can express their claim in equation (i) as $w'(v, e)$, where e is the exchange rate of the precapitalist sector's currency vis-à-vis the capitalist sector's and $\delta w' / \delta e > 0$. (A more elaborate discussion taking explicitly into account the price-formation rules in both sectors is given in Patnaik 1997.) It can be seen that when the markup rule is *not* being applied, a depreciation of the exchange rate lowers the terms of trade, since the increase in the money claims of the primary producers is less than the increase in the price of the capitalist sector's product. When the markup rule is *being* applied, an exchange-rate depreciation lowers the steady inflation rate for a given v. This is likely to bring the *new* steady inflation rate below the original inflation rate, which is likely to have been equal to the *old* steady inflation rate. Given the ratchet effect on the inflation rate, therefore, the terms of trade would move against primary producers since the increase in their money claim would be less than the increase in the price of the capitalist sector's product. It follows that an exchange-rate depreciation of the precapitalist sector's currency would lower the terms of trade of the primary producers, whether or not the economy is following the markup rule.

This model of price formation, which combines Kalecki-type markup pricing with a ratchet effect (which Kalecki himself occasionally mentioned [1971, 50–51]), may be criticized on the grounds that according to it the rate of inflation (calculated from period zero) can never fall. This criticism, however, can be met through a more complex formulation of the ratchet effect. For example, the floor to which the inflation rate can fall in (i) may itself be made a function of v. As long as there are suitable restrictions, that is, the floor does not fall too rapidly with a decline in v (in which case the whole point of the ratchet effect gets lost), all the preceding conclusions would remain more or less intact.

Notes

Introduction

1. It may be thought that a world of paper money and a world of gold money are vastly different and that conclusions derived from one cannot be used in the context of the other. There is no doubt a major difference between the two, namely, that the value of paper money can fall to zero, unlike the value of gold money, since gold itself has a use-value other than in its role as money. Correspondingly, the social sanction that underlies the role of gold as money is very different from the social sanction that underlies paper money. But analytically, the principle determining the value of gold vis-à-vis nonmoney commodities is no different from the principle determining the similar value of paper money.

2. There is a view that even in a world of perfectly flexible prices, price expectations may be inelastic because of the legacy of experience. A stable equilibrium today becomes possible, in other words, because a stable equilibrium existed yesterday. This, however, is a non-explanation since it assumes in effect what it sets out to prove. It proves the existence of a stable equilibrium in a world of flexible prices (today) by assuming the existence of such an equilibrium (yesterday).

3. This does not necessarily mean that there is no price flexibility according to this tradition. Marx, a pioneer of the propertyist tradition, distinguished between "market prices," "prices of production," and "labor values," the first of which was determined by demand and supply. Nonetheless, he emphasized overproduction crises—that is, the fact of *ex ante* overproduction turning into actual output adjustment (accompanied by "depreciation of capital"), owing to, among other things, inherited debt commitment, which is a phenomenon facilitated by the fixation of the *value of money* from outside the realm of demand and supply (by the relative quantities of labor embodied in his view), and hence by a certain invariance of this value.

4. The term *deindustrialization* is used throughout this book not in the sense of a decline in the proportion of the workforce engaged in industry, but rather in the sense of a reduction in overall employment in the economy, through a replacement of domestic output by imports. Deindustrialization is used for this general phenomenon of contraction because such contraction typically occurs in the industrial sector. It does not necessarily presuppose an import surplus for the economy as a whole; it can happen with balanced trade or even with a trade surplus (Patnaik 2004).

5. To talk of "workers" earning "wages" being located within the precapitalist environment of the capitalist sector at the core points to the existence of a capitalist sector within the periphery itself. Even if this latter sector is called "capitalist" (which may not always be a valid description; see U. Patnaik 1991), it is certainly disjointed from the capitalist sector at the core, in the sense of the conditions of the two sets of workers being different, with the peripheral workforce also including pauperized poor peasants.

6. Of course, with large, distantly located labor reserves, even if there is a domestic wage push, accelerating inflation can still be prevented, as we saw earlier, via a suitable and spontaneous shift of the terms of trade against the primary producers. But the domestic labor reserves are being emphasized here because the weight of primary commodities (except oil) in the value of gross output of the metropolis has gone down greatly in recent years, so that the efficacy of such terms of trade in preventing accelerating inflation has diminished.

1. The Great Divide in Economics

1. On Smith's theoretical objective, see Marx 1969b and Dobb 1973.

2. See Lukacs 1975.

3. Marx distinguished between "classical political economy" and "vulgar economy" in his "Afterword to the Second German Edition" of *Capital*; see Marx 1974a, 24–25.

4. In the context of criticizing the "vulgar economy" of Lexis, Engels (1974, 10) writes, "It is just as easy to build up an at least equally plausible vulgar socialism on the basis of this theory, as that built in England on the foundation of Jevons' and Menger's theory of use-value and marginal utility. I even suspect that if Mr. George Bernard Shaw had been familiar with this theory of profit, he would have likely fallen to with both hands, discarding Jevons and Karl Menger, to build anew the Fabian church of the future upon this rock."

5. This issue is discussed in greater detail in chapter 2.

6. It may be thought that in a world of endogenous money, since banks are willing to make money supply adjust to the demand for it, a crisis of generalized overproduction cannot arise. But endogenous money implies banks' willingness to supply unlimited money at a given interest rate. At this interest rate, and with the money wage rate given (without which there can be no determinate amount of money supply or demand in an endogenous money world), *ex ante* generalized overproduction can certainly arise. It could possibly be avoided if banks maintained both endogenous money and the particular interest rate at which "full employment" could be reached under the given circumstances (especially expectations about the future). But this "full employment interest rate" is not known beforehand; and any attempt in practice to approximate such a target interest rate is likely to affect expectations and hence shift the target itself. Besides, even if such a "full employment interest rate" is known beforehand, it will still not always be possible to achieve it—if, for example, this rate is below what is needed to cover the minimum lenders' risk.

2. The Monetarist Theory

1. Monetarist literature traditionally has postulated a proportional relationship between money demand and money income. That the former is merely an increasing but predictable function of the latter is quite sufficient for the monetarist argument about the value of money being determined by demand and supply. The criticism made in the text against this proportional relationship holds equally for the more general case of an increasing function.

2. Marshall puts the matter as follows: "In every state of society there is some fraction of their income which people find it worth while to keep in the form of currency; it may be a fifth, or a tenth, or a twentieth. A large command over resources in the form of currency renders their business easy and smooth, and puts them at an advantage in bargaining; but on

the other hand it locks up in a barren form resources that might yield an income of gratifica-tion if invested, say, in extra furniture; or a money income, if invested in extra machinery or cattle" (1923, I, IV, 3). Immediately after this statement, however, Marshall goes on to sug-gest that the "ready purchasing power" kept by the "inhabitants of a country" may consist of two parts, one linked to income and the other to property. But in Pigou's subsequent rigor-ous development of this "Cambridge" idea, the part linked to property dropped out (though the assumption of an additional component of demand for money being linked to property, apart from that linked to income, does no damage to the logic of monetarism, provided it is a fixed ratio). On Pigou's "fundamental equations" (in Keynes's words), see Keynes 1979, 1:205–208.

3. Used by Baran and Sweezy 1966, this term refers to the *ex ante* savings at full employ-ment over and above what may be needed in the form of additional money stock in keeping with the increase in income.

4. The typical mechanism postulated, of course, is through movements in the interest rate, but this issue need not detain us here.

5. Postulating a plausible mode of entry of money into the economy has been one of the weak points of monetarism, especially when we move away from the simple case of commodity money. This is because in a world of "deposit money," the entry of money itself would normally be through banks' purchase of securities, which directly and immediately affects the interest rate, which can no longer then be assumed merely to be equilibrating sav-ings and investment as in standard monetarist theory. The mechanisms thought up by mone-tarist writers for introducing money into the economy (without affecting the interest rate), accordingly, have often been quite strange and amusing. Friedman had imagined a helicop-ter dropping money from the skies and augmenting everyone's money stock. An influen-tial textbook by Blanchard and Fisher (1992) visualizes the government handing over fixed amounts of money to all newborn babies. Such assumptions, often glossed over as simplifi-cations, actually hide serious conceptual problems.

6. The reverse, however, is not true. There can be a logically consistent story of a Wal-rasian equilibrium where money, as money, does not figure at all (Arrow and Debreu 1954). But since money *is* a social reality, any such version of Walrasianism has little relevance as social theory.

3. Equilibrium and Historical Time

1. Following the lead of Malinvaud 1977, some may prefer to call the case of Keynes-ian involuntary unemployment a non-Walrasian general equilibrium; see Mukherji 1990. But what Malinvaud calls "Keynesian unemployment" is not strictly Keynesian. Malin-vaud's world is fixed-wage, fixed-price, while Keynes's world was fixed-wage, flex-price. The Keynesian equilibrium, therefore, is not a "rationing equilibrium." But no matter how it is characterized by mainstream economists, they are unanimous in their belief that it entails only a change in Walrasian *assumptions*, not an assault on the logic of the Walrasian system. The argument of this book is that it essentially represents the latter.

2. The real-balance effect, it may be seen, ensures the satisfaction of the gross-substitute assumption, since a reduction in the money wage and price reduces the excess demand for money. It constitutes an attempt, in short, to buttress monetarism without assuming a

constant ratio between money income and the demand for money balance. An important part of the argument of this book consists in the claim, discussed later, that the real-balance effect is logically flawed.

3. For a discussion of some of these issues, see Mukherji 1990, Mukherji and Sanyal 1986, and Patnaik 1997.

4. This was explicitly assumed away in chapter 2.

5. It may be thought that commitments are simply negative endowments. This is not correct. A liability is a negative endowment, and it is not synonymous with a commitment in our sense. The latter entails an obligation to pay a certain sum by a certain date, while a liability does not necessarily entail any such *time-bound* payment obligation.

6. This last statement may appear to contradict what we have assumed regarding expectations about equilibrium. If these are such that each individual correctly forecasts the equilibrium, then surely each knows the other's plans; how, then, can we talk about atomistic individuals? There is in fact no contradiction between assuming that each agent correctly forecasts the equilibrium and asserting that each agent acts as an atomistic individual. It is as if each agent is simultaneously an atomistic individual and an auctioneer. This does not come in the way of his acting as an atomistic individual; on the contrary, he is able to do so all the better in so far as he has a lot more information at his command. Putting it differently, my assumption that each agent correctly forecasts the equilibrium is analogous to the assumption that recontracting can be carried out any number of times. My assertion that each agent acts as an atomistic individual is by no means contradicted by the assumption that recontracting among the agents is possible any number of times.

7. The one-good and identical input and output assumptions make input purchase by firms, strictly speaking, unnecessary; but one can think of both the input and the output as vectors, the former in fixed proportions and the latter in variable proportions but with the rates of transformation among the different items being fixed and equal under all alternative techniques, and the same as the proportion of the input vector.

8. We can also arrive at such a stationary equilibrium by assuming rational expectations, that is, perfect foresight about the future, subject to random errors, and except in so far as completely novel circumstances arise. Indeed, the argument of this chapter, as we will see, remains unaffected whether we assume static or rational expectations. There is, however, a point about the rational-expectations assumption that is often not appreciated, namely, that for perfect foresight to be logically tenable, economic agents imbued with perfect foresight must not be tempted to become free riders in any sense in the belief that what they do would make no perceptible difference to the denouement which they have so perfectly foreseen. This assumption of cooperative rationality marks a significant break from methodological individualism. This assumption, however, is essential for all models of rational-expectations equilibria, which is why, as I argue in a later chapter, these models are based illicitly on a simultaneous espousal and denial of methodological individualism.

9. I am assuming that the economy begins on this stationary equilibrium just for the convenience of exposition; the assumption is not necessary for the validity of the argument.

10. Since the whole thrust of the argument in this chapter is that monetarism is logically untenable in a world with inside money, I deliberately begin at the other end by assuming the exclusive prevalence of outside money and then show that inherited payments

commitments—and hence, by extension, inside money—cause logical problems for the monetarist model.

11. Throughout this discussion I have assumed that money does not constitute a form of wealth holding, which is why it appears as if the change in money stock, which can have a disturbing effect, can come about only exogenously. But once we recognize that money is also held as wealth (which of course would entail setting up the basic model differently from what has been done here), then any increase or decrease in the desire to hoard money out of a given stock would ipso facto alter what is available for meeting the fixed-payments commitments and advancing wages to workers. It would therefore have the same effect as the exogenous change in money stock discussed earlier. This is exactly the way that Marx set out his theory of crises.

4. The Modus Operandi of Monetarist Theory

1. Strictly speaking, as already mentioned, at zero value of money there would be zero demand for money, but that is a matter pertaining to a discontinuity in the function. As the value of money approaches zero, the demand for money, in the monetarist perception, becomes infinitely large.

2. See Hahn 1984.

3. The classic work by Oskar Lange (1944) preceded Patinkin, but Lange was more concerned with answering a particular, though crucial, question—whether price flexibility increases employment—than with setting up a theoretical structure per se.

4. This is arrived at as follows. Each young person will be carrying into the next period an amount that is the sum of two components: $b \cdot m^1_0$ for bequeathing to progeny at the time of death and $m^1_0 (1- b) / 2$ for his or her own consumption in the next period. (This is in accordance with the optimization exercise.) This sum is nothing else but $m^1_0 (1 + b) / 2$.

5. The model presented in chapter 2 was of this sort, where there was no wealth carried over after a person's death.

5. The Cash Transactions Approach to Monetarism

1. This means only that *a* consistent monetarist story can be told, not that the setting of the story corresponds to the monetary institutions of a bourgeois society. Since monetarism requires (see chapter 2) that money supply be exclusively linked in equilibrium to the value of goods and services (and hence money income) and not the interest rate, the attempts to ensure that the interest rate is kept insulated from money supply are frantic and often amusing, even among those following the Clower approach. Thus, Blanchard and Fisher, in an influential textbook (1992), create a fantastic monetary universe for this purpose, while developing a general-equilibrium Baumol-Tobin model. In this world, all money is outside money, gifted to babies by the government. Everyone in addition has some goods that can be exchanged against bonds with firms, in whose possession goods grow at a certain (profit) rate. These bonds can be exchanged at will against money with banks, and vice versa. In this world, surely, the banks must have excess reserves (to provide money at will against bonds). But then why should banks not get rid of their excess reserves by buying bonds in the market, thereby driving down the interest rate, instead of meekly waiting for individuals to come to them? While

this question is never answered, Blanchard and Fisher's assumptions make the interest rate independent of the demand and supply of money (and equal to the profit rate). Banks are thus brought in as a deus ex machina, with no objective function of their own, merely ensuring that the interest rate remains outside the purview of the demand and supply of money.

2. In fact, the constant time-lag assumption is exactly analogous to the assumption, in a different context, of a constant (Cambridge) k. It lacks justification for exactly the same reasons that k lacks justification.

3. The assumption that a desire for changing the initial commodity stock is necessarily accompanied by a desire for *some* change in the money stock ensures uniqueness of the equilibrium, which alone makes it meaningful. With this assumption, the *ex ante* and the *ex post* volumes of commodity transactions are necessarily equal in equilibrium.

4. Such a notional division, of course, cannot be made in practice, but it is useful for purposes of exposition.

6. An Excursus on Rational-Expectation Equilibria

1. See Dobb 1969 for a review of the entire debate.

2. This would be true, even if it is the case that implicit in the rational expectation assumption is not necessarily any knowledge about the expectation-formation rule of everyone, but only the belief that all economic agents follow, and assume everyone else to be following, a Ramsay-type optimizing rule. While the latter belief simplifies the problem of prediction, it still does not rule out the need for solving "thousands of equations" since each agent has different endowments, even if we assume that they all have the same utility function.

3. Ramsay 1928.

4. Ramsay (1928) had taken the "bliss" level of utility as the ultimate goal of the optimization exercise. An alternative singular point, suggested by Koopmans (1965), is where the marginal product of capital is zero (for a stationary labor force), or equals the rate of growth of the labor force in efficiency units (which is the golden-rule path). Since the concept of "bliss" from the consumption side is problematical, the Koopmans route is the one more commonly followed, in which case B is the level of utility associated with per capita consumption on the golden-rule path. (Appropriate adjustments would have to be made if social consumption fund is taken as the argument of the utility function.)

5. Throughout this section, I assume that this is what the rational expectation theorists actually believe, even though there is no explicit discussion of such problems in the rational-expectation literature.

6. See chapter 3, note 8.

7. An Excursus on Methodological Individualism

1. Marx, as is well known, had accused Malthus of plagiarism in all his works, including his work on glut (Marx 1975, 61–62).

2. "It is only in a highly authoritarian society, where sudden, substantial, all-round changes could be decreed that a flexible wage policy could function with success" (Keynes 1949, 269).

8. An Excursus on Walrasian Equilibrium and Capitalist Production

1. For further discussion of these issues and their bearing on the possibilities of achieving a socialist society, see Patnaik 1991.

2. Michael Kalecki writes, "Indeed under a regime of permanent full employment, 'the sack' would cease to play its role as a disciplinary measure" (1971, 140).

3. In Marx's words, "Taking them as a whole, the general movements of wages are regulated by the expansion and contraction of the industrial reserve army" (1974, 596). For Marx, real wage and money wage movements always went together, a view reflected in Goodwin's (1967) attempt at developing a spontaneous growth cycle of a Marxian kind along these lines. The inflationary consequences that arise owing to a reduction in the reserve army, when money and real-wage movements are dissociated, are discussed at great length in Patnaik 1997.

4. This point is made by Robert Eisner (Baker, Epstein, and Pollin 1998, 388), who, however, calls NAIRU a "dismal doctrine," suggesting that it is possible to achieve near-full employment under capitalism. For a contrary position to Eisner's in this respect, and one closer to mine, argued in the concrete context of postwar capitalism, see Glyn's essay in the same volume.

5. "In all such cases, there must be the possibility of throwing great masses of men suddenly on the decisive points without injury to the scale of production elsewhere. Overpopulation supplies these masses" (Marx 1974a, 592).

6. This point was made by Oskar Lange (1941) in his review of Schumpeter's *Business Cycles* (1939).

7. For a critique of these claims, see Patnaik 1997.

8. This would be my response to the kind of position Eisner articulates.

9. A Critique of Ricardo's Theory of Money

1. Marx (1969b, 97) had talked of Smith's tracing out "in general form the origin of surplus value and of its specific forms." "But then," Marx added, "he takes the opposite course and seeks on the contrary to deduce the value of commodities . . . by adding together the natural prices of wages, profit, and rent."

2. On these issues, see also Dobb 1973.

3. Quoted in Marx 1971, 174n.

4. Quoted in ibid., 180.

5. Of course, the equilibrium values would depend upon the money wage rates across countries, assuming that capital mobility equalizes the rate of profit. Let us assume here for simplicity that the money wage rate is identical across countries. The violation of this assumption, which entails the existence of a set of equilibrium prices in the world market based on *unequal wage rates* across countries, each of which remains specialized in the production of a particular commodity, is symptomatic of unequal exchange (Emmanuel 1972). Since we are not concerned here with the problem of unequal exchange, we assume that the money wage rate is the same across countries.

6. Hume's proposition was so telling a refutation of the mercantilist doctrine that Adam Smith quoted it most approvingly in his early lectures. Hume, he said, "proves very

ingeniously that money must bear a certain proportion to the quantity of commodities in every country; that whenever money is accumulated beyond the proportion of commodities in any country, the price of goods will necessarily rise; that this country will be undersold at the foreign market, and consequently the money must depart to other nations" (Cannan 1896, 197, quoted in Dobb 1973, 58).

7. If wages are supposed to be at some real subsistence level, then a change in the money prices of commodities automatically entails a corresponding change in money wages.

8. The only uncertainties in their minds would be about how rapidly this convergence would occur and whether some fresh disturbance would come in the way of this convergence. But fresh disturbance is not germane to the present discussion, and no matter whether the convergence is rapid or slow, there could never be, on Ricardo's own premises, any doubt about the direction of movement of the short-run value of money whenever it diverges from its equilibrium value.

10. Marx on the Value of Money

1. This fact keeps the value of money relative to the nonmoney commodities bounded away from zero. The fact that the money commodity has a use-value independent of its functioning as money ensures that, even though the demand for money falls to zero when its value falls to zero, the value of the money commodity can never fall to zero. The view sometimes held in Marxist circles that the money commodity is a commodity whose exchange value is its use-value is therefore not correct. The money commodity must have a use value independent of its exchange value if it is to function at all as a repository of exchange value.

2. The term *average velocity* may give the impression that Marx, like Ricardo, is assuming a constant income velocity of circulation of the total money stock. But that is not correct. His assumption of "average velocity," even if we were to take it to be constant (which would be justified under "normal" circumstances), refers only to that part of the money stock that is used for circulation purposes. It does not refer to the total money stock of which a part is held as a hoard and not used for circulation.

3. This fact was adduced by Rosa Luxemburg (1963) as constituting one of the reasons why looking at the process of capital accumulation as solely an interaction between the two great departments of production within a closed capitalist sector was fundamentally incorrect. See Patnaik 1997 for a discussion of her views.

4. Of course, it may be asked: even if the short-run quantity theory of money is rejected, why can not the exchange ratio between money and commodities, both in the short and in the long run, still be equal to their relative prices of production? The point is that there is no necessary reason for this to happen, which is what is meant by saying that money is outside the equal rate of profit rule. Some rule for determining this exchange ratio has to be specified, but this rule has no particular justification. Since Marx takes the labor-embodied rule as underlying the commensurability between commodities and between commodities and money in general, in the absence of the equal-profit-rate rule supervening, the labor-embodied rule is what remains for him as the determinant of the exchange ratio between money and commodities.

5. The argument of this paragraph can be put as follows. Let us assume for simplicity that the economy consists of n single product industries, each producing through the application

of labor on a machine that is itself a produced good (the machines may be different for different goods). If the machine for the jth sector is produced by the ith sector, then the machine input per unit of output (at "normal capacity" use), divided by the turnover period of the machine, may be denoted by a_{ij} and the matrix of such coefficients by A, which has only one positive entry per column. Let us define $E^* = l'(I - A)^{-1} \cdot Q^* / l$, when l' is a row vector of labor coefficients, Q^* the output vector that would be produced when the machine in each sector is working at normal capacity, and l the labor embodied in a unit of the money commodity. When the actual expenditure $E = E^*$, then, since E necessarily equals $p' \cdot Q$ (the actual market value of produced output), $l' (I - A)^{-1} \cdot Q^* / l$, which by assumption equals $p^* \cdot Q^*$ (the normal-capacity-output value at equilibrium prices), must also equal $p'Q$. We thus have two separate reasons why the sum of market prices may differ from the sum of values: (1) $E \neq E^*$, which is an aggregate demand problem; (2) $E = E^*$ but $Q \neq Q^*$, which is the particular mismatch problem. We will discuss the former problem, assumed away in the discussion of this paragraph.

6. Saying this is very different from the proposition, advanced by Grandmont and others in the context of contemporary monetarism and discussed earlier in this book, that money has a positive value in any period because it has always had a positive value historically (which introduces something akin to inelastic price expectations and therefore keeps the value of money bounded away from zero). The positivity of the value of money here arises because it is a *produced* commodity, though several considerations enter into the determination, historically, of what that value is (rather like the case of another produced commodity, oil). Here (present) positivity is not being explained by (past) positivity per se.

7. Conditions of production are defined in terms of production coefficients per unit output (the unit may be the entire output produced) when this output is the normal-capacity output.

8. The conclusion that follows from this is somewhat staggering: almost the entire literature not just on Marx's theory on money (which is small anyway), but even on Marx's theory of value and price has been totally off the mark. It has not understood the sui generis nature of Marx's writing and hence not really understood that writing at all. We return to this question in the next chapter.

9. The existence of idle money balances implies that there can be both *ex ante* excess demand and *ex ante* deficient demand for commodities compared to full capacity output. In the discussion that follows, I will concentrate only on the case of *ex ante* deficient demand, that is, on *ex ante* overproduction crises (in Marxist terminology). I will take up the more general case later.

10. It is another matter that changes in expectations would normally encompass commodity markets, and hence have an effect on commodity prices and output; in other words, in the matter of disturbances, the "how" and the "where" questions *are* related. But the fact remains that it is the "where" question that is of decisive importance.

11. In presenting the foregoing argument, I have assumed that there is always a hoard, that is, the amount of money stock always exceeds what is required for circulating the amount of commodities produced at "normal" capacity use at equilibrium prices. What happens if this assumption does not hold? The very fact that wealth holders would expect disturbances arising from the money side to be self-liquidating would mean that they would never allow a situation to arise where the hoard would disappear, that is, where these disturbances

would not be self-liquidating. Paradoxically, therefore, an argument derived on the assumption that the hoard always exists itself ensures that the hoard always actually exists. (In the extreme case where the output of the money commodity becomes inadequate, token money will be used to make good the deficiency.)

12. Strictly speaking, the inherited payment commitments in real terms have to be obtained by dividing the commitments in money terms by the equilibrium price corresponding to full capacity output, that is, the equilibrium price derived from the production coefficients that would prevail when the economy is at full-capacity output. Since the real value of these commitments enters into the definition of full-capacity output, it follows that this definition has a self-referential character. While we have defined it in the text, for simplicity, by abstracting from this fact, it must not be forgotten.

13. This incidentally is just one possible interpretation of Marx's concept. An alternative interpretation would suggest that j is fixed, with capital having a fixed lifespan, and hence only a certain amount of employment can be provided in any period. The excess of the available labor force over this amount is the reserve army of labor, whose relative size determines the wage rate; but this wage rate has no effect on j. See Patnaik 1998 for this alternative interpretation.

14. Today it would be more appropriate to take the money wage rate as being affected by the size of the reserve army rather than the real wage rate, no matter whether we take the simple Phillips-curve formulation or "augment" it with price expectations (Patnaik 1997). Indeed, one of the criticisms one can have of Goodwin (1967) is that he makes the real wage rate dependent on the size of the reserve army. But such a formulation is perfectly justified in the context of Marx whose universe is one of commodity money, where money and real wages necessarily move together.

15. The following quotation is just one among the many that can be given to establish the point that Marx visualized quantity adjustments, occurring together with price adjustments, in response to increases in demand: "And if the demand is so great that it does not contract when the price is regulated by the value of commodities produced under the least favourable conditions, then these determine the market value. This is not possible unless demand is greater than usual, or if supply drops below the usual level. Finally, if the mass of the produced commodities exceeds the quantities disposed off at average market values, the commodities produced under the most favourable conditions regulate the market-value. . . . What has been said here of market-value applies to the price of production as soon as it takes the place of market-value" (Marx 1974a, 179). The term "usual" used by Marx in this passage is precisely what we have tried to capture through the notion of normal-capacity output.

11. An Excursus on Marx's Theory of Value

1. For a demonstration that Marx's transformation results hold under conditions more general than the economy's being in von Neumann proportions, see Patnaik 1990.

2. Alternatively, we can, as in the previous chapter, assume n single product industries, each producing through the application of labor on machines (one type for each industry, though the same type can be used in more than one), which are themselves produced goods. The machine quantity for unit production in each sector, divided by the turnover period of the machine concerned, can then form the element of the A-matrix. We have, however, taken

the A-matrix as one of current inputs exclusively, in order to make a comparison with the Sraffa discussion easier.

3. When this happens, then, formally, the results are exactly what were derived in the previous section with the wage rate a pure number. But since wages are actually paid in money, underlying this pure number is the specification of an exchange ratio between money and the world of commodities without which the prices of production cannot be derived.

4. Strictly speaking, it is enough for price determination that the money value added per unit of labor in the production of nonmarketed commodities, should be some given magnitude. But it is reasonable to assume that this magnitude should equal some average figure for the economy as a whole, rather than being a purely arbitrary figure.

5. Once we reinterpret Marx's value theory as we have done, there would be many more instances where Marx's specific conclusion that the rate of profit remains unchanged between the value and the price systems would be valid. Consider one such instance. Suppose we have a completely decomposable production system (not a single basic good), where each separate subsystem (that is, sector) has n goods, of which $n - 1$ are intermediate goods and only the nth good is a final good. It has an input matrix where the only positive entries are $a_{11,}$ and $a_{i, i+1}$ with $i = 1, \ldots n - 1$, (all other entries are zero); that is, good 1 enters into its own production and that of good 2, good 2 enters into that of good 3, good 3 into that of good 4, and so on until good n, which enters into no production but is the only good of the sector that is sold in the market as a final good. The prices of production based on the equalization of the profit rate and the money wage rate across subsystems (sectors), and on the nonmarketed commodity pricing rule specified earlier, will give the same rate of profit as $S / (C + V)$ of the value system. Marx's transformation procedure, in other words, would have been totally vindicated. The Austrians also assume such hierarchical production structures, but the Austrian results do not hold in such cases, as Sraffa has shown.

12. Marx's Solution to a Dilemma

1. This problem, of course, would arise in a crisis, no matter what the cause of that crisis, but the system in equilibrium could never be demand-constrained according to this conception. In Bukharin's language, "temporary general overproduction" was possible, but not "permanent general overproduction."

2. The text of the *Manifesto* used here is contained in Karat 1999.

13. Alternative Interpretations of Keynes

1. Precisely because of this belief in an unchanged liquidity preference schedule (when money wages and prices changed), which entails that a fall in money wages and prices would raise employment, Hicks (1967) suggested that the strongest case for Keynesianism arose when the marginal efficiency of capital schedule was vertical, that is, when the world was characterized by oligopolies. My argument here is that this belief in a liquidity preference schedule that remains unchanged when money wages and prices fall, a belief shared by even Hicks, is itself untenable.

2. Of course, if the producible commodity, for which there is *ex ante* excess demand, has nonaugmentable output in the short run, then it is de facto nonproducible. In that case, if

relative prices are sticky, the *ex ante* excess demand for it (and hence the *ex ante* excess supply for the other producible commodities) is eliminated through quantity adjustment, and the need for any future augmentation of the output of this "excess-demanded" commodity also disappears. This, as discussed in chapter 10, is why general overproduction arises in the Marxian system, even though the money commodity there is producible.

3. Modigliani 1944, the standard interpretation of Keynes, proceeds along these lines.

4. True, the increase in money supply through a "central Bank under public control" would not have the effect of increasing the real value of inherited debt payment obligations, and hence be preferable on that score. But if the central bank increases money supply at some fixed interest rate, which is typically what happens in endogenous money regimes, then again there is no necessary achievement of full employment. If the central bank were to make money supply elastic at an interest rate appropriate for full employment (with the money wage rate given), this would succeed only if this appropriate interest rate is approachable, that is, it not only exceeds the "liquidity trap rate" but also covers the minimum lender's risk (which itself varies with changing perceptions). In short, the bearishness of the public can be counteracted through the bullishness of banks only within limits, since the latter, after all, are only financial intermediaries.

5. Rakshit 1989 gives this interpretation of Keynes.

6. Interestingly, this is also the way Kaldor (1978) interprets Keynesian theory even while moving away from it. After arguing that the determination of output by a "multiplier" occurs only in a world of fixed relative prices, he illustrates his point by saying that the Keynesian multiplier arises because of the fixity of the interest rate (and, hence, by inference, not of money wages as is commonly supposed).

7. A detailed discussion of the substantive question can be found in Patnaik 2007.

14. A Digression on a Keynesian Dilemma

1. We are, of course, looking at the effects of the state of credit only on those who place orders, not on the suppliers of these orders. The implicit assumption is that in their case supply is never credit-constrained.

2. Schumpter (1939) adopted the idea of investment being spontaneously discouraged by accelerating inflation from Machlup. Lange (1941) discussed it in his review of Schumpeter's work. For a detailed discussion, see Patnaik 1997.

3. By exogenous stimuli here, and in this chapter generally, I obviously mean exogenous stimuli specific to the closed self-contained capitalist economy, such as innovations, since that is my focus of analysis.

4. An additional factor has to be considered here, namely the long-term tendencies under capitalism. The emergence of oligopolistic collusion on one hand and of trade unions on the other has the effect of lowering the upper threshold level of activity. Oligopolistic collusion may have the effect of reducing the lower threshold as well. Above all, however, it makes the task, of keeping the economy within the viable range, more difficult. I discuss this in chapter 17.

5. This is because the net rate of profit is simply $[I / (1 - c)] / K - \delta$, which equals in a state of simple reproduction $[\delta / (1 - c)] - \delta$, or $\delta c / (1 - c)$.

6. Keynes (1919) did address himself to this problem briefly and found the basis of the high level of activity under nineteenth-century capitalism in the expansion of its frontiers in the New World. But this perception does precisely what we have been arguing: it locates the source of the stability of the system not within the immanent logic of its own spontaneous functioning as a closed system but outside of it. Keynesianism, in short, cannot theoretically explain the system's stability, but it does not theorize about this lack of explanation.

15. Marx, Keynes, and Propertyism

1. The term "full capacity use" in this paragraph can be substituted by "normal capacity use."

2. This definition is not identical with that of Keynes, that is, it is not synonymous with the absence of "involuntary unemployment" as defined by Keynes.

3. "Capitalism" here means a model of a capitalist economy. In the real world, the existence of full employment in some capitalist economies in this sense may be possible if vast labor reserves needed for the stability in the value of money are preserved elsewhere. The fact that some capitalist countries in the postwar years of Keynesian demand management achieved near-full employment is therefore not a refutation of the proposition advanced in the text. See Patnaik 1997 for a fuller discussion of these issues.

4. This is essentially the model of Goodwin 1967.

5. For the role of fascism in "achieving" full employment, see Kalecki 1971.

16. The Incompleteness of Propertyism

1. At full employment, too, there is no fixed pool of savings, since savings can increase through "profit inflation." But even those who do not accept profit inflation must concede the effect of output on aggregate savings.

17. A Solution to the Incompleteness

1. There is no obvious reason why an increase in the degree of monopoly per se should alter the interest rate. In any case, the argument presented here requires only that there should be no tendency for a secular decline in the interest rate with a rise in the degree of monopoly.

2. This can be easily checked as follows. Let us take the system of equations given in 14.3 with only one change. Equation (i) becomes

$$n_{t+1} = n_t + b(v_t - v_0) \cdot n_t + \varepsilon \ldots \tag{i$'$}$$

in order to introduce the effect of exogenous stimuli available within the system. Again there would be two roots, both positive, with the smaller one representing a stable trend. An increase in μ can be seen to lower the value of this smaller root.

3. If the physical composition of exports happens to be different, then the same result will still hold, but after peasant agriculture has adjusted its product composition.

18. Capitalism as a Mode of Production

1. The parallel between Marx's and Naoroji's writings is drawn in Ganguli 1965. Naoroji's book, originally published in 1901, was republished in 1962. For a discussion of Indian nationalist writings on the economics of colonialism, see Chandra 1965.

2. True, there are a number of concrete remarks made about colonialism throughout *Capital*; moreover, a certain role is assigned to colonial trade in the discussion of the "counteracting tendencies" to the "tendency of the rate of profit to fall." Later Marxist writers have taken a cue from this and developed theories of imperialism in which imperialism is seen as bringing about one or the other "counteracting tendency." But since the "falling tendency of the rate of profit" itself requires rather strong assumptions for its validity (see Patnaik 1997) and has a rather ambiguous status within the corpus of Marx's theory (Lenin scarcely made any use of it other than referring to it in his *Encyclopaedia* article on Marx), the theories of imperialism built on it can scarcely be seen to be incorporating imperialism into the "law of motion" of the capitalist mode of production.

3. Irfan Habib (1995), to my knowledge, was the first to raise this issue.

4. There is a hint in volume 2 of *Capital* that Marx sees the precise problem that was later to occupy Rosa Luxemburg, but he resolves the matter by bringing in exports to the "gold-producing sector" within capitalism. This, however, is patently unsatisfactory. Marx himself saw paper money under certain circumstances as being a substitute for gold (that is, a universe of commodity money, such as was assumed by him, did not have to have only the money commodity functioning physically as money); and if this money is issued by the government, then in effect an export surplus to a destination outside of the mode of production proper, namely to the government, is being talked about. See Dobb 1973.

5. This is true of what Marx calls the "latent" form of relative surplus population.

6. Of course, it does not have to be labor power; the relative value of any commodity that enters into the production of other commodities, and that cannot become a "free good" with respect to other commodities, being fixed in terms of money would do. But this latter fixity must ipso facto entail a certain restriction on the degree to which the money wage rate of the workers engaged in the production of this commodity can vary.

7. A detailed discussion of the matter is contained in Patnaik 1997.

19. Money in the World Economy

1. It is a remarkable fact that even after the end of the Bretton Woods system, the relative values of the major currencies have remained secularly unchanged, notwithstanding fluctuations. For the period since 1980 this is certainly true of the U.S. dollar, the pound sterling, and the yen. (We are not considering here the very recent decline in the dollar.) In the case of the euro, which came into being only recently, it is too early to talk of "secular movements" with respect to any other currencies.

2. It would appear from the recent experience of some Asian countries that their currencies have moved out of this vulnerable group, though the group still includes the vast majority of third-world currencies. But even among the Asian countries, a distinction must be drawn between those, like China, that have strong current account surpluses, and those,

like India, whose recent currency appreciation is based on financial inflows. A question mark still hangs over whether the latter countries have moved out of the vulnerable group. Even in their case, the need for capital controls remains, though for a different reason: to prevent domestic deindustrialization and peasant distress caused by currency appreciation, financed by a rise in external indebtedness.

Bibliography

Althusser, L. 2003. *The Humanist Controversy and Other Writings*. London: Verso.

Arrow, K. J., and G. Debreu. 1954. "Existence of an Equilibrium for a Competitive Economy." *Econometrica* 22 (July): 265–290.

Bagchi, A. K. 1972. "Some International Foundations of Capitalist Growth and Underdevelopment." *Economic and Political Weekly* 7, nos. 31–33: 155–170.

———. 1982. *The Political Economy of Underdevelopment*. Cambridge: Cambridge University Press.

Baker D., G. Epstein, and R. Pollin, eds. 1998. *Globalization and Progressive Economic Policy*. Cambridge: Cambridge University Press.

Baran, P. A., and P. M. Sweezy. 1966. *Monopoly Capital*. New York: Monthly Review Press.

Blanchard, O. J., and S. Fischer. 1992. *Lectures on Macroeconomics*. Cambridge, Mass.: MIT Press.

Bukharin, N. I. 1972. *Imperialism and the Accumulation of Capital*. In Tarbuck 1972.

Cannan, E., ed. 1896. *Lectures on Justice, Police, Revenue, and Arms by Adam Smith, reported by a Student in 1763*. Oxford: n.p.

Chandra, B. 1965. *The Rise and Growth of Economic Nationalism in India*. Delhi: People's Publishing House.

Clower, R. W. 1967. "A Reconsideration of the Microfoundation of Monetary Theory." *Western Economic Journal* 6:1–9.

Dobb, M. H. 1969. *Welfare Economics and the Economics of Socialism*. Cambridge: Cambridge University Press.

———. 1972. *On Economic Theory and Socialism*. London: Routledge and Kegan Paul.

———. 1973. *Theories of Value and Distribution Since Adam Smith*. Cambridge: Cambridge University Press.

Eisner, R. 1998. "The NAIRU: Is It a Real Constraint?" In Baker, Epstein, and Pollin 1998.

Emmanuel, A. 1972. *Unequal Exchange: A Study of the Imperialism of Trade*. London: New Left Books.

Engels, F. 1974. Preface to Karl Marx, *Capital*, vol. 3. Moscow: Progress Publishers.

Feinstein, C. H., ed. 1967. *Capitalism, Socialism and Economic Growth: Essays Presented to Maurice Dobb*. Cambridge: Cambridge University Press.

Foley, D. K. 1982. "The Value of Money, the Value of Labour-Power, and the Marxian Transformation Problem Revisited." *Review of Radical Political Economics* 14, no. 2: 37–47.

Friedman, M. 1966. *Essays in Positive Economics*. Chicago: University of Chicago Press.

Galbraith, J. K. 1968. *American Capitalism*. New York: Pantheon Books.

Ganguli, B. N. 1965. *Dadabhai Naoroji and the Drain Theory*. Delhi: Asia Publishing House.

Glyn, A. 1998. "Internal and External Constraints on Egalitarian Policies." In Baker, Epstein, and Pollin 1998.

Goodwin, R. M. 1951. "The Non-linear Accelerator and the Persistence of Business Cycles." *Econometrica* 19:1–17.

———. 1967. "A Growth Cycle." In Feinstein 1967.

———. 1991. *Chaotic Economic Dynamics*. Oxford: Clarendon Press.

Grandmont, J. M. 1982. "Temporary Equilibrium Theory." In K. J. Arrow and M. D. Intrilligator, eds., *Handbook of Mathematical Economics*, 2:879–922. Amsterdam: North-Holland.

Gurley, J. G., and E. S. Shaw. 1960. *Money in a Theory of Finance*. Washington, D.C.: Brookings Institution.

Habib, I. 1995. "Problems of Marxist Historiography." In *Essays in Indian History*. Delhi: Tulika Books.

Hahn, F. H. 1984. *Equilibrium and Macroeconomics*. Oxford: Clarendon Press.

Hansen, A. H. 1938. *Full Recovery or Stagnation?* New York: Norton.

———. 1941. *Fiscal Policy and Business Cycles*. New York: Norton.

Harrod, R. F. 1939. "An Essay in Dynamic Theory." *Economic Journal* 49:14–33.

Hayek, F. A., ed. 1935. *Collectivist Economic Planning*. London: Routledge.

Hicks, J. R. 1937. "Mr. Keynes and the Classics." In Hicks 1967.

———. 1950. *A Contribution to the Theory of the Trade Cycle*. Oxford: Clarendon Press.

———. 1967. *Critical Essays in Monetary Theory*. Oxford: Clarendon Press.

———. 1974. *The Crisis in Keynesian Economics*. Oxford: Clarendon Press.

Hool, B. 1979. "Liquidity, Speculation and the Demand for Money." *Journal of Economic Theory* 21:73–87.

Johnson, H. G. 1958. "Monetary Theory and Policy." *American Economic Review* 52:351–354.

Kahn, R. F. 1931. "The Relation of Home Investment to Unemployment." *Economic Journal* 41 (June): 173–198.

———. 1954. "Some Notes on Liquidity Preference." *Manchester School of Economic and Social Studies* 22 (September): 229–257.

———. 1972. *Selected Essays on Employment and Growth*. Cambridge: Cambridge University Press.

Kaldor, N. 1945. "Speculation and Economic Stability." *Economic Journal* 7:1–27.

———. 1964. *Essays on Economic Stability and Growth*. London: Duckworth.

———. 1976. "Inflation and Recession in the World Economy." *Economic Journal* 86:703–714.

———. 1978. *Further Essays in Economic Theory*. Cambridge: Cambridge University Press.

Kalecki, M. 1954. *The Theory of Economic Dynamics*. London: George Allen and Unwin.

———. 1962. "Observations on the Theory of Growth." *Economic Journal* 72 (March): 134–153.

———. 1971. *Selected Essays on the Dynamics of the Capitalist Economy, 1933–1970*. Cambridge: Cambridge University Press.

Karat, P., ed. 1999. *A World to Win: Essays on the Communist Manifesto*. Delhi: Leftword Books.

Keynes, J. M. 1919. *The Economic Consequences of the Peace*. London: Macmillan.

———. 1949. *The General Theory of Employment, Interest and Money*. London: Macmillan.

——. 1951. *Essays in Persuasion*. London: Macmillan.

——. 1979. *The Collected Writings of J. M. Keynes*. London: Macmillan.

Koopmans, T. C. 1965. "On the Concept of Optimal Economic Growth." *Pontificiae Academiae Scintiarum Scripta Varia* 28:225–300.

Kornai, J. 1979. "Resource-Constrained Versus Demand-Constrained Systems." *Econometrica* 47:801–819.

Lange, O. 1938. *On the Economic Theory of Socialism*. Minneapolis: University of Minnesota Press.

——. 1941. "Review of Joseph Schumpeter's *Business Cycles* (2 Volumes)." *Review of Economic Statistics* 23:9.

——. 1944. *Price Flexibility and Employment*. Bloomington, Ind.: Principia Press.

——. 1963. *Political Economy*. London: Pergamon.

Lenin, V. I. 1975. *Selected Works*, vol. 3. Moscow: Progress Publishers.

Lewis, W. A. 1978. *Growth and Fluctuations 1870–1913*. London: Allen & Unwin.

Lukacs, G. 1975. *The Young Hegel*. London: Merlin.

Lutz, F. A., and L. W. Mints, eds. 1951. *Readings in Monetary Theory*. New York: American Economic Association.

Luxemburg, R. 1963. *The Accumulation of Capital*. London: Routledge and Kegan Paul.

Malinvaud, E. 1977. *The Theory of Unemployment Reconsidered*. Oxford: Basil Blackwell.

Marshall, A. 1923. *Money, Credit and Commerce*. London: Macmillan.

Marx, K. 1969a. *Pre-Capitalist Economic Formations*. London: Lawrence and Wishart.

——. 1969b. *Theories of Surplus Value*, Part I. London: Lawrence and Wishart.

——. 1971. *A Contribution to a Critique of Political Economy*. London: Lawrence and Wishart.

——. 1974a. *Capital*, vol. 1. Moscow: Progress Publishers.

——. 1974b. *Capital*, vol. 3. Moscow: Progress Publishers.

——. 1975. *Theories of Surplus Value*, Part III. Moscow: Progress Publishers.

Modigliani, F. 1944. "Liquidity Preference and the Theory of Interest and Money." *Econometrica* 12:45–88.

Morishima, M. 1973. *Marx's Economics: A Dual Theory of Value and Growth*. Cambridge: Cambridge University Press.

Mukherji, A. 1990. *Walrasian and Non-Walrasian Equilibria*. Oxford: Clarendon Press.

Mukherji, A., and A. Sanyal. 1986. "Price Flexibility and Unemployment: Microeconomics of Some Old Fashioned Questions." *Keio Economic Studies* 23:19–35.

Naoroji, D. 1962. *Poverty and Un-British Rule in India*. Delhi: Commonwealth.

Patinkin, D. 1965. *Money, Interest, and Prices*. New York: Harper & Row.

Patnaik, P. 1972. "External Markets and Capitalist Development." *Economic Journal* 82 (December): 1316–1323.

——. 1990. "Marx's Transformation Problem and Ricardo's Invariant Measure: A Note." *Cambridge Journal of Economics* 13:555–562.

——. 1991. *Economics and Egalitarianism*. Delhi: Oxford University Press.

——. 1994. "Disproportionality, Crisis and Cyclical Growth." In D. Nayyar, ed., *Industrial Growth and Stagnation*, 18–35. Delhi: Sameeksha Trust and Oxford University Press.

——. 1997. *Accumulation and Stability Under Capitalism*. Oxford: Clarendon Press.

——. 1998. "Unemployment as Failure to Exchange." In D. Nayyar, ed., *Economics as Ideology and Experience*, 3–17. London: Frank Cass.

———. 2002. "Globalization of Capital and Terms of Trade Movements." In V. K. Ramachandran and Madhura Swaminathan, eds., *Agrarian Studies*, 94–110. Delhi: Tulika Books.

———. 2004. "On the Economics of Open Economy Deindustrialization." *Indian Journal of Labour Economics* 47, no. 1 (January–March): 39–47.

———. 2006. "The Other Marx." In Iqbal Husain, ed., *Karl Marx on India: From the New York Daily Tribune*, lv–lxviii. Delhi: Tulika Books.

———. 2007. "Land Preference and Productive Investment: A Theoretical Note." In A. Vaidyanathan and K. L. Krishna, eds., *Institutions and Markets in India's Development*, 95–108. Delhi: Oxford University Press.

Patnaik, U. 1991. "Capitalist Development in Agriculture: Note." In U. Patnaik, ed., *Agrarian Relations and Accumulation*, 38–56. Delhi: Sameeksha Trust and Oxford University Press.

Pigou, A. C. 1937. *Socialism Versus Capitalism*. London: Macmillan.

Rakshit, M. K. 1989. Introduction to M. K. Rakshit, ed., *Studies in the Macroeconomics of Developing Countries*. Delhi: Oxford University Press.

Ramsay, F. P. 1928. "A Mathematical Theory of Saving." *Economic Journal* 38:543–559.

Robertson, D. H. 1940. *Essays in Monetary Theory*. London: Staples.

Robinson, J. 1960. *Collected Economic Papers*, vol. 2. Oxford: Basil Blackwell.

———. 1966. *Collected Economic Papers*, vol. 3. Oxford: Basil Blackwell.

Rowthorn, R. E. 1977. "Conflict, Inflation, and Money." *Cambridge Journal of Economics* 1:215–239.

Samuelson, P. A. 1957. "Wages and Interest: Marxian Economic Models." *American Economic Review* 47 (December): 884–912.

———. 1971. "Understanding the Marxian Notion of Exploitation: A Summary of the So-called Transformation Problem Between Marxian Values and Competitive Prices." *Journal of Economic Literature* 9, no. 2: 399–431.

Saul, S. B. 1970. *Studies in British Overseas Trade*. Liverpool: Liverpool University Press.

Schumpeter, J. A. 1939. *Business Cycles*. New York: McGraw-Hill.

———. 1952. *Ten Great Economists*. New York: Oxford University Press.

———. 1961. *The Theory of Economic Development*. New York: Galaxy Books.

Solow, R. M. 1956. "A Contribution to the Theory of Economic Growth." *Quarterly Journal of Economics* 70:65–94.

———. 1990. *The Labor Market as a Social Institution*. New York: Oxford University Press.

Solow, R. M., and J. E. Stiglitz. 1968. "Output, Employment and Wages in the Short Run." *Quarterly Journal of Economics* 82, no. 4: 537–560.

Sraffa, P. 1951. Introduction to P. Sraffa, ed., *Works and Correspondence of David Ricardo*. Cambridge: Cambridge University Press.

———. 1960. *Production of Commodities by Means of Commodities*. Cambridge: Cambridge University Press.

Strachey, J. 1959. *The End of Empire*. London: Gollancz.

Sweezy, P. M. 1946. *The Theory of Capitalist Development*. London: Dennis Dobson.

Tarbuck, K., ed. 1972. *Imperialism and the Accumulation of Capital*. London: Allen Lane.

Tobin, J. 1958. "Liquidity Preference as Behaviour Towards Risk." *Review of Economic Studies* 25:65–86.

Index